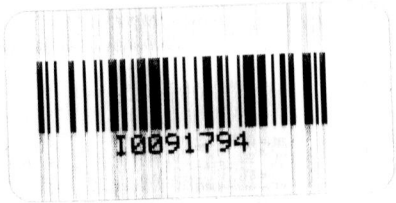

Health Apps, Genetic Diets, and Superfoods

Contemporary Food Studies: Economy, Culture and Politics

Series Editors: David Goodman and Michael K. Goodman

ISSN: 2058-1807

This interdisciplinary series represents a significant step toward unifying the study, teaching, and research of food studies across the social sciences. The series features authoritative appraisals of core themes, debates and emerging research, written by leading scholars in the field. Each title offers a jargon-free introduction to upper-level undergraduate and postgraduate students in the social sciences and humanities.

Emma-Jayne Abbots, *The Agency of Eating: Mediation, Food, and the Body*

Terry Marsden, *Agri-Food and Rural Development: Sustainable Place-Making*

Peter Jackson, *Anxious Appetites: Food and Consumer Culture*

Joanne Hollows, *Celebrity Chefs, Food Media and the Politics of Eating*

Philip H. Howard, *Concentration and Power in the Food System*

Tania Lewis, *Digital Food: From Paddock to Platform*

Hugh Campbell, *Farming Inside Invisible Worlds*

Henry Buller & Emma Roe, *Food and Animal Welfare*

Kate Cairns and Josée Johnston, *Food and Femininity*

Claire Lamine, *Sustainable Agri-food Systems: Case Studies in Transitions Towards Sustainability from France and Brazil*

Eva Haifa Giraud, *Veganism: Politics, Practice and Theory*

Health Apps, Genetic Diets, and Superfoods

When Biopolitics Meets Neoliberalism

Tina Sikka

BLOOMSBURY ACADEMIC
LONDON • NEW YORK • OXFORD • NEW DELHI • SYDNEY

BLOOMSBURY ACADEMIC
Bloomsbury Publishing Plc
50 Bedford Square, London, WC1B 3DP, UK
1385 Broadway, New York, NY 10018, USA
29 Earlsfort Terrace, Dublin 2, Ireland

BLOOMSBURY, BLOOMSBURY ACADEMIC and the Diana logo are trademarks of
Bloomsbury Publishing Plc

First published in Great Britain 2023
Paperback edition first published 2024

Cover design: Terry Woodley
Cover image © rashmisingh/Adobe StockCaption: Baobab Tree Vector Painting.
Aboriginal dot art vector background.

A catalogue record for this book is available from the British Library.

Library of Congress Control Number: 2022948388

ISBN: HB: 978-1-3502-0203-0
         PB: 978-1-3502-0207-8
         ePDF: 978-1-3502-0204-7
         eBook: 978-1-3502-0205-4

Series: Contemporary Food Studies: Economy, Culture and Politics

Typeset by Integra Software Services Pvt. Ltd.

To find out more about our authors and books visit www.bloomsbury.com
and sign up for our newsletters.

Contents

List of Figures

Acknowledgements

I would like to thank my parents and sister, first and foremost, for their love and support. I would also like to extend my appreciation to Bloomsbury Press, my University colleagues (Media, Culture, and Heritage – Newcastle University), and the scholars throughout my academic career that encouraged me – specifically, the late Roman Onufrijchuk, Gary McCarron, and Andrew Feenberg.

Acknowledgements

Introduction

'Good health' is one of those fuzzy, mutable phrases that resists clear, stable definition as a result of its imbrication in social processes that are 'notoriously vague [and exceedingly] interpretive' (Winter and Kron 2009, 301). It is something I think about regularly having grown up first as a figure skater then as an avid consumer of media through which expectations around health, bodily comportment, and responsibility were first constituted and then reinforced by family and peers. This book is aimed at making sense of the discourses and structures that constitute 'good health' in the first instance, by excavating and determining what it means to be in 'good health' on an embodied and visceral level. Here, 'health' is defined as a powerful, internalized, and normative technology, what Foucault refers to as a 'technology of the self', that is both discursive and material (Foucault 1988). Health and healthy bodies are not just products of how we talk about them (i.e. social constructions), but embodied states – what Haraway refers to as material-semiotic agents – that are both energetic and meaning-producing (Haraway 1988).

In this book, I make several analytic moves in order to provide a critical account of what it means to be healthy and achieve 'good health', in today's contemporary media saturated, bio-technological, and hyperconsumerist environment. To that end, I apply a novel materialist, intersectional, and critical health science and technology studies (STS) lens to prise open and lay bare what I believe are some of the harms that make up our contemporary health ecosystem. This includes how we talk about health as well as how we inhabit and embody modern health subjectivities.

The first move sets out the context by demonstrating the ways in which contemporary health identities are constituted by a dual movement towards: 1. personalized nutritionism, defined as a curated and individualized approach to health which sees particular, genetically aligned nutrients and foodstuffs as a health panacea (PN) (Lupton 2014b; Sander 2017); and 2. genetic biomedicalization (GB). GB fuses genetic determinism with the medicalization of life such that engineering one's biocapacities through diet, gene therapy, and pharmaceuticals is seen as necessary (Rose 2007; Bliss 2018). In addition to disparities with respect to access and cost, personalization and biomedicalization impact bodies hailed into contemporary health subjectivities based on one's ability to conform to what are largely Western, heteronormative, and ableist conceptions of health (Hale, Wein-Ying, Cotton, and Khilnani 2018; Welhausen 2018).

Additionally, I trace how PN and GB have impacted those multiply marginalized in disproportionate ways. For example, I unpack the ways in which the values underlying GB are racialized and racializing since it assumes that technological and medical interventions that are aimed at racialized minorities will address health disparities rather than reinscribe racial hierarchies and stereotypes (Kruper and Ehlers 2013; Godsland 2017). GB also relies on a neoliberal conception of health wherein one's genetic destiny is seen as fungible *if* consumer-citizens commit to self-initiated change. As such, much of this book focuses on examining sites of embodied and constructed marginalization as it relates to PN and GB inclusive of race, gender, class, dis/ability, and sexuality.

The second move this book makes is in developing the tools needed to argue that PN and GB co-constitute *the* dominant knowledge regimes from which to examine our contemporary health ecosystem. It is important to point out that this ecosystem, or 'assemblage', includes health and health adjacent corporations for whom profit is the central motive. Health apps, monitoring devices, targeted genetic testing, personalized diets, superfoods, and functional foods dominate this sector. I call this the 'dietary-genomic-functional/superfood industrial complex' which, in addition to being founded on questionable scientific assumptions, reinscribes racial categories through personalization and appification; perpetuates a privatized and neoliberal conception of health (in which the onus is on the individual to enact a 'healthy' lifestyle); extends an impoverished and instrumentalized relationship to food; normalizes harmful body regulation and fat stigma; and commodifies health and food (via the postcolonial fetishization of Otherness (superfoods) and adoption of strict wellness regimes).

Taken together, this scaffolding sets the stage for a considered diagnosis and mapping of our contemporary health assemblage. It is from this that I then construct a possible alternative to this understanding of 'good health'. By applying STS, critical health studies, and an intersectional lens to the study of 'good health', it becomes possible to formulate avenues for change. Namely, an interpretation of health that is prosocial, biodiverse, public, and grounded in the principles of health justice and sovereignty.

In Chapter 1, I lay out the theoretical foundations of the book from which this dominant conception of good health is based. I also unpack and describe its genesis and make the case that it constitutes *the* dominant understanding of health where the descriptor 'hegemonic' is used to refer to the definitions of social and ideological dominance. I use the terms 'hegemonic health' and 'good health' interchangeably as the latter is how it is referred to in media and corporate literature whereas the former is used in more scholarly work. Either way, I argue both are indicative of the same phenomenon. As such, I define hegemonic 'good' health as *a co-produced state of idealized expectations, performances, embodiments, and patterns of consumption dominated by gendered, raced, and classed technophilic knowledge regimes that reproduce regimented and coercive Western standards of health and wellness.* This definition is historically informed, supported by rigorous theoretical and empirical analysis, and comprehensive in its remit.

Throughout the book, I engage with the works of Michel Foucault (1984), Nikolas Rose (Rose and Rabinow 2006), and Deborah Lupton (2016) for their examination of biopolitics, biomedicalization, and neoliberalism; Karen Barad (2007), Donna Haraway (2004), and Jane Bennett (2010) for their scholarship on materiality and gender; Julie Guthman (2011), Alison and Jessica Hayes-Conroy (2015), and Jonathan Metzl (Metzl and Kirkland 2010) for their research examining the intersections between health, diet, and social relations; Lundy Braun (2014), Troy Duster (2003), and Jonathan Kahn (2012) for their work on race, technology, and health; as well as literature on food justice, health sovereignty, and intersectionality (Mullings and Schultz 2006; Alkon and Agyeman 2011; Werkhseiser 2014). The first chapter provides a genealogy of my definition of hegemonic 'good' health as it exists today, keeping in mind that health remains open to discursive re-articulations – ones that break 'suturing ... over-determination' and where there 'is always "too much" or "too little" – an over-determination or a lack, but never a proper fit, a totality' (Hall 2006, 3). In addition to its discursive dimension, this definition is also intentionally attuned to health materialities and embodiments, wherein health and wellness are seen as relational and emergent states of being and where the body is always implicated in relations of power and understood as a site of emotion and affect (Deleuze 1988; Coole and Frost 2010).

In Chapter 2, I provide an overview and political economic analysis of our existing hegemonic health ecosystem. This involves a detailed mapping of existing health technologies including: 1. monitoring technologies; 2. tracking technologies; 3. health-oriented genetic technologies; and 4. dietary techniques and products. Many readers will recognize some of the brands but be surprised to learn about their business and labour practices and the influence they have in defining hegemonic good health.

It is notable that some of the technologies and categories I engage with overlap with one another (i.e. some apps and devices both monitor and proscribe) and are constantly morphing to adjust to user expectations, market signals, and corporate objectives. The corporate tactic of planned obsolescence is particularly relevant in this context (Spinks 2015). Overall, it is important to think about this chapter as providing a snapshot of the health market ecosystem by connecting corporate entities to health ideologies. Additionally, a large portion of this book employs a practice of 'snapshotting' or, in more formal terms, instituting 'agential cuts' as a way of momentarily stabilizing the changing and complex assemblages of norms, values, technologies, laws, policies, institutions, and knowledge regimes that constitute hegemonic good health. The companies and technologies that have become dominant are agential actors with affordances and capacities that make certain relations and norms knowable and hegemonic. As Lupton argues, what many of these technologies enact, in conjunction with all the other human and nonhuman actants, is a 'desire to control and manage the body and conform to norms and ideals about good health and body weight' (Lupton 2018b, 2). This is very much in line with the definition of 'hegemonic good health' I have articulated.

In Chapters 3 to 6, I return to my central definition of hegemonic good health and use it to examine these three biomedical and surveillant technologies in more detail: Aduna, a superfood company; GenoPalate, a biogenetic personalized nutrition outfit; and GetFit, a fitness tracker.

Methodologically, I begin with an analysis of the device/technology/ foodstuff using a political economy of culture framework which applies an economic lens, inclusive of labour relations, organization, profitability, etc., to understand these technologies as social and economic phenomenon. This allows for the examination of these three companies and their products/ services as economically productive forces that give rise to hegemonic health norms (Calabrese and Sparks 2004; Mosco 2014). While physically separated as chapters, these three case studies should be thought of as synergistically intra-acting with one another. Their particular attributes and effects, taken together, produce a unique accounting of the world as 'intra-acting "agencies"' that demand fluid study and analysis (Barad 2007, 139). Users who consume superfoods, apps, and genetic diets, for example, will have to contend with the specificity of how they intra-act with one another in their own lives. The fact that I found adopting one technology at a time so fraught leads me to believe that there are likely to be even more formative insights to be gleaned from how these technologies work together.

The factors that connect these case studies together are threefold. First, Aduna's baobab superfood, GenoPalate's genetic testing kits, and GetFit's app are popular and economically successful products with high rates of adoption and use. Thus, they have comparable levels of consumer penetration as well as similar objectives (both implicit and explicit) around health, wellness, and wellbeing. Second, each of the technologies represents one dominant sector in our hegemonic health ecosystem (food, genetics, and trackers) and examining them together provides both a meta- and micro-level snapshot of our health ecosystem in action. Third, it is the case that users (mostly the affluent 'worried well') will often consume and/or employ these technologies in tandem. As such, placing them alongside one another helps readers envision and grapple with the ways in which power, gender, race, materiality, class, ideology, dis/ability, fatness, and justice work in and through these health assemblages and, in doing so, makes it possible to locate sites of fracture where social change can occur.

I then draw on inductive thematic and discursive analysis coupled with new materialism and phenomenology to posit embodiment as co-constituted with discourse – what Haraway (1997) refers to as the natureculture or, for Barad (1997), the material-discursive. Specifically, I use critical discourse analysis to examine the assumptions, values, and norms circulating within the official presentation of products and services (e.g. websites, promotional materials, app stores, media coverage). This extends the insights around culture and health that emerged out of the section on political economy (Fairclough 2001). One of the central bits of analytic work this does is to: one, establish the modalities of hegemonic food health (and where GB and PN apply); and, two, demonstrate how representation, health provisioning, and embodied experience work to produce the kinds of inequalities described above. Specifically, to reinscribe racial difference, privatize healthcare, impoverish our relationship to food, instil gendered modes of body regulation, and intensify pervasive commodification. These socio-cultural and economic norms work in material-discursive service of the hegemonic definition of good health. It is thus important to keep in mind that, in actuality, health is multidimensional, processual, and reflective of embodied experience (Fullagar 2019).

Next, the application of 'agential cuts' is used to home in on two chains of relations in order to, *momentarily*, stabilize indeterminacy for the sake of analysis and intelligibility (Barad 2007). It is from here that power, body norms, consumerism, inequality, intersectional identity (race, class, gender, sexuality, dis/ability), and self-subjectification come to the fore and are examined in a manner that takes the agency of nonhumans seriously. This manoeuvre allows for an understanding of, as Holford puts it, 'how as knowers, [we] negotiate between actual phenomena (reality) and our subjective understandings of them (across cuts), all the while also reminding us that we are part of the phenomena in question. These negotiations are ongoing and ceaseless, in that depending on contexts, points of views and practices/actions at hand, we can reconfigure cuts with one key condition – accountability' (Holdford 2018). Finally, I close these chapters by engaging in an auto-ethnographic accounting of my personal experience engaging with these technologies for a period of two weeks each. These auto-ethnographic interludes provide a window into the embodied experience of the citizen-consumer.

Vis-à-vis the case studies, Aduna is a superfood company and lifestyle brand focused on selling health-oriented products, baobab fruit specifically, sourced from small-scale farmers in West Africa. It has a £100,000 a year turnover and is carried by retailers in the UK and Europe including Whole Foods (Murray 2014). Aduna describes itself as a socially and environmentally aware and active company. Two of its primary selling points are its ethical and sustainable sourcing and just labour practices. GenoPalate, on the other hand, is a niche company that is popular in the health and nutrition world. It also is considered to be one of the most innovative in the industry (it received $4 million in equity financing in December 2020). GenoPalate specializes in genetically based dietary programmes and promotes itself as a locus of health pedagogy, scientific expertise, and wellness/wellbeing. GenoPalate allows users to upload their raw DNA data from any other services (including the popular 23andMe) which, they claim, results in precise diet plans. The third company, GetFit, is a privately held and 'AI-driven' app development company that produces semi-personalized popular fitness and diet apps aimed at supporting health transformations. While housed in Belarus, GetFit has an office in New York and has cultivated a sizable following. Its claim to fame is the use of ECG monitoring to produce personalized fitness and dietary advice. The app works with the Apple watch and provides a programme that allows users to 'get fit' at home without the need for any equipment.

Taken together, these three cases form a constellation representative of the industry I map out in Chapter 2 (the 'dietary-genomic-functional/superfood industrial complex'). They function as a rich store of textual, normative, scientific, and embodied manifestations of hegemonic good health and all that it entails. These companies are also representative of personalized nutritionism (PN) and genetic biomedicalization (GB) articulated above. This analysis goes beyond a critical health studies discussion of wellness, personalization, and genetification or an STS-focused examination of technologies that co-construct hegemonic health culture (whether in the form of digital trackers, genetically based diets, or superfoods). In addition to a close examination of these technology's discursive and thematic constructions, I also take on and examine the ways in which marginalized individuals and groups are impacted by each along the mutually constituted axes of race, gender, class, disability, and sexuality. This intersectional approach situates social categories within larger socio-structural forces and conjunctures such as capitalism, neoliberalism, and settler colonialism (Crenshaw 2017; Rice, Harrison, and Freedman 2019; Hill Collins 2019). When health becomes a central locus of marginalization on the basis of access to technology, expensive foodstuffs, knowledge/pedagogy, social location, and bodily comportment, what becomes apparent is that these forces impact health much more intensely than an individual tracker, diet, or superfood might. And yet these trackers, personalized diets, and functional/superfoods continue to act as important neoliberal handmaidens through which citizens are encouraged to consume and surveil their way to good health.

Forming the final two elements of this book is an examination of the treatment of these technologies and objects as agential, vibrant, and capable of expressing a kind of selfhood that makes them visible and knowable (Lupton 2020b). This requires a materialist and corporeal understanding of the users of these devices, services, and products whose affective experiences are inextricably linked to the discourses that make them meaningful. I argue that we must consider the pre-cognitive sensations that these technologies ignite and the bodily experiences they enact: basically how they make users feel. As Grosz argues, it is not only important to think about how bodies are 'always irreducibly sexually specific, necessarily inter-locked with racial, cultural, and class particularities' (Grosz 1994, 19–20), but also how these differently situated bodies experience the social, technological, and symbolic on a level that is visceral, 'carnal', or 'enfleshed' (Braidotti 2006, 182).

This is where my auto-ethnographic work comes in. As stated, I incorporated each of these devices/services/products into my own life for two weeks during which time I took copious notes to extract insights based on my own experiential knowledge and detailed reflections on the themes of health, personalization, genetification, biomedicalization, and neoliberalism (Roth 2005; Denshire

2014). In doing so, I assessed whether my definition of hegemonic good health as *a co-produced state of idealized expectations, performances, embodiments, and patterns of consumption dominated by gendered, raced, and classed technophilic knowledge regimes that reproduce regimented and coercive Western standards of health and wellness* resonated with my experience of these technologies. To be clear, auto-ethnography, as a method, is utilized in order to draw the researcher into closer relation with these non-human actants in order to generate 'thick descriptions' based on knowledge that is often overlooked (the experiential) (Geertz 1973). It also involves connecting personal reflexive insights to larger social and cultural themes by actively situating myself in the research. As Peseta puts it, 'Without these intimate and detailed evocations of life and professional practice, our knowledge of those [more intimate] worlds would be severely diminished' (Tai Peseta as cited by Denshire 2014, 838). Autoethnographies also work to add an experiential and grounded layer of analysis and insight into traditional case studies. While formative case studies are helpful in producing robust investigations of a bounded phenomenon from the outside, I argue they are less capable of providing rich analysis from the inside. I thus use autoethnography to attend to this shortcoming and push myself, as a researcher, to 'open up conversations and evoke emotional responses' from my readers (Ellingson and Ellis 2008, 445). Autoethnographies are also helpful methodologically in that they shift one's research lens from diagnosis, analysis, and critique to the overlooked areas of experience, affect, and context.

It was these grounded reflections that forced me to think critically and reflexively about my own positionality in relation to health, these three technologies, and to being a scholar of health. My identity as a South Asian, straight-sized woman with no discernible disabilities, raised in a middle-class Canadian immigrant home, currently holding a PhD and a stable university position, inevitably shapes my observations, insights, and conclusions. However, rather than serving as barriers to 'objective knowledge', I argue my positionality and background have allowed me to write in ways that 'elicit emotional identification and understanding' (Denzin 2001, 12), and 'bring life to the research [and] research to life' (Ellis 1998, 4). This is done by thoughtfully integrating relevant scholarships and my own experiences of racialization, immigration, gender bias, size bias, and class to craft a novel perspective. Also of note is my role as a critical researcher whose chosen methods subvert how these technologies are traditionally used (i.e. with a real desire to improve health). I argue my approach, while critical, is still able to generate important insights of significance to a wider audience by wedding the experiential with the critical/theoretical. This allows for a wider discussion of discursive power, consumer appeal, engagement, as well as resistance.

It also allowed me to form an intimate relationship with the technologies as well as with health as a phenomenal subject-object. It also afforded me the ability to shift positionalities and move from describing and investigating an assemblage (the case study), to exploring my embodied experiences of it (auto-ethnography). I feel strongly that becoming intimately familiar with the objects one studies is critical and an example of good research practice. STS, as a field, has also come to embrace this kind of multimodal, complex, and noisy research.

The two-week window during which I produced the autoethnographies posed its own set of limitations since, because it is bounded, did not permit the kinds of analysis a more sustained and committed form of engagement (say over six months) might offer. It does, however, allow for sufficient time to generate a substantive and nuanced analysis of several real-world situations. Being emersed with these technologies and the socio-cultural infrastructures that surrounded them for six weeks resulted in several notebooks of notes and hours of voice notes being produced, which served as a rich store of primary data resulting in robust findings (Ghita 2019).

This four-pronged approach (discourse/thematic, political economic, material, auto-ethnographic) is novel and meant to offer an original reading and accounting of our dominant health assemblage. One that 'Brings biopolitics, critical geopolitics, and political economy together with genealogies and phenomenologies of everyday life' in a manner that is open, contingent, and reflective of 'the ongoing processes within which social actors ... are irredeemably immersed' (Coole and Frost 2010, 28).

A final issue related to methodology has to do with questions around the perceived lack of generalizability, universalizability, rule-governed inferences, and systematized analysis. I, along with a myriad of qualitative researchers, contend that quantitative, positivist analysis is not the only way to generate valuable knowledge and that qualitative case studies and autoethnographies can and do produce significant findings and generate hypotheses that are concrete, complex, and provide rich insights into important areas of social life (Atkinson 2006; Noor 2008).

Chapter 4 takes on what is probably one of the most difficult aspects of this research: namely, possible solutions. Specifically, I ask what a health ecology that eschews the hegemonic norms laid out in the rest of the book might look like. In describing several possibilities, I also unpack the assertion that popular conceptions of 'hegemonic good health' are, at least in part, socially constructed phenomenon that could be constructed differently. On a technological level, this means thinking about how it might be possible to use the affordances of our existing technologies to circumvent the raced, classed, and gendered exploitation of users. Technofeminism offers a way to do this by approaching health technologies as open to intervention and rearticulation – or what Judy Wajcman describes as engaging in the feminist political practice of fundamentally 'reshap[ing] the networks of science and technology' (in this case health technology) (Wajcman 2004, 127). It is thus worth asking whether tracking technologies, personalized health regimes, and functional/superfoods could be transformed in ways that are consistent with more emancipatory ends. Also considered are alternative health pedagogies that have emerged in the past decade and that have begun to chip away at our dominant health regime. This includes health sovereignty, holistic health, Health at Every Size (HAES) health justice, and fat justice (Ruger 2004; Morello-Frosch et al. 2006; Metzl 2010; Weiler et al. 2015). These models are critical of neoliberal personalization, genetic reductionism, the functionalization of food, fat stigma, and the gendered racialization of health. What is important about this last full chapter is the articulation of the beginnings of an emancipatory health discourse and practice that is contingent, embodied, intersectional (as well as anti-racist and anti-colonial), ecological, and community-oriented.

Finally, I conclude the book with a summary of its most salient points followed by a brief return to a more speculative practice. Specifically, I engineer a fictive health assessment based on the beginnings of a new definition of 'good health' discussed in the preceding chapters. I probe how our criteria might change, what our new indicators might be, how novel data might be gathered, and what kind of health advice could be given. Basically, how health might be enacted within a realigned assemblage – one with new affective capacities and priorities, transformed institutions, and new norms (Fox 2017; Lupton 2018a).

1

Good health and technology

In order to better understand and contest hegemonic conceptions of good health, it is necessary to consider health as an assemblage, a term Jane Bennett uses to think about complex social phenomenon as a multispecies entanglement of ideas, data, technologies, institutions, and objects/artefacts. For Bennett,

> Assemblages are ad hoc groupings of diverse elements, of vibrant materials of all sorts. Assemblages are living, throbbing confederations that are able to function despite the persistent presence of energies that confound them from within. They have uneven topographies, because some of the points at which the various affects and bodies cross paths are more heavily trafficked than others, and so power is not distributed equally across its surface.
>
> (Bennett 2010b, 23–4)

Thus, we can think about our current hegemonic health assemblage as a contingent amalgamation of discourses, actors, and actants that have congealed around the norms, institutions, and technologies we are familiar with today. Namely, a *co-produced state of idealized expectations, performances, embodiments, and patterns of consumption dominated by gendered, raced, and classed technophilic knowledge regimes that reproduce regimented and coercive Western standards of health and wellbeing.* This understanding of 'hegemonic good health' has its own valences, norms, and assumptions. In a recent chapter on the 'social construction of good health' (Sikka 2022), I define hegemonic health as 'a co-produced state of idealized expectations, performances, embodiments, and patterns of consumption dominated by gendered and technophilic knowledge regimes that reproduce regimented and coercive Western standards of health *and beauty*'. I remain wedded to much of that analysis and definition but have since replaced 'beauty' with 'wellbeing' as wellbeing better represents current interests in mental health, spirituality, and sensory care (Lupton 2017b). I have also expanded my analysis to include specific technologies as well as behaviours and discourses.

In this chapter, I perform a deep exegesis of this definition of 'hegemonic good health' following some necessary context, thereby establishing a baseline for the case study-driven analysis in later chapters and the solutions posed further on. I also unpack the role played by personalized nutrition (PN) and genetic biomedicalization (GB), which I argue form the material-discursive scaffolding of this health assemblage.

Methodologically, foreshadowing some of the emancipatory themes I take up in the final chapters, this approach leaves space for seeking out fissures and openings for more pro-social forms of technological becoming. This consists of moves that are posthuman, dissymmetrical, minoritarian, material, and in which molecular and genetic science is used to amplify the power of living matter and nonunitary subjectivity (Braidotti 2011). In doing so, GB has the capacity to crack open possibilities for becomings that take on the human but are also embedded in 'specific material configurations of the world … and specific material phenomenon (relations rather than "things")'. This causal relationship between the apparatuses of bodily production and the phenomena produced is one of 'agential intra-action', 'a relation that explains how actants, both human and non, are ontologically inseparable' (Barad 2003, 814). If we think about our genes in this way, I contend it may be possible to find ways to reconfigure and rethink their role in understanding health as a set of relations that reflect a more capacious conception of science, technology, identity, and the material-discursive.

Hegemonic good health: Some context

Using a biomedical lens, 'good health' is most often used to describe one's clinical status as it relates to disease. Thus, being given a clean bill of health means that the routine disease markers a physician or nurse might test you for, e.g. diabetes, cholesterol, deficiencies, blood pressure, etc., have either come back negative or are within the normal range (Wyle 1970; Ereshefsky 2009). Consistent with this model, medical knowledge is filtered through a curative lens in which 'the patient's embodied being is disavowed in favour of the "healing" of illness, and eradication of pathogens' (Murray 2008, 168). This is an important point in that it draws attention to how undervalued embodied experience is in the medical model and the extent to which personal experience is eschewed in the production of medical knowledge. Also standard in the medical model is the source of the remedy wherein the cure to health problems is believed to lie in the individual and their personal actions/choices. Conrad refers to this as (neoliberal) healthicization – an understanding of health that moves us away from base 'biomedical causes and interventions' and towards a focus on 'lifestyle and behavioural causes and interventions' (Conrad 1992, 22).

At the same time, as health has become 'healthified', 'good health' has also expanded its remit to include consideration of one's overall state of wellbeing. In reflecting this trend, the WHO (World Health Organization) now defines health as 'a state of complete physical, mental and social well being and not merely the absence of disease or infirmity' (WHO 2021). Health as wellbeing aims to (re)connect the mental with the biophysical and reconsider one of the organizing principles of Western thought – namely, that reason (i.e. the cogito) is the locus of knowledge and that this all-powerful mind sits in opposition to the material body. In challenging this, biostatistics and absence of disease, while still important, have begun to give way to a wider discussion of mental and physical wellbeing as an important social, spiritual, and environmental indicators of health. One that is kaleidoscopic rather than unipolar.

Calogero and Thompson (2010) refer to wellbeing as the process of feeling at home in one's body as a result of conditions that allow for spiritual, environmental, emotional, and physical flourishing. This approach places affect and embodied knowledge front and centre which, in the context of health, had traditionally been seen as secondary to expert knowledge and evaluation. However, discourses of wellbeing can also work to reinforce the operating logic of neoliberal conceptions of health – namely, as an individualized and singular responsibility. As such, it becomes important to highlight the ways in which hegemonic understandings of 'health and wellbeing' are shaped by corporations who have worked to commodify 'good health' as a medical outcome that can be bought and sold in the form of diets, technologies, medications, and exercise programmes. I call this economic chain of goods, services, and imaginings the 'dietary-genomic-(super)functional food industrial complex'.

In the remainder of this chapter, I unpack the definition of hegemonic good health (*a co-produced state of idealized expectations, performances, embodiments, and patterns of consumption dominated by gendered and raced technophilic knowledge regimes that reproduce regimented and coercive Western standards of health and wellbeing*) and its use while also foreshadowing the possibility for alternatives. This definition is will require some effort and theoretical work to explain as it incorporates both established and more recent thought-provoking research from feminist science studies, cultural theory, phenomenology, materialism, political economy, critical technology studies, and gender studies.

The definition: Hegemonic good health

The most straightforward way in which to parse out and explain the historical, social, cultural, political, and scientific dimensions of 'good health' is to go through it step by step. As such, in order to understand hegemonic good health as *a co-produced state of idealized expectations, performances, embodiments, and patterns of consumption dominated by gendered and raced technophilic knowledge regimes that reproduce regimented and coercive Western standards of health and wellbeing*, we need to unpack the role played by: 1. co-production; 2. idealized expectations, performances, embodiments, and patterns of consumption; 3. gendered, raced, and technophilic knowledge regimes; and 4. Western standards of health and wellbeing.

Co-production

Co-production is an analytic tool that speaks to the ways in which phenomenon, forces, technologies, and norms are part of a process of dialectical shaping and mutual constitution. First and foremost, when applied to health, it becomes important to think about the relationship between our myriad artefacts and this particular health hegemony.

Technofeminist studies makes the best use of co-production and draws on it to refer to the mutual shaping of gender and technology in which 'technology is both a source and a consequence of gender relations' (Wajcman 2004, 7). Drawing on this approach, we can think about the ways in which gendered stereotypes and norms are embedded in technology and then perpetuated by them as they are taken up and used in everyday life. The technologies of our current health assemblage reflect this mutualism through design – the majority of which are surveillant, structured, centralized, and opaque (i.e. algorithms) and whose uses feed back into and perpetuate dominant structures and norms. These technologies also shape subject positions (i.e. the empowered patient or autonomous subject) that comply with the institutions they rely on (Harbers 2005). As Ferreira argues, these norms are a consequence of existing power relations enacted through technology – meaning that they are both 'a source and consequence' of hegemonic health norms that are then 'materialized in technology' (Ferreira 2017; see also Wajcman 2004; Smelik and Lykke 2010).

Idealizations

Next are the 'idealized expectations, performances, [and] embodiments' that form part of this definition which, as its primary subjects, rely on the experiences of white, heterosexual, cis, slim, conventionally attractive men and/or women whose attainment of desirable health metrics are believed to be achievable through self-discipline. For women, this often involves the careful and taxing social balancing of outward displays of enjoyment vis-à-vis food (e.g. as in the case of parties and gatherings), and the performance of feminine self-restraint necessary to maintain a certain bodyweight. Kate Cairns and Josée Johnston call this the 'do-diet' – a regime that requires that women 'should know what foods make her fat, but also avoid the appearance of "dieting" ... Perhaps most importantly, she understands how to control her body but also knows when to indulge' (Cairns and Johnson 2015, 153). For men, this involves a semiotics of food wherein meat and meat eating are seen as an especially masculine practice tied to health and the performance of appropriate gender roles (Rothgerber 2013). It is significant that meat eating has been linked to larger dynamics of patriarchy, control, and the subordination of nature and women as argued by Carol Adams (2015) and Amy Calvert who demonstrate how 'consuming meat ... [became] linked to becoming masculine, and to embodying power, while alternative dietary practices are marginalised, mocked and maligned' (Calvert 2014, 19). The equation of health with meat consumption finds its justification in things like men's health magazines, which studies have found discursively construct and perpetuate a positive correlation between masculinity, health, and meat eating (Stibbe 2004; Rothgerber 2013).

Embodiment in this definition refers to the fact that bodies and health are viscerally felt and inhabited. New materialism and phenomenology make it clear that the body and the myriad affective states it finds itself in are not solely sites of discursive struggle and inscription. While health is, to a large extent, a product of disciplinary practices and knowledge regimes, it is also something that is lived (Foucault 1988; Wright 2012). New materialism connects the very real way in which health subjectivities are born out of the biopolitical, normalizing, and regularizing of healthist discourses (ones that encourage self-surveillance, discipline, and the display of neoliberal individualism), while also being grounded in a *robust theory of the body* (Lupton 2016a; Ajana 2017). Health is always already inextricably tied to our body's materiality, its plasticity, and its relation with other humans and nonhumans and the natural world. It thus enfolds discourse into the affective producing of *lived* health ideologies (Hite 2019). Using the moniker of the posthuman, new materialism considers the ways in which bodies are also 'potentially unruly … agentive "entities" (or assemblages) in themselves' – ones that are gendered and racialized but not entirely disconnected from discursive relations (Hinton 2015, 2; see also Haraway 2010).

Patterns of consumption

The 'patterns of consumption' aspect of hegemonic good health refers to our growing hyperconsumerist engagements with different forms of packaged and 'chosen' personalized diets and technologies that promise 'good health'. This consumer promise is rendered legible through the deification of the neoliberal, entrepreneurial subject bent on personal improvement through self-discipline – what Mitchell Dean refers to as the 'reflexive project of the self' (Dean 1996; Till 2014). Importantly, this ethos is classed and raced in particular ways such that, vis-à-vis race, the ideal consumer subject is seen as white, Western, and heterosexual (Noble 2018). As I make clear throughout this book, this default is anything but neutral, it has real material consequences reflected in health disparities that are tied to 'racial discrimination, social stratification … and mistrust of the scientific establishment [that] feeds back into the health of individuals' (Fujimura and Rajogopalan 2011, 6). It is important to keep in mind that the corporations which give rise to the tools used in the maintenance of this ethos are tremendously profitable with, for example, CNBC estimating that the personalized nutrition industry will reach profits of $64 billion by 2040 (Fitzgerald 2020), the superfoods and functional foods sector earning $137 billion in 2018 (Grand View Research 2019), and digital health trackers expected to take in $54 billion by 2023 (Barkho 2019).

Gendered, raced, and technophilic knowledge regimes

The next element of this definition of 'hegemonic good health' consists of specific norms, behaviours, performances, and embodiments shaped by 'gendered and raced technophilic knowledge regimes'. The example noted above vis-à-vis femininity/masculinity and health norms is just one way in which health has become a locus through which to express and enact gender. Another is through 'thin femininity', which is justified by postfeminist enactments of health defined by individual choice. Postfeminism's emphasis on health through self-discovery is justified by a feminist politics that relocates empowerment to the body so that the choice to enact normative health regimes is seen as agential because it is chosen. It also involves a myriad of 'self-monitoring practices' inclusive of 'the diary, the life-plan' and 'choosing' to remain slim (McRobbie 2009, 19; also see O'Neill 2020). The fact that these decisions are made within a context of unequal power relations, however, is often ignored.

Men have also had to contend with knowledge regimes that encourage them to strive for desirable bodies through exercise and diet plans coded as masculine (e.g. supplements for muscle mass, protein-rich diet (paleo), and taxing exercise (Crossfit)) (Robertson 2007; Calogero and Thompson 2010; Norman 2011). Men's fitness magazines, for example, play an important part in constructing ideal embodiment – one that is focused on risk mitigation, disease prevention, and attaining that 'traditional young, lean, muscular male body' (Boni 2002, 470). The fact that men are being increasingly drawn into performing health hegemonies more explicitly – i.e. through consumer practices – is notable. They too are having to walk a nutritional tightrope by being 'simultaneously compelled to both achieve culturally privileged male bodies at the same time that they are interpellated to maintain a functional, aloof, and distanced relationship to their bodies' (Norman 2011, 432). I would point out that this focus on bodies is functional and pragmatic as the material body comes to be seen as emblematic of good health, thus allowing for the accumulation of health capital that is then used in everyday life.

Also of note is the fact our understanding of gendered bodies and health must go beyond the male/female binary and consider intersex and trans bodies as well as different kinds of masculine/feminine/nonbinary embodiments. Unfortunately, central to the hegemonic definition of 'good health' is the fact that bodies that resist male/female binary are almost always ignored or erased. Recently, however, important work has emerged challenging this, such as insightful analysis on the masculinization and/or feminization of gay male bodies in terms of desired muscularity and thinness which challenge traditional gendered expectations (Lakkis, Ricciardelli and Williams, 1999; Tiggemann and Isabella 2020). What is not clear, however, is how closely these desires are associated with an intentionally performed and communicated *health* status.

On the subject of race, hegemonically defined 'good health' hinges on standards and norms that appear neutral but hide assumptions that are far from 'objective'.

Western medical science has been used to naturalize racial difference dating back to the eighteenth century in which, for example, perceived differences in lung capacity and crania were used to justify slavery by relying on a discourse of biological inferiority and nonhumanness (Blakey 1999; McWhorter 2017). Early genetics were also deployed to concretize the belief that phenotypical whiteness, and thus white bodies, were superior. This assumption was justified by racially biased scientific processes that relied on the elevation of selective measurement and overdetermined causal logic as *the* source of knowledge (Nelson 2016; Voléry and Julien 2020). This structural bias continues today in the form of algorithms that reinscribe race as a biological fact as well as through race-based medicines, race-specific diets, and adjustments to health metrics based on race (Ferdinand and Ferdinand 2008; Kahn 2012). So-called 'race neutrality' also functions to replicate these hierarchies.

In this book, I make the case that health as a biomedical outcome must resist reinscribing race and, instead, acknowledge the ways in which racialization has produced unequal health outcomes by marginalizing certain groups on the basis of perceived phenotypical difference (Frieze 2015). Addressing this will require attending to racist ideologies and entrenched structural racism in ways that make it clear that, for example, a particular woman is more at risk of heart disease not because she is phenotypically Black, but because that phenotypical difference has led to her being more likely to live in a segregated and polluted part of a city, have less access to quality education and healthcare, have stressful caring responsibilities, and engage in unstable, low-paid work (Roberts 2011; Hinze, Lin, Anderson 2012). This, to be clear, is an imposed oppression – one that is smoothed over in our media and discourse but which is lived and experienced on a visceral level by those who are marginalized.

Finally, it is important to emphasize how deeply the image of the fit, white, able-bodied, middle class, and youthful body is rooted in colonial imaginaries. As Warwick notes, this ideal is reflected in stereotypes about the health of racialized bodies as well as the ongoing neocolonial exploitation of genetic data, tissue samples, and local knowledge (Anderson 2009). Gutin locates this socio-historically in early assumptions about Blackness, blood, and purity wherein 'dark skin [was seen] as a marker of innate unhealthiness' and the 'persistent interest in attributing a biological origin to racial difference and disparities in health' which has continued (Gutin 2019, 224).

This part of my definition of hegemonic health also speaks to how it is gendered, with slimness elevated as an ideal for women and muscularity for men. Further intersections between race, gender, and other identity positions, inclusive of sexuality, dis/ability, and class, are also important. Black women and women of colour, for example, experience the pressures of health expectations differently since raced, particularly Black, bodies are often seen as dangerous, unwieldy, and sexually available (Shilling 2012). The stereotype of the obese Black woman also overlaps with class and is solidified in what Sabrina Strings identifies as the 'social dead weight' stereotype that 'is largely a reproduction of the trope of the diseased black woman that has been used throughout American history' (Strings 2015, 107). Proportions, bodily comportment, and clothing size thus become signifiers of health which is inscribed *on* the body. Yet, as we well know, bodily comportment is not always the best indicator of one's wellbeing (Watkins 2015). Fat activists have for decades challenged the causal link asserted between fatness and ill health, arguing that fatness is neither pathological nor an indicator of illness (Guthman 2011; Ernsbergrer 2012).

Finally, it is important to note that in our contemporary environment, medical, nutritional, and health advice continues to be disproportionately dispensed by white and Western experts based on data gathered from a less than representative group and without due attention to context, culture, and lived experience (Hayes-Conroy and Hayes-Conroy 2013). Strings, in her book *Fearing the Black Body: The Racial Origins of Fat Phobia*, traces how whiteness as an indicator of health and beauty developed such that stereotypically white characteristics became elevated, along with thinness, as part of a national project to (re)produce desirable citizens (Strings 2019). 'Western' is thus not only spatially and temporally specific but is also ontological in its imprinting of the health values of a particular group onto the rest of the world.

Turning to technophilia, there is an underlying set of technophilic knowledge regimes that ground this contemporary understanding of 'good health' worth unpacking further. By technophilic I mean to express an enthusiastic embrace and support for technologically based interventions into health both as it relates to individuals and populations. On the one hand, technophilia is a sentiment, one that 'assumes future technological improvements can [and will] outpace historical experience' (Mitchell 2012, 24). On the other, technophilia also captures the force of supportive discourses by governments, health professionals, corporate actors, and the media who have worked to construct citizens that are open to, if not demanding of, technological solutions. Late capitalism's profit and production bias, especially when coupled with neoliberal individualism, works through these technologies to cultivate and extract biological tender in the form of data and communication (Banner 2017). This is evident in the Quantified Self (QS) movement, as well as through mobile and eHealth technologies (Saron 2017).

Technophilia is also reflected in the normalization of a certain kind of masculinity – one that reifies the dominance of men and reflects the belief that the 'interests and competencies inscribed in the design of ...' technologies are '... predominantly masculine' (Ourdshoorn et al. 2004, 53; Jensen 2008). These regimes are also racialized at the point of access, design, and infrastructure since 'assumptions about whiteness [are] embedded in the infrastructure and design' of these technologies (Daniels 2013, 696). While I discuss the subject of race and design in each of the case studies and in the final chapter, it bears noting here that digital health technologies already reflect existing social biases as in the case of health monitoring devices like pulse oximeters for whom the form of light signalling used have been found to 'not [be] as accurate, and may not work at all, in people with darker skin tones' (Shcherbina et al. 2017; Colvonen et al. 2020). Also of note are the risk assessments scores compiled by insurance companies and public health bodies who rely on scoring mechanisms that include health tracking data which then feeds into their algorithms. These algorithms have been found to give Black patients a lower starting score than white patients, based on the assumption that they are sicker, meaning they need to reach a higher threshold in order to obtain care (Boyd and Crawford 2012; Ho, Ali and Caals 2020).

Returning to neoliberalism, technophilic health knowledge regimes also reflect the widespread belief that health is a state that can be successfully intervened and improved upon with the use of trackers, technologies, apps, and enhanced foodstuffs. Availing oneself of these products and services functions as a signifier of accumulated health capital and reflects one's duty to build said capital as a good, agential citizen. Societal and environmental determinants of health, inclusive of barriers to access, poverty, unemployment, as well as discrimination, are often left unaddressed.

This regimentation-orientation of the hegemonic definition of 'good health' functions on the level of parsimony and control as well as coercion. Regimentation reflects a biopolitical understanding of health in which bodies and populations are seen as sites of management. Drawing on Rose and Rabinow, this approach attends to the forces that seek to 'maximise its [the body's] forces and integrate it into efficient systems' as well as 'a biopolitics of the population, focusing on the species body, the body imbued with the mechanisms of life: birth, morbidity, mortality, longevity' (Rabinow and Rose 2006, 196). Health thus becomes a commodity, a vital capacity that must be surveilled and controlled. Ultimately, this means that health requires a commitment to accumulating biomedical knowledge and using health technologies to construct bodies that are enhancement-oriented. This orientation aims at cultivating a kind of being that, according to Foucault, requires 'him [her/they] to act upon himself, to monitor, test, improve, and transform himself' (Foucault 1992, 28).

I use the term regimentation to reflect the orientation to life and the body needed for this particular kind of subjectivity. The requirement that we transform care of the self into compelled self-knowledge (through routine, informatalization, and regimented discipline) has an outsized impact on lived bodies. For instance, this ethic can be psychologically and physiologically exhausting, requiring constant vigilance resulting in a sense of the embodied self as decontextualized, ahistorical, and machinic (Mayes 2015; Morris 2019b). It can also result in feelings of failure, self-alienation, and somatic detachment. Scholarship in fat studies has taken up this kind of analysis such that the body is seen as an active ledger, one that is situated and constantly changing. As Rice argues, it is through 'infolding, everything that happens to people – accidents, insults, or pleasures' that then 'becomes an ingredient in the history and development of ... bodies' (Rice 2015, 393; see also Grosz 1999; Colls 2007). This, I contend, includes the accumulated pressure to conform.

Regimentation also reflects the rise of nutritionism (which is distinct from healthism – to which I return later), which grounds health in the perceived nutritional value of food (Dreher 2018). Nutritionism embraces regimented optimization in which nutrients dominate. It also encourages the application of a techno-managerial gaze vis-à-vis food and a personal commitment to tabulating calories, fats, and micronutrients in pursuit of self-mastery. According to Scrinis, nutritionism is constituted by,

> [the] precise understanding of how foods and nutrients affect biochemical processes; the simplification of the understanding of these biomarkers and their relationship to bodily health; the differentiation of biomarkers into 'good' and 'bad' types; and the tendency to undermine and erase the distinctions between types of foods in terms of food quality.
>
> (Scrinis 2012, 274)

This perspective is particularly salient as it relates to superfoods, which I take up in Chapter 3.

Western standards of health and wellbeing

The final two components of this definition are that of coercion and 'Western standards of health and wellbeing'. While powerful in its traditional usage, the term coercion is taken up here in a slightly less visceral manner and, instead, is illustrative of the dual-role capillary power plays in health discourse and embodiment (Foucault 1980a). Coercion should thus be thought of simultaneously as imposed, e.g. by medical professionals, employers, and insurance companies, and internalized through 'a complex and expanding apparatus of control, discipline and regulation that involves micropolitical processes whereby the individuals ... [are] encouraged to conform to the morals of society' (Petersen and Lupton 1996, 4). In my final analysis, I build upon this approach by disclosing how coercion is materially and agentially enacted by technologies, and unpacking how this operates in practice through my own accounting of the toll it takes using personal auto-ethnographies.

While I have covered the role of 'the West' as forming *the* spatial and ontological foundation of hegemonic health as it relates expertise, science, race, and gender, there is one further aspect worth exploring. Namely, the precise nature of said 'Western standards of health and wellbeing'. I argue that these standards, contemporaneously, are based on an amalgamation of numerical indicators (BMI, body fat, blood pressure, cholesterol), bodily comportment (thin for women, muscular for men), and whiteness which, at least for the former two, are seen as achievable through hard work and individual acts of striving – what Brown describes as the imperative of 'rational, calculating creatures whose moral autonomy is measured by their capacity for "self-care" – that ability to provide for their own [health] needs and to service their own ambitions ... [an] individual who is fully responsible for her/himself' (Brown 2003 42). This is a very specific conception of good health – one that is depoliticized and dismissive of alternatives like those found in indigenous health and foodways, alternative food networks, health justice movements, and community conceptions of good health (Daniels 2001; Shattuck 2013).

Connected to this is the embracing of 'wellness culture', which reflects the merging of neoliberalism with hyperconsumerism. Wellness or wellbeing culture thus becomes yet another source of health capital accumulated through participation in particular kinds of consumer practices such as in the conspicuous display of health accoutrements. This can occur through the purchase of specific kinds of apparel and equipment, participation in costly classes, consumption of particular kinds of food (inclusive of superfoods), and involvement in health and fitness subcultures. Terminologically, wellbeing has begun to replace wellness in discussions of work and health resulting in the latter's (wellness's) growing association with crass capitalism while retaining its framing 'as a quality inhering in the liberal individual' (Smith and Reid 2018, 808). Wellness discourses are often normalizing, moralizing, and self-objectifying in ways that 'instrumentalize the self-regulating propensities of individuals in order to ally them with [neoliberal] socio-political objectives' (Miller and Rose 1990, 28l; see also Purser 2019). Wellbeing, on the other hand, has tended to be used by oppositional, holistic, health justice, and new materialist movements to signify a state of health that is cooperative across species, rooted in community, and integrated with the environment (Braidotti 2013b). However, wellbeing has, in some instances, also been used in the context of hegemonic good health as I define it (Wiest et al. 2015).

Similarly important is how tightly wellness and wellbeing are tied to healthism – a framework I return to throughout the book and which is used to describe, as Crawford puts it, 'the preoccupation with personal health as a primary – often the primary – focus for the definition and achievement of well-being; a goal which is to be attained primarily through the modification of lifestyles' (Crawford 1980, 366). Healthism is constituted by moral claims and neoliberal subjectivities that see health as controllable, supported by the state, and constantly to be strived for (Skrabanek 1994; Lupon 2013). These judgements and norms, as Metzl (2010) asserts, are manifested in hierarchies and structures of power and privilege experienced in and through bodies. Significantly, the emotions associated with the failure to live up to these ideals, e.g. shame, stress, displeasure, discomfort, and worry, also have an impact on health (Fullager 2019). Ongoing research in Fat Studies, for example, unpacks how,

> markers of the good and bad forms of life under the notion of deficit are not only felt on the body, but also embodied and transferred via affective tendencies. What is embodied, is the sense of not being good enough or, in liberal humanist parlance – not quite human and/or nonhuman.
>
> (Bahra 2018, 193; see also Lupton 2018c;
> Rich and Mansfield 2019)

This represents a troubling and harmful division which is magnified when those designated as 'nonhuman' are also racialized, classed, and/or gendered. Thinking critically about how these overlapping and intersectional forms of oppression function within the context of hegemonic health norms is thus essential (Schulz and Mullings 2006). This is especially the case if we are to take the material understanding of bodies and subjectivities as emerging out of changing systems of intra-activity, agencies, and forces seriously and move our understanding of health in new directions.

Cumulatively, this definition of good health speaks to the dominant norms, pathologies, and practices that constitute how we relate to and categorize bodily states and how said states are enmeshed in relations of power/knowledge and shaped by race, gender, sexuality, dis/ability, and class relations. There are, however, two further elements that need to be unpacked as they relate to the particular kinds of technologies being used to buttress this conception of hegemonic good health. Specifically, nutritional personalization and genetic biomedicalization.

Personalized nutritionism and genetic biomedicalization are the two most significant technological 'trends' I argue constitute the socio-technical scaffolding of hegemonic good health. PN and GB operate as part of this health assemblage by quantifying and monetizing bodies, fetishizing individual choice, and placing both trust and hope in technologies to solve social problems. I define PN as the celebratory desire to adopt new nutritional techniques and technologies that promise a more personally curated health habitus resulting in enhanced overall medical health and a better life. Nutritional personalization is often technophilic and manifest in dietary, fitness, and sleep tracking apps as well as portable and digital medical devices capable of monitoring states of illness (e.g. diabetes, blood pressure, etc.) as well as everyday activities. What is most important about these devices is their role in constructing an ideal 'digitally engaged patient', one who is agential, empowered, and responsibilized to enact care based on collected and algorithmically analysed data (Lupton 2017a). These technologies also encourage the adoption of wider 'cultural practices and processes of identifying, augmenting, and codifying the [individual] body through technology' (Hood 2020, 158). It is the intersection of nutritional data with technology that is significant to PN since it depends on the parsimonious collection of information about one's life in order to make dietary personalization useful. It is important to note, however, that this personalization, while presented as facilitating personal empowerment, also functions as a technology of normalization by constructing certain dietary practices and bodily states as desirable (Ivancic 2018).

These ideal bodies are disciplined, hierarchized, and judged in accordance with a biopolitical self that is white, male, and, more often than not, heteronormative. Techno-nutritional hegemony imposes a social order that benefits from naturalizing difference, including racial difference, through personalized diets, exercise regimes, and, most importantly, by comparatively ranking bodily states in order to market lucrative products e.g. (vitamins, meal plans) and services (Hite 2019). PN exploits biopolitical modes of surveillance and control using technologies that co-produce the ideal participatory biocitizen in service of population-level public objectives (Burchell, Davidson and Foucault 2008; Ross 2018). Rabinow and Rose refer to this dual track as the disciplining anatamo-politics of the body which, when coupled with the biopolitics of population, enacts,

> one or more truth discourses about the 'vital' character of living human beings; an array of authorities considered competent to speak that truth; strategies for intervention upon collective existence in the name of life and health; and modes of subjectification, in which individuals work on themselves in the name of the individual or collective life or health.
>
> (Rabinow and Rose 2006, 195)

Exemplary citizenship, to which I return later, constitutes another plank of PN wherein dietary action in pursuit of 'good health' (especially practices which feed into an atomized collective and shifts responsibility away from the state), are executed in order to perform health as part of conscientious, self-aware citizenship (Sharon 2015). Being healthy thus becomes part of a national project that places importance on projecting a country's strength and vitality, often resulting in the stigmatization of those who do not conform (i.e. fat bodies, queer bodies) and plays into modern forms of hyper-nationalism (Ayo 2012). At its most basic level, this model of healthy citizenship acts as a self-disciplining technology through which engaging in nutritional health practices is seen as a duty of citizenship and a site of judgement.

Overall, what becomes clear in this description of PN is that it is divorced from any sense of what its impact is on one's sense of self – a self that feels the weight of dietary surveillance, dataveillance, expectations, rules, and normalizing discourses. The merging of faith in technology (technophilia) with personalized rules and regulations (dietary personalization) and 'objective' science works to entrench commitment to a technoscientized life. One that trusts in modern science and technology to fix large-scale social problems despite its tendency to instrumentalize bodies and justify racial and gender oppression (Harding 2008). New materialism and phenomenology offer ways to (re)conceptualize the material-discursive as co-constituted rather than binary and applies this lens to the study of science and technology. Rosi Braidotti, in her work, demonstrates the ways in which technomaterial-discursive assemblages are processual, materially embedded, and exist *in relation to* material bodies, environments, affordances, and knowledge. These forces, or 'lines of flight', act viscerally on the subject. Braidotti characterizes this 'as a relational embodied and embedded, affective and accountable entity and not only ... a transcendental consciousness' (i.e. as posthuman) (Braidotti 2019a, 31; see also Braidotti 2019bb). I return to the material-discursive effect PN has on our bodies and our sense of self in later chapters.

PN works synergistically with GB (inclusive of tracking), however, GB focuses more on extending a scopic, surveillant, and genetic lens to diagnoses, treatment, health policy, and individual health regimes. Thus, GB includes ancestry testing, disease profiling, and genetic tinkering. Its objective is to reveal avenues of intervention so that individuals can live longer, healthier lives. This form of biomedicalization builds upon traditional medicalization by opening up more and more parts of one's lifeworld to reflection and control using a medical lens. Medicalization is one of several healthways discussed throughout this book which works to buttress our modern hegemonic health regime by encouraging patients to achieve statistically 'normal' functioning, in line with markers articulated by health experts and institutions. This often involves calls for more intensive forms of self-monitoring, medicating, and management (Kukla 2014). Biomedicalization takes things one step further through the introduction and integration of normalizing rhetoric and regimes that act both on the individual *and* population level. Biomedicalization is defined by Clarke et al. as 'the increasingly complex, multisited, multidirectional processes of medicalization that today are being both extended and reconstituted through the emergent social forms and practices of a highly and increasingly technoscientific biomedicine' (Clarke et al. 2010, 55).

The objective of this biomedical turn is to encourage the use of disciplining *biological* technologies to regulate the species body as well as the individual body for purposes of capitalist reproduction via the accumulation of biovalue (Novas 2006). What is most significant about biomedicalization is that its' technologies and techniques are applied at the molecular level (i.e. on the level of genes, metabolic pathways, and proteins) which, it is thought, will increase useful knowledge and, in time, detect/treat genetic diseases (Willmes 2020). Other scholars focus more on genetic biomedicine's profitability, arguing that it is simply a new form of biogenetic capitalism. Niche desires for individual, genetically specific health profiles, dietary advice, exercise plans, and lifestyle regimes opens us up as sources of profit. Chapter 2, which outlines a political economy of this sector, makes the significance of this move clear. It is worth emphasizing here, however, that genetic biomedicalization draws into its orbit strategies that, on a material level, have been transformative – especially as it relates to the treatment of life. These processes, as Braidotti asserts, render 'The self-generative power of living matter ... [to be] ... both denied and enhanced by patenting and branding for the sake of corporate profit' (Braidotti 2007, 71).

With regard to GB, there is a core tension around the meaning and value of biomarkers as it relates to genetic thinking. My focus, however, is on the specific ways in which health is intertwined with biomedical genetification while keeping in mind that there are other ways in which this science can be used. For example, I would note that the mythology behind the all-powerful gene (master molecule), when coupled with the promise of biomedicine, has become culturally imperative. This mythos feeds into desires for acceptance, belonging, and healing as well as for safety and security (i.e. risk mitigation). GB also fits nicely within a neoliberal understanding of health wherein individual biology, rather than social determinants, is the cause of illness. This leaves sufficient room for investment in determining health status through tests, engaging in lifestyle practices to mitigate illness, and performing the kind of health subjectivity and citizenship that is expected of all good citizens. GB includes the innovation of new technologies including pharmacogenomics, genetic engineering, tissue banks, metabolic regulation, and biobanking. Power, in this context, is exerted on individuals horizontally through the circulation of explicit and implicit expectations and the internalization of the expectation that we must 'exercise responsibility and self-control to restore and maximize ... life potential via biomedical [and genetic] expertise' (Fullagar, 2009 403). The addition of the digital and nanotechnological to the bioinformational and genetic intensifies this.

GB also reflects the move by corporations, researchers, and governments to (de)code risks related to health through the lens of criminality, intelligence, and ideology. This is often referred to as the 'new eugenics' and risks supporting even more racialized forms of risk assessment. Since the early 2000s, there has been a concerted effort to use genetic technologies to map human difference and superimpose those differences onto populations (where 'populations' serve as proxies for race). This permits, and even encourages, the retention of racial categories that are subsequently used to produce race-based medicines, diets, and analytics as in the case of BiDil – a heart failure drug whose patent was extended through its reclassification as a medication that worked particularly well on Black patients (despite major flaws in the methodology and evidence it works\ed on everyone) (Roberts 2011). This research continues despite scientific and sociological consensus that race is not biological but socially produced (Hatch 2016; Masuoka 2019). Race-based medicines, health advice, and interventions reify the assumption that there is something biological and genetically essential about race. This belief persists despite the fact that it has been developed and sold under the pretence of attending to persistent racial inequalities by focusing on the needs of racialized communities (which risks reinscribing race as natural/genetic rather than social and cultural). It also conceals other, more profit-driven motivations for racializing health (Duster 2003; Peters and Venkatesan 2010). GB also, as Bonham, Callier, and Royal put it, 'ignores the many underlying social and biologic factors that influence both the development of disease and response to treatment' (Bonham, Callier, and Royal 2016). This includes access to quality healthcare, education, stable work and income, sustainable food, housing, and safe community spaces. Scholars of STS, of which I include myself, have been quick to point out that the use of GB to attend to these inequalities, e.g. by personalizing healthcare at the molecular level – as many new methods and technologies promise to do, brings us dangerously close to doing the opposite. Namely, by indemnifying 'the biological reification', 'biological rewriting', and 'genetic reinscription' of race (Hatch 2016, 112). Another risk worth noting over and above providing fodder to race realists is that the assembled normative assumptions drawn from GB could be used to justify the increased surveillance and stigmatization of marginalized groups.

It is important to point out that my explanation of GB thus far is circumscribed and reflective of a meta-discursive analysis that leaves out the body almost entirely. My auto-ethnographic chapters make up for this by allowing for a much-needed reflection on how genetics, biomedicine, and the body intersect with agential informatic technologies to (re)produce a relation to the self that is fragmented, medicalized, and marketable. It could also, however, potentially encourage the application of techniques of the body in order to amplify and extend its capacities in line with the duty to perform health for both self and society. Yet, GB, in producing this static and circumscribed conception of self, also leaves room for limited agency through acts of individualized lifestyle change (i.e. 'if you know you have a genetic propensity for heart disease, change your habits'). I argue these cracks are not sufficiently open to allow for a more capacious understanding of health in which bodies, genes and all, are understood as part of an assemblage in which the thing-power of human and non-human actants pushes up against the network of relations in which they reside (Bennett 2004).

GB should therefore be examined through the lens of material theory in three ways: 1. as fluid and relational rather than discrete and unmediated – thus allowing for future posthuman transformations; 2. as situated in a technocratic technological environment that reduces and commodifies life and health for profit (despite the fact that real life 'exhibits both recalcitrance and resilience in response to interventions that attempt to finetune the molecular functions of organisms' (McAfee 2003, 206)); and 3. as exerting their own generative power in ways that shape embodied experience. To be clear, by embodiment I mean the sensorial, experiential, affective, and corporeal happenings that occur from being part of a technical assemblage in which biomedically extracted and processed genetic information intra-acts with knowledges and discourses about health as well as with the engaged biological and social body. This kind of analysis requires a socio-material lens, one that considers how these technologies work with embodied selves to change what is sensible to us outside of traditional binaries. Thus, to better understand GB and PN, I draw on new materialism to think about how these new biomedical and genetic assemblages shape phenomenal lived bodies that are always situated, gendered, raced, classed, and sexed. What is useful about this approach is that it is both anti-humanist and sensorial. Scholars of affect have taken great pains to emphasize how there is a particularity to human embodiment, thereby rejecting flat ontologies. What new materialism adds to this approach is a consideration of embodiment rooted in emancipatory politics (Grosz 1994). It also allows for an understanding of GB and hegemonic health as something which excites and impacts structures, subjectivities, surfaces, as well as the material specificities of biological functions and 'consequently … the space and matter-ing of the organic, fleshy and visceral endosoma' (Richardson and Harper 2006, 3).

There is always a danger that genetic biomedicalization and nutritional personalization will persist in extending the curation of informatic body objects wherein bodies are transformed into 'digital and mathematical constructs that can be redistributed, technologized, and capitalized' (Prentice 2012, 20). This negative potentiality, in addition to those listed above, is reflected in my definition of hegemonic 'good health' and are taken up in the case studies.

Overall, GB and PN promote an approach to the self that speaks to the desire to make the body understandable and transparent. This is done in pursuit of political economic objectives, namely profit, both in the form of expanded sites of commodification and the discursive and material production of healthy nation states supported by citizen subjects capable of working within these spaces. Also of note are the normative socio-cultural dimensions of GB and PN which are expressed in the elevation of white, male, cisgender, and able-bodied bodies as well as a belief in technology's capacity to 'make' health, as I have defined it, a reality for us all.

In this chapter I have articulated, unpacked, and justified in detail my definition of hegemonic 'good health' as *a co-produced state of idealized expectations, performances, embodiments, and patterns of consumption dominated by gendered and raced technophilic knowledge regimes that reproduce regimented and coercive Western standards of health and wellbeing.* GB and PN provide necessary ideological scaffolding in the form of technoscientific regimes that support this definition. Before engaging in a material-discursive, embodied, and auto-ethnographic examination of some of these technologies, in the next chapter I provide a necessary political economic overview of what I have termed the 'dietary-genomic-functional food industrial complex'.

2

Political economy of culture and the bio-techno-health industry

In this chapter, I provide a critical overview of the highly lucrative bio-techno-health sector using political economy of culture as the basic framework. As an erstwhile scholar of communication and culture, I argue that it is helpful to use some of the analytic tools in communication and media studies in executing this work. This approach requires mapping out the features of this sector, inclusive of its political and economic consequences, as well as the associated assumptions and ideologies about health and society that are being reproduced (Murdock and Golding 1973). Political economy of culture, as a method, facilitates this by accounting for how prevailing ideologies are concretized into objectifying ideas and transmitted through culture – i.e. through advertising, product placements, social media, news programming, and influencer tie-ins (Nixon 2012).

This approach is indebted to a Marxist understanding of how economic structures shape privileged ideologies. As such, it requires scrutinizing the way in which these structures connect to socio-economic interests – i.e. through ownership, market share, concentration, capitalization, etc. Put another way, the study of the political economy of culture consists of 'viewing culture from political economy, from the perspective of analysis of the system of production and distribution [which] may disclose how the culture industries reproduce the dominant corporate and commercial [health] culture, excluding discourses and images that contest the established social system' (Kellner and Durham 2012, xii). When applied to health, what becomes clear is that the capitalist economic structures that make up the health and wellness industry intersect with media technologies and other modes of representation in ways that perpetuate hegemonic and neoliberal health ideologies.

In what follows, I begin by engaging in some necessary infrastructural mapping followed by a general overview of what I have termed the 'dietary-genomic-functional (super)food industrial complex.' Next, I undertake a more focused analysis of the three sectors (health trackers, personalized diets, superfoods) that are applicable to this research. The products and services I draw on as case studies have been chosen because of their: 1. market share; 2. popularity (purchases, growth); 3. media coverage and media hype; and 4. corporate backing (i.e. through mergers/acquisitions, etc.). In addition to informing the reader of the corporate state of play, I also probe more deeply into the companies that stand out in order to make the case, in line with a political economy of culture approach, that the structure and organization of these firms perpetuate capitalist and neoliberal objectives. Which is to say that they do not operate in silos but are synergistically productive of ideologies and meanings reflected in hegemonic understandings of health (Garnham 1990; McChesney 2006). As Graham puts it, studying economic formations in this way allows for a better understanding of how 'values of all kinds are produced, distributed, exchanged, and consumed ... how power is produced, distributed, and exercised ... and how these aspects of the social world are related at any given place and time' (Graham 2006, 494). While scholars in this area, inclusive of Graham, Garnham, McChesney, and Mosco, all discuss the political economy of culture in relation to media specifically, I argue that a political economy of 'health' also benefits from this approach.

Overview

The number of technologies and companies that constitute the 'dietary-genomic-functional (super)food industrial complex' is enormous and covers corporate wellness, fitness, nutrition, supplements, beauty, selfcare, and foodstuffs. In 2018, what has come to be known as the 'health and wellness economy' was valued at $4 trillion – roughly 5 per cent of the world's economic output (Nelson 2019). The 2018 Global Wellness Trend Report puts the industry's valuation at $3.72 trillion where 'wellness' is used as an umbrella term to include everything from superfoods to athleisure as well as experiential and immersive fitness, personalized medicine, and wellness tourism. The report highlights the increasing significance of personalization, optimization, and biomedicalization stating that 'Our future will not be built on fossil fuel but on biology, and the wellness industry has a huge opportunity to lead the way' (Welltodo 2018, 6).

Homing in on some of the details, preventative and personalized medicine is currently estimated to generate $500 billion a year and includes genetic biomedicine as well as other associated lifestyle technologies (Raphael 2018). Notably, these numbers do not include health trackers and healthy eating – which pulls in upwards of $800 billion a year (note that healthy eating is generally not broken down by types of diets or foodstuffs in industry reports) (Statista 2021). As stated, the sectors that are of most interest to me with respect to health are personalized diets, health trackers, and superfoods. In the following sections, I investigate each of the sectors with particular attention paid to their production and reproduction of co-constructed hegemonic health ideologies.

Personalized diet industry

The personalized diet industry is profitable in its own right and is projected to be worth at least $11.5 billion by 2025 (Cavanah and McGroarty 2019). As stated in Chapter 1, most of the companies that sit within this sector use genetic testing or external DNA ancestry profiles to provide users with a diet and exercise plan that is tailored to their individual genetic makeup. These diets form part of a larger industry that fuses genetic biomedicalization with personalized nutrition. What makes these technologies so interesting is that they provide users with individual programmes, ostensibly customized for their biology, so that they can make the best use of their inheritance. This framing allows for the retention of the individual as the prototypical health subject capable of pursuing 'good health' by working within the limits set by their genetics (which are not seen as 100 per cent determining) (Henderson et al. 2009).

The major players in the personalized diet industry include Amway, Viome, Persona, Vitagene, Zipongo, Panaceutics Inc, Habit Food Personalized Inc., DNAfit, Mindbodygreen, Bayer AG, Bactolac Pharmaceutical Inc., Nutritional Genomix, and Biogeniq. Some of these companies fall within the domain of the personalized diet industry but do not rely on genetic testing as their primary method. This is the case with Bayer AG, the global pharmaceutical firm, who recently acquired Care/of – a company that is described as a personalized nutrition startup that relies on quizzes and questionnaires to produce a diet plan and which sells their own branded vitamins and supplements (Bayer Global 2020). While interesting in their own right, my focus is less on these kinds of firms and more on companies that use genetic data.

Like the superfood industry, personalized nutrition firms have been experiencing a boom period. Two of the most popular are DNAfit and Habit (or Habit Food Personalized). Habit is likely the most well-known personalized nutrition company that uses direct to home DNA kits as well as other measurements (of the body and some environmental metrics) to produce a unique nutritional profile for its users. Propensity for weight gain, sensitivity to caffeine, and food intolerances are some of the indicators reflected in their dietary plans (which also comes with recipes supported by AmazonFresh meal kits) which are used to place users with their appropriate 'food tribe' via the tracking app (personal support is also available). The company relies on SNPs (single nucleotide polymorphisms) to reach conclusions about customer responses to certain nutrients. Remember, however, that these findings have been reached based on the company's (limited) collection of other genetic profiles and population data. Moreover, this approach also elides nutrient gene interactions and assumes a linear model of gene expression (San-Cristobal, Milagro and Martinez 2013; Mutch et al. 2018). According to the *Academy of Nutrition and Dietetics*, many of the findings from services like Habit are 'not yet ready for routine dietary practice' largely because they are not sufficiently robust in assessing other factors that determine health and risk profiles (Camp and Tujillo 2014; also see Collier 2017). It is also important to keep in mind that DNA kits are only as good as the data they are compared to and that SNPs do not reflect the complexity of one's full genome. Concerns about how disease propensities are determined and how they are taken up by consumers, despite caveats that individuals should consult their physicians, can also pose ethical problems (Katwala 2019).

In 2019, Habit was acquired by Viome Inc., a health and personalized nutrition company focused on gut biome health. Habit is prototypical in reflecting the trend towards the integration of diet and nutrition with community and support. Corporate synergies, mergers, and horizontal integration allow for and encourage the centralization and concentration of capital while maintaining enough flexibility to take advantage of niche markets (Wayne 2003). This move creates the structural conditions for the reproduction of health norms that are ideologically in line with the neoliberal objectives necessary to keep corporations profitable (Fuchs 2009). The affordances of digital media supports this philosophy via their ability to capture the attention of users and organize digital spaces into 'institutional ecologies' that prioritize certain kinds of interactions, knowledge (i.e. through surveillance), conversations, and consumer habits. In this case, it includes ones that fit ideologically within the hegemonic model of good health. Habit's website, for example, promises to 'translate insights from your body into personalized nutritional recommendations to help address the root cause of inflammation, biological aging, and chronic disease' by 'decoding your body'. This is necessary, according to Habit, because 'our body's individual needs are far more unique to you than you could have imagined' (Viome 2021). The themes of personalization, genetic datafication, neoliberal responsibility, and technification can be found throughout much of the website's materials. What is important, and what this chapter aims to demonstrate, is that the structure of our new techo-health ecosystem, inclusive of its incentives, motivations, and reach, works to reinscribe our dominant health assemblage – one that fortifies capitalism, genetic biomedicalization, and personal nutritionism by setting out the appropriate background conditions and 'many other institutional arrangements that are needed to make [health] capitalism actually work' (Wright 2010, 35).

DNAfit is another company worth noting as an exemplar of this industry and which, similar to Habit (now rebranded 'Viome'), focuses on providing individual health and nutrition information using DNA testing kits (DNAfit 2021). DNAfit promises to provide actionable advice for an optimal diet – one that considers caffeine and carbohydrate sensitivity, food intolerances, and nutrient needs coupled with fitness-specific information like recovery, aerobic potential, and endurance. Also of note is DNAfit's launch of Elevate, an online fitness platform purportedly tailored to their customer's genes creating a tight synergy between health, diet, and fitness. Significantly, DNAFit's reports also includes disease risk and family planning. Taken together, their service is packaged in such a way so as to 'genetify' almost every aspect of their customer's lives in pursuit of, in their own words, 'smarter, easier and more effective solutions to health and fitness …' – ones that are 'entirely unique to your DNA profile' and personalized to offer 'a healthier and happier life' (DNAfit 2021). From a political economy of culture perspective, DNAfit, which was bought in 2018 by a larger firm headquartered in Beijing with offices in California and Massachusetts (showing how global these firms are), is organized so that one's socio-biological lifeworld entirely open for re-engineering. This re-engineering, to be clear, supports behaviours that reaffirm contemporary ideals of efficiency, profitability, and neoliberal human subjectivity. The 'dietary-genomic-functional (super)food industrial complex', of which DNAFit is a part, has the effect of enfolding our conceptions of good health into the objectives of industrious global capital. What should be made clear is that these firm operate in ways that reproduce social and economic norms around health by acting as 'shaping agents' – ones that 'favour certain interests, identities, agents, spatiotemporal horizons, tactics, strategies, and projects over others' (Sum and Jessop 2013, 48). They also form part of a health assemblage constituted by a turn to biogenetic and informational codes. Using new materialism, in which structures (political economy) and discourses are enmeshed into a new kind of ethico-onto-political epistemological practice, what becomes clear is how complex and confounding material entanglements are as well as the importance of thinking about the rise of dominant, materially resonant norms as products of affective forces, bodies, technological affordances, and agentially vibrant flows that coalesce in ways that can be shaped and re-shaped. 'Cutting together-apart', according to Barad, becomes a way to exert responsibility and 'act, together even if through fluid, fleeting, and constantly revised moments in motion' (Berbary 2020, 3; also see Barad 2014). Moreover, as Bennett, Cheah, Orlie, and Grosz argue, as much as 'we might welcome a broad transformation in lifestyle ... the norms, incentives, and identities people adopt inevitably become part of new disciplinary formations whose contours need to be specified and traced' (Bennett, Cheah, Orlie and Grosz 2010, 23). I have attempted to do precisely this here and will apply a similar approach in the following discussion of health trackers.

Health trackers

Health trackers constitute a substantial portion of the 'dietary-genomic-functional (super)food industrial complex' and tend to focus specifically on the dietary and functional dimensions of our contemporary hegemonic good health assemblage. Their focus on diet in the form of food intake and functional movement (through calories burned) works to enrol consumers into a hegemonic health philosophy. As it stands, the fitness tracker market is often described as a 'growth industry' and is projected to bring in just over $90 billion by 2027 (Fortune Business Insights 2020). These tools are most widely used by customers in the form of apps which can be downloaded to a smart phone/watch but can also exist as a standalone device – the latter of which tend to be used in the context of medical monitoring. My focus here is on health apps and watches (often tethered to smartphones) that function in a similar vein (i.e. they track and surveil).

The companies that comprise this sector are the largest in terms of profit, as well as being tightly integrated horizontally and vertically. The big players vis-à-vis activity and fitness include Apple, Google – inclusive of the Fitbit (which it bought in 2019 and Pebble Technology Corporation whose watch technology Fitbit bought prior to that), Samsung Electronics, Nike, Garmin (which leads on fitness and activity trackers as well as in location and mapping), and Xiaomi Technology (which manufactures wearable technologies as well as fitness and health trackers) (Allison 2018). These companies are structured for maximum profitability through lean supply chains, low pay, exploitative working conditions, and high prices as Daniel Cooper notes in his exposé on the industry titled, 'You Can't Buy An Ethical Smartphone Today' (Cooper 2018). While Cooper's analysis focuses on smartphones specifically, health trackers follow this business model closely and are often owned by the same company. Xiaomi is an interesting case in that its popularity and profitability is a result of their low-cost and large product range supported by low labour costs. Know the Chain, a not-for-profit corporate tracking group, notes this in its profile of the company in which states that Xiaomi 'does not disclose a commitment to addressing forced labour, nor does it have a policy prohibiting forced labor in its supply chains' (KnowTheChain 2020; also see Kronfli 2021).

This is also in keeping with Google's product line, which has been found to be produced under exploitative conditions including overwork, underpay, and unsafe working conditions by its own internal eight-country investigation (Wong 2021). Also of note is the controversy surrounding Google's acquisition of Fitbit, which consumer advocacy groups, academics, and activists fear will result in the further monetizing of citizen health data and cause harm through a form of 'platform envelopment' leading to the 'extension of monopoly power and consumer [data] exploitation'. Other concerns include worries that the 'combination of Fitbit's health data with Google's other data' will create 'unique opportunities for discrimination and exploitation of consumers in healthcare, health insurance and other sensitive areas, with major implications for privacy too' (Bourreau et al. 2020). This is a significant and pervasive concern – particularly under conditions of digital capitalism in which antitrust laws are rarely applied and issues of data privacy accede to profitability and the objectives of the digital economy (Foster and McChesney 2014; Fuchs 2020). While I return to the subject of privacy later, it is important to note that the access Fitbit has to sensitive health data, when coupled with the vast trove of information Google already has on the general public, is troubling. This collection, as Shoshana Zuboff argues, amounts to an epistemic coup in which data is used 'for the sake of predictions that become more lucrative as they approach certainty' (Zuboff 2020).

Fitbit is also marketed as 'innovative', 'motivational', and '*mindful*' – with endorsements from noted health gurus like Deepak Chopra. Their website greets users with the statement: 'meet the app that puts a world of health & fitness in your hands' and emphasizes that it is supported by a company for whom 'health and fitness come first' (Fitbit 2021). Fitbit represents a prototypical example of a company that has successfully integrated economic consolidation with semiotic encodings that inscribe the hegemonic good health assemblage. One that relies on a neoliberal responsibilization of the individual, focuses on technological solutions, emphasizes ideal bodily comportment, and grounds wellbeing in consumption and consumerism. As Fotopoulou and O'Riordan argue, there 'is more at stake than behavioural change and individual well-being ... these are normative devices ... aimed at teaching users how to be [particular kinds of] good consumers and biocitizens' (Fotopoulou and O'Riordan 2017, 55). A lot has been written about Fitbit as a technology of health using biocapitalism and/ or subject producing discursive enrolments as its analytic lens (Banner 2017; Owens and Cribb 2019). The size, popularity, and branding of this technology mean that it cannot be ignored. My focus in the case study chapters however, focuses on some of the more emerging technologies which I contend have been overlooked vis-à-vis their impact on health norms despite having a growing user base.

There are a host of other trackers on the market that are more affordable and accessible than Fitbit and which do not require more than a smartphone. The food trackers include apps like MyFitnessPal, Calorie Counter Pro, Healthy Out, and Noom – all of which focus on monitoring nutrition. Noom is an interesting case since it is currently in the top five of the 'most downloaded health apps' list and the only one that the CDC has certified to provide virtual health services like diabetes monitoring. The app I find most interesting is MyFitnessPal, an app that provides access to a detailed database of nutritional metrics for various food and funnels this data into goal-specific calculations of users' daily intake, meals, and activity levels. It also allows for the scanning of barcodes and has cultivated a space for an expansive social community of users (upwards of 200 million) where they can engage, share and support one another. MyFitnessPal was owned by the large sport and clothing company Under Armour in 2014 but was then sold to an investment firm, Francisco Partners, shortly thereafter (Evans 2016; Muolo 2020).

MyFitnessPal's priority, as articulated on their website, is to allow users to 'Take control of your goals. Track calories, break down ingredients, and log activities' (MyFitnessPal 2021). Motivation, understanding, and goal achievement are highlighted, as is their community which is grounded in an ethic of 'feeling better, looking better, and living better' (MyFitnessPal 2021). This discursive framing of the app is supported by persistent self-responsibilization which involves enrolling users into health subjectivities grounded in quantifiable data and numbers. It also encourages a form of interpersonal surveillance, what Kent calls 'intervisibility', as a core part of identity construction (Kent 2020). The production of this kind of subjectivity is essential for the functioning of the capitalist system – one that is productive, performance-oriented, and gathers over mineable data. The disciplining MyFitnessPal engenders is consistent with the biopolitical scientization of food and movement which prioritizes quantification over other kinds of knowledge, producing what Mudry calls 'a new ontology of food' and exercise rooted in nutritionism (Mudry 2009).

The platform itself, while permitting user interaction, is structurally oriented to the aggregation and selling of personal data and is interoperable with larger companies and services in order to capture market share (Smicek 2017; Williams, Will, Weiner and Henwood 2020). Hegemonic good health is constructed through these kinds of structural economic imperatives and discursive articulations that 'operates by abstracting human bodies from their territorial settings and separating them into a series of discrete [and profitable data] flows' (Haggerty and Ericson 2000, 606). This latter phenomenon, which results in the production of even more lucrative data doubles (where data doubles are defined as datafied digital doppelgangers capable of being reflected upon and exploited), draws us back into a discussion of how new materialism is best suited to re-articulate these economic-discursive insights into a framework that also pays attention to the onto-epistemologies of matter and the possibility for change. This includes the consideration of contingent and unpredictable forces, gendered and raced intra-actions, and the exploration of platforms as agential (Warin and Hammarström 2018). Spliced into this assemblage are the cuts I have made which provide an opening for an even more embodied (and later auto-ethnographic) accounting of techno-human intra-actions. One that see emotions, affect, and experience not as the property of a contained self, but as emerging out of relations between the forces, objects, and artefacts in this health assemblage (Braidotti 2013b). This approach, as Fox and Aldred put it, 'establishes a perspective upon the world as continuously *emergent* via a series of interactive and productive events/assemblages, rather than founded upon stable structures or systems' (Fox and Aldred 2019, 4).

What is important to keep in mind for all these technologies is the pervasiveness with which hegemonic good health is embedded into these technological assemblages and the significance of learning about how economic structures and imperatives shape health norms. Remember, however, that, in line with new materialism, this is not a unidirectional mode of shaping but one that elicits phenomena that emerge out of a complex, rhizomatic network of actors, agents, humans, non-humans, and objects. From this assemblage, what has materialized are companies that reflect values, motives, and agendas consistent with capitalist exploitation and neoliberal individualism. This is the result of an alignment of forces that function best under our current socio-economic conjuncture. Political economy of culture, functioning as a particular kind of cut, allows for a momentary stabilizing of these forces so that power and ideology can be focused on. I argue that this is an important part of understanding the micropolitics of hegemonic good health and its emergence as a health norm that facilitates capitalism's functioning while also being co-constituted with capitalism.

Before moving on to superfoods, a short aside is needed vis-à-vis one of the most telling instantiations of economic imperatives acting as a force via *discourse* as it applies to health trackers – namely, the Quantified Self (QS) movement. Self-identified 'Quantified Self-ers' constitute a subculture complete with a robust online community and in-person gatherings. They adhere to a philosophy of intensive self-tracking in order to achieve health transparency and optimization through digital feedback loops and biohacking (Wired 2009). In essence, 'QS supports the notion that various self-tracking tools and applications, including emotion trackers, food trackers, and pedometers, offer an effective opportunity for people to understand their bodies, minds, and daily lives as a series of quantifications that can be examined and acted upon' (Ruckenstein and Pantzar 2017, 402). The reason I bring it up here, in addition to setting up its significance for the case studies, is to make clear how movements like QS function as hegemonic health force multipliers wherein users perform free labour by carefully imputing data and forming communities useful for marketing purposes. As Barta argues, 'Members are savvy enough to understand the enormous market potential for personal data (health or otherwise) and are yet optimistic about how such data is transformed within sharing communities, either ones of their own choosing and making, like QS Meetups, or of network effects' (Barta and Neff 2014, 4). This is an important insight in that it thematizes user agency which, in the context of some of the analyses of economic forces, makes resistance possible.

In the next section, I provide an overview of the superfood sector including the major actors, economic interests, and prevailing discourses necessary to understand the case studies in later chapters. It also demonstrates how a hegemonic conception of good health, as I have defined it, emerges out of our contemporary assemblage of vital intra-acting forces that have aligned in particular ways. Central to this movement, according to Lemke, 'is the extension of the concept of agency and power to non-human nature, thereby also calling into question conventional understandings of life' (Lemke 2015, 4). I demonstrate how this works in practice through new materialist auto-ethnographic studies of these technologies.

Superfoods

Superfoods are image-rich, highly mediated, and Western-centric consumer products represented in specific ways inside the of the global north. Earlier, I shared some statistics about the rise in their consumption and market share which sits in the billions. The major players include smaller firms, such as OMG! Organic Meets Good, Healthy Truth, and Nutiva Inc., as well as ones attached to larger 'known' conglomerates such as Del Monte Pacific Limited, and General Mills (Intrado 2020). Unfortunately, some of the best breakdowns of the industry (in industry reports) are paywalled. Added to this barrier, in relation to accessing information, is the fact that many of these companies, in particular startups, are not listed and therefore are not required to be as financially transparent. There is also a distinction that needs to be made between the most profitable and well-known companies versus the most highly regarded (as in transparent, 'ethical'). The latter companies rest much of their reputation on ethical sourcing and quality, while those that are much smaller tend to make lighter claims (Papacharalampous 2017). Many individual countries have their own local brands and superfood products whose popularity, and profitability, waxes and wanes (Meyerding, Kürzdörfer, and Gassler 2018; Peña-Lévano, Adams and Burney 2021).

As a sector there are hundreds of superfood companies globally, with a jumble of names (many of which overlap), and, as stated, changing ownership structures. They are also structured to pivot quite quickly based on trends which makes providing a stable snapshot of the field rather difficult. Take, for example, the case of popular Australian superfood company Slendier Slim which began by selling products that incorporated the vegetable Konjac into wheat-based products and which quickly grew into a multi-million dollar company with ambitions to expand globally. The company itself, which front-ends its own origin story of health and wellness, now *appears* to have expanded to also sell muscle stimulation machines as part of a health package to 'help you with your fitness goals' and 'achieve the break you deserve from dieting' (Brett 2012; Slendier Slim 2021). And yet, it is unclear whether the stimulation machines are part of the superfood company, whether there is a distinction between Slendier and Slendier Slim, and who now owns the company. After some digging, it appears that Slendier, owned by Erica Hughes, is distinct from Slendier Slim which is a separate health and wellness company. I include this solely to illustrate the 'messiness' of this sector which, appropriately, pairs well with its discursive/ definitional messiness (i.e. vis-à-vis what is a superfood).

An important uniting trend in this sector is that of creeping corporate consolidation. There have been a host of mergers and acquisitions over the past few years in the superfood industry. This includes Nestle's purchase of Terrafertil, a superfood company specializing in Andean goldenberries, Archer Daniels Midland acquiring Yerbalatina Phytoactives, which produces plant-based extracts, and General Mills forming a partnership with GoodBelly, a probiotic and cereal firm (kbv research 2020; O.W.N. News Network 2018). From a political economy point of view, this pattern of larger companies acquiring smaller ones is in keeping with a monopolistic corporate strategy that will inevitably lead to a few corporate giants dominating the superfood landscape. Importantly, this domination spans the tangible *and* the semiotic. PepsiCo's 2018 acquisition of Health Warrior, a superfood snack company, acts as a prime example of this phenomenon. Symbolically, it serves to displace some of PepsiCo's bad press as it relates to the healthfulness of its key products by diversifying into more 'health conscious' product lines.

Health Warrior is a relatively new company (founded in 2010) that uses superfoods (chia seeds, pumpkin seeds, dark chocolate) as key ingredients in its energy bars. Unlike other companies, Health Warrior minimizes the exoticism of superfoods and, instead, plays into hegemonic good health by arguing that its bars aim to 'fuel the world's health momentum with delicious, seed-forward foods' (Health Warrior 2021a). Its literature features busy working parents and emphasizes their use of authentic, quality ingredients which can be eaten 'between matches, meets and games to meetings and day care pick-ups' (Health Warrior 2021b). What is important to point out here is that what remains constant – namely, health as something you can, and must, consume. Josée Johnston, Andrew Biro, and Norah MacKendrick call this the 'corporate-organic foodscape' and, in their research, call for a more 'sophisticated understanding … of the complex relationship between social movement innovation [e.g. the rise of health oriented companies] and market adaptation [e.g. conglomerates buying them up]' (Johnston, Biro, and MacKendrick 2009).

A different strategy is taken by Teraferil's Nature's Heart Superfoods (of which Nestlé now holds a majority stake). The company was founded in Ecuador by five entrepreneurs in the early aughts and expanded quickly throughout parts of South America. The company prides itself on working with small farmers, being recognized for its positive social impact, and highlights that its founding members, who are still involved, continue to reside in Ecuador (Nestlé 2018). What is most interesting about Nestlé's acquisition, in addition to exemplifying the trend towards deeper corporate consolidation, is the very different symbolic coding the company relies on as compared to Health Warrior. Currently, Nature's Heart (2020) draws heavily on an idealized construction of the proximate Global South as untouched, pristine, 'serene, sun-blessed'. Their website feature images of lush farmland and highlights the company's use of family farmers, 'who sell us their freshly picked goldenberries in return for a regular and sustainable second income'.

In engaging with this part of their website, two things immediately come to mind: first is the disclosure of the irregular nature of the employment they offer, since the producers all appear to be contractors (which is a problem in and of itself), and second is the discursive treatment of their goldenberries, maca, cacao, and chia products, which act as synecdoches for the authentic, back to nature ethos of the company. Discursive constructions of this sort are not new and are rooted in a form of engagement with the Other that is, 1. controlled, 2. reflective of mythical origin stories, and 3. enactive of a kind of enlightened moral cosmopolitanism (Emontspool and Georgi 2017; Finn 2017). These foods thus become indigenized as markers of local cuisine in ways that construct distant cultures as static and open to profitable co-optation. Engaging with Otherness through food thus becomes a way in which to control and render the Other intelligible by 'making subjects by means of objects' (Comaroff and Comaroff 1997, 218; also see Counihan and Van Esterik 2012). Real people engaging in labour are thus invisibilized as is the social contexts in which superfoods are consumed. For superfood scholars like Jessica Loyer, this impulse is deeply imbricated in colonialism and cultural imperialism in ways that 'celebrate cultural continuity but do not account for the way in which poverty [for example] developed in the region' (Loyer 2016, 132).

Additionally, the company's description of superfoods as 'antioxidant rich, "equivalent of a multivitamin" and "brimming with nutrients"' works to decontextualize food and health and reduce the former to the latter. This continues despite the fact that, as Mintz puts it, 'cherished tastes are rooted in underlying economic and social conditions … [that] … are surely far more than simply nutritive' (Mintz 1996, 24). From this analysis, what becomes clear is that the appropriative control of food chains constitute an important site of research – particularly as it relates to the oligopolistic control of what foods are available and how this has hindered innovation, inflated prices, pushed out local producers, and endangered the resiliency of food systems (Dixon 2003; Gillespie and Van den Bold 2017). A robust understanding of the dialectical between superfood-specific symbolic formations and intra-acting economic structures explains the emergence of health nature–culture matterings that are neoliberal, technophilic, colonial, and racialized (Haraway 2013).

Significantly, drawing out a few more points vis-à-vis corporate consolidation, the very properties and characteristics that have made superfoods popular, including transparency, personal connection, rootedness, and 'naturalness', tend to be watered down when they are acquired by larger firms. Dean Foods, for example, when it acquired Silk – the organic soymilk company – in 2009 began using non-organic soybeans to control costs and, while it removed the 'organic' label, 'kept the same Silk packaging and the same universal product code so most consumers and retailers did not know the difference' (note that Silk is now owned by Danone) (Woodall and Shannon 2018, 218). The promise of quality as it relates to superfoods is important since it is this property that is their principal selling point (Dreher 2018).

Another important aspect of the political economy of superfoods worth returning to briefly is reflected in the drive to consolidate and is expressed in the fate of local producers – many of whom live in the Global South. This organizational accretion impacts the symbolic value of superfoods whose effects are felt on several levels – beginning with commercialization. Many of the foods we think of as superfoods are traditional, Indigenous, and meant to be consumed under certain conditions for a local population. When a particular superfood gains popularity, they begin to be produced on a larger scale, resulting in inflated shipping costs, higher CO_2 emissions, possible soil depletion, land clearing (as in the case of the Mexican avocado), and the very real possibility of extinction (particularly superfoods in their natural/wild form, e.g. morel mushrooms and American ginseng) (Global Forest Watch 2019; Gilford 2020). Local supplies can dwindle, since regional markets are no longer seen as viable, and prices tend to increase – which is what occurred with Peruvian and Bolivian quinoa in producing countries at the height of its boom about a decade ago (Parker-Gibson 2015; Gamboa et al. 2017). Consequently, many of these crops (which are niche in the west) and the farmers who produce them suffer from boom and bust cycles – especially with superfoods that have a faddish quality to them. This occurred with quinoa when demand dropped slightly in 2015 and which, when coupled with global oversupply, had an overall negative effect on the financial stability of farmers (AFP 2018).

Yet, it should be noted that some retrospective analyses of the quinoa case have challenged the more negative conclusions. A study using data from a national survey in Peru, for example, revealed that, overall, farmers had benefited socio-economically from the quinoa superfood trend (Bellemare, Fajardo-Gonzales and Glitter 2018). Suffice to say, each individual superfood paints a different picture requiring an examination of their conditions of cultivation, procurement, transport, purchase, and consumption. This is something political economy is well placed to do. For now, what is important to keep in mind is how the economic organization of superfoods as an industry, with its creeping concentration, profit focus, exploitation, and expansion of consumer centrism, has contributed to the hegemonic ideology of good health I have been so critical of thus far.

A further issue of significance is that of labour practices in the form of low pay, overwork, child labour, and land grabs (Govinnage 2014; Billon and Shykora 2020). While mechanisms have been implemented to certify the ethicality of superfood production (often industry-led), these products remain fetishized and function as ethical signifiers irrespective of how they are actually produced. Superfood companies are quick to highlight their social justice bona fides which allows consumers to 'self-identify as people who resist the inequality of the free market and who wish for a more just world' – yet remain implicated in cycles of exploitation based on an underlying economic structure that fragments, disconnects, and drives consumption (Loyer 2016, 133; also see Scheiemer 2018).

A couple of more general notes on the settler colonial dimensions of superfood economies that deserve to be highlighted include, first, the ideological repackaging of old stereotypes of the exotic Other as untouched by hypercapitalism and thus more connected with nature and the secrets of the good life (Hussey and Curnow 2013; Loyer and Knight 2018). This assumption is folded into discourses of ancestry (i.e. this food is our common heritage since we all come from the same place) and is discursively packaged as consistent with contemporary society's post-racial social order. Moreover, as Brondizio argues, these articulations are tied to discourses of development in which consumption of superfoods (acai in their article) is seen as key to combatting underdevelopment (Brondizio 2004).

Second is an update to an older idea related to difference that facilitates 'safe' contact with the 'Other' as a 'cultural resource always available to be consumed by more power members of the geo-political core' (Johnston and Baumann 2010, 102). bell hooks' canonical concept of 'Eating the Other' describes this phenomenon which operates by 'dull[ing] [the] dish that is mainstream culture' in ways that 'not only displaces the Other, but denies the significance of that Other's history through a process of decontextualization' (hooks 1992, 21–31). Generally, superfoods are consumed as prototypical consumer products and used as a means through which to facilitate self-development in line with hegemonic health norms. Yet, it should be noted that not everything about superfood consumption can be reduced to the agency of economic structures, their discursive articulation, or the synergistic intra-action between the two. In subsequent chapters I leave ample room for an exploration of the ways in which pleasure and engagement might result in spite of these forces.

Updates to hooks' framework by scholars like Lisa Heldke and Lucy Long expand its focus by examining the exoticization of the Other through food as in the case of food tourism and food adventurism which often ends up with customers experiencing healthified exotic difference in the form of a smoothie rather than through relations of sharing, care, and respect (Long 2008; Heldke 2015). Examining superfoods through a political economic lens requires that we examine the semiotic meaning of superfoods as substances and services that purport to help mould one's body to conform to neoliberal definitions of the good life. Again, it remains the case that these ideals often reflect the priorities of existing capitalist economic structures. Also important are the myriad means through which these messages are able to stabilize and replenish the prevailing economic order. Taken together, I argue that commercialism, concentration, and capitalist commodity (superfood) fetishism adds an important layer of complexity to south–north commodity circuits and supply chains made legible by culturally infused political economic analysis. This schema takes as its operating assumption that contemporary hegemonic conceptions of good health (constituted by commodity fetishism, neoliberal individualism, consumerism, whiteness, and Western-centrism) have emerged as our culture's dominant health assemblage because of the particular alignment of flows, vitalities, objects, humans, structures, and nonhumans that have become dominant.

Conclusion

In this chapter, I have provided an analysis and overview of what I have termed the 'dietary-genomic-functional (super)food industrial complex' using a political economy of culture approach. I have grounded this standpoint on a new materialist scaffolding in which the co-constituting structures and ideologies highlighted form an important part of our hegemonic health assemblage. The trackers, biogenetic diet services, and superfoods discussed above, as categories and individual companies, draw much needed attention to the impact of corporate consolidation, monopolies, supply chains, north–south relations, profits, and capitalism in producing our contemporary health subjectivity. Hegemonic good health, along with these technologies co-construct an ideal subject that is efficient and industrious as a worker; effectively responsibilized; quant-inclined and techno-curious as a health subject; and ethical and mindful as a cosmopolitan consumer. In the following chapters, I draw on a similar framework in the first instance before turning to one rooted in new materialism and posthuman auto-ethnography to provide an affective and embodied account of hegemonic health using a health tracker, personalized diet, and superfood to ground this analysis before exploring possible alternatives.

3

Case study one: Aduna's baobab fruit

In this chapter, I take a deep dive into Aduna (2021a), a UK-based superfood company. I begin with a political economic-discursive examination of the company, drawing on publicly accessible information, its website, and the case it put forward to prospective investors in 2018. As laid out in my overview of the methodology, I use a political economy of culture approach combined with discourse analysis in order to intensify ideology critique and construct a comprehensive account of how our contemporary health hegemony 'shows up' and intra-acts within and through this particular assemblage. Tracing how contemporary health ideologies emerge out of the production of superfood commodities becomes the basis from which a robust analysis of the presence and salience of our dominant good health hegemony is made manifest. Also part of this chapter is a deep analysis of two agential cuts in which I examine issues of subcultures, health norms, the environment, and social justice as well as a set of auto-ethnographic reflections based on my two-week consumption of this product. Here, I discuss issues around Otherness and exoticism, the performance of food choice, community, health vulnerabilities, and neoliberalized personal responsibility.

Baobab: Political economy of culture and discourse analysis

Aduna is a small but thriving private, 'later-stage' VC (venture capitalist) firm founded in 2011 with its primary office in London. It retails a wide range of superfood products from nutritional bars to supplementary powders. Its owners and co-founders, Andrew Hunt and Nick Salter, are 'reformed' corporate execs whose experiences in Senegal and The Gambia inspired them to establish the company. It is telling that the company's 'founding story' (as chronicled on its website) is grounded in Salter and Hunt's own personal narratives of self-discovery and redemption. Hunt, for example, spent several years in Senegal working with farmers before coming together with Salter to work out how they could, in their own words, 'transform this obscure product [baobab] into a globally-recognised superfruit that could provide a sustainable income to an estimated 10 million rural households' (Aduna 2021b).

Aduna's valuation, prior to its latest round of equity crowdfunding (EQ), was £3.7 million. In the most recent round, in July of 2018, Aduna attracted $449.4K of investment. EQ allows investors to get in early on emerging, unlisted companies in which shares are traded in exchange for monetary investment. EQ offerings are often couched in the language of democratic participation (anyone can invest) through which industriousness and ingenuity are rewarded. Adjacent trends include that of crowdsourcing, the sharing economy, and co-production in which 'ideas, knowledge and otherwise idle assets are made available and accessed by geographically distributed online communities' (Langley 2016, 304). Scholars of political economy have been critical of this kind of platformization (Casilli and Posada 2019). This is because, despite claims of openness and its association with charity and the gift economy (i.e. crowdfunding, peer to peer business lending, alternative finance), equity crowdsourcing is dominated by the usual actors – mostly male, white, Western, and affluent investors – and is constituted by circuits of exchange that tend to resemble that of traditional market economies. Which is to say that it is just as abstract, extractive, and reflective of conventional capitalist relations (Baeck, Collins and Zhang 2014; Langley 2018).

This is important from a political economy perspective because it reveals a tension between narratives that legitimize the objectives of purportedly post-capitalist, care-oriented companies and the reality of their market orientation. This tension is addressed directly by Aduna on its crowdsourcing listing (on the Seedrs website), in which it states that it, as a company, works hard to pursue 'ethical profitability'. They promise investors direct access to a company in which 'profit meets purpose' and for whom 'conscious consumerism', in the form of 'positive social and environmental impact', is part of their corporate ethos.

This represents a transparent use of discursive framing in that it seeks to communicate the objective of the company – to make a profit – but in a way that is more palatable to socially conscious investors. Their intention (again, from the Seedrs listing) is to combine 'major commercial opportunity with social impact – in equal measure' (Seedrs 2018). This assertion of an equivalency between economic interest and ethics is a discursive frame popular in environmental communication (i.e. sustainable development) which, when examined closely, reveals itself to be contradictory since it relies on the belief that capitalist economic formations can be both sustainable *and* economically rational. This involves, particularly with superfoods, a redefining of foodstuffs and nature as 'an element of valuable capital, present within the world productive system, and itself to be rationally managed as a productive enterprise' (O'Connor 1993, 10). The power required to maintain this assembled dispositif, and ensure its acceptance, is based on its knowledge-producing capacities such that the power to articulate it ensures that it becomes hegemonic (Jäger 2001; Foucault 2007).

It is important to remember that Aduna exists as part of a larger constellation of similar companies that rely on analogous discourses to ensure stability of meaning. As Weiss and Wodak argue, these dominant discourses help 'to sustain and reproduce the social status quo … that is, they can help produce and reproduce unequal power relations between (for instance) social classes, women and men, and ethnic/cultural majorities and minorities through the ways in which they represent things and position people' (Fairclough and Wodak 1997, 258). This exemplifies the process by which hegemonic good health becomes entrenched since '*text production equals [capitalist] system reproduction*' (Weiss and Wodak 2007, 10 italics in original). I would add a caveat, however, by underlining the fact that while discourse forms part of a larger constellations of structures, relations, objects, humans, and norms, it is important to remember how economic structures work dialectically with discourses to co-produce dominant values such as those contained within our current health hegemony. It is not insignificant that hegemonic health (reminder: *a co-produced state of idealized expectations, performances, embodiments, and patterns of consumption dominated by gendered and raced technophilic knowledge regimes that reproduce regimented and coercive Western standards of health and wellbeing*) has been able to maintain a tight control on health norms and values. I contend that this is due, in large part, to a fortuitous alignment of prevailing discourses and capitalist political economic formations.

The majority of discourse analysis I performed on Aduna centres on its website since it is the most forward-facing manifestation of the company. The analysis completed thus far lies more squarely with its economic imperatives which fits nicely with a political economy of culture approach. In examining the website, hegemonic good health is used as the guiding discursive frame through which to study Aduna's emergence as a company for whom health has become a site of neoliberal, consumer-centric, and functional practices supported by political economic structures that facilitate system stabilization.

To begin with, Aduna's baobab product should be seen as part of a constellation of identified and idealized practices consistent with health-centric 'expectations, performances, embodiments, and patterns of consumption'. It does not, as new materialism makes clear, exist independently or outside of a larger network of forces, institutions, structures, norms, and ideologies. The place in which hegemonic health makes itself most felt is on the product's purchasing page where details about the fruit, inclusive of health claims, are first asserted. For example, a piece titled, '5 reasons to love baobab powder' is presented so that states of being are connected directly to the consumption of nutrients. Arrows pointing to the packaged product proclaim its link to immunity, gut health, energy, skin health, and impact. Connected to each of these are corresponding nutrients: vitamin C for immunity, prebiotic fibre for gut health, vitamin C for energy, antioxidants for skin health (collagen formation), and, for good measure, sustainable incomes for impact. Hegemonic health's reliance on a discourse of nutritionism, or what Loyer calls 'nutritional primitivism', fits seamlessly into Aduna's construction of baobab as a nutritional powerhouse 'rich in fibre and vitamin C' (Loyer 2016). Yet, the company also strives to balance this nutritionism by paying attention to social context, which Biltekoff et al. argue tends to be left out of hegemonic health's 'Overton window'.

This nutritional qua lifestyle breakdown (or reductionism) is in keeping with larger desires and expectations reflected in hegemonic good health; namely, the 'simultaneous aspiration to achieve aesthetic refinement, nutritional superiority, ethical and ecological responsibility, and cosmopolitan chic' (Finn 2017, 19). Health regimes that include superfood products tend to be taken on by individuals with ample disposable income for whom, as Finn elaborates, sophistication, thinness, purity, and cosmopolitanism are important values.

Race and racialization are particularly important factors to consider with respect to how health is constructed by Aduna and the role it plays in reproducing racial knowledge regimes and 'Western standards of health and wellbeing'. On the level of straightforward *representation*, not much can be said as there are no images of board members or employees available to get a sense of the company's racial or gender diversity. What is clear, however, and worth repeating, is that both co-founders – who serve as the forward-facing representatives of the company – are white men. While I return to the significance of representation further on, I would be remiss if I did not mention here that mere diversity, i.e. bodies in chairs, is limited in its capacity to challenge the [health] status quo (Lee 2003). Drawing in people of colour to operate within a system that is hostile and exploitative can function as a box-ticking exercise, or what Nirmal Purwar calls 'the inclusion of people who look different' without 'changing values, cultures, and priorities' (Puwar 2004, 1; also see Wills 2001; Ahmed 2007).

As stated, racialization should be understood as a process through which racial difference is (re)produced and used to justify unequal power relations. Race, as a discourse *and* material relation, circulates throughout Aduna's website via text and images in ways that are difficult to capture. Examining the presence and absence of race through CDA required a close reading of text and image in order to reveal the presence of racialization, how it is embedded, how it functions, and the ways in which it reproduces inequality. It is important to keep in mind that examinations of racialization through discursive analysis cannot be disconnected from material forces. New materialism requires that racial 'spacetimematerrings' are cut in ways that highlight its fluidity and multi-dimensionality (Henderson and Solutions 2015).

The places in which people (largely women) of colour *visually* appear on the website are concentrated in three areas. First, is in the 'Our Mission' section in which smiling Black African women are shown carrying baobab in a basket on the heads. Also on this page is a sole Black male employee who is posing for the camera with the founders and holding up a sign that says 'feel good' in a forward-facing shot. On another page, we see a gallery of clickable images that introduces consumers to the producers – all of whom are smiling and in traditional dress. Even more images of (Black women) producers with embedded interviews (in text) can be found on a page titled 'Meet the Producers'. Questions posed to the women include the number of members in their households, life before and after they began to work for Aduna (all very positive), and their favourite use of baobab. Second, situated below the founders' story and acting as a sort of banner image on most pages, is an image of a Black woman in traditional, brightly coloured dress lying down in front of a tree, laughing, with a container of baobab powder placed on her stomach. Directly below is a link to the company's mission statement, which contains a host of assertions worth noting in the context of race and health (discussed below).

The significance of these visuals vis-à-vis race and hegemonic health is rooted in their implicit claims to represent a movement away from modern and despoiling forms of being, inclusive of health, and towards an existence that is prosocial, organic, and emergent. Here, racialized Otherness intersects with gender in rendering positive the acts of those who purchase baobab by intimating that support for this company will identify consumers as ethical, social, and healthy subjects. The use of these kinds of images for commercial purposes transfers moral capital onto Aduna's products so that they function as signifiers of social change. However, Mohanti, in a trenchant critique of this kind of instrumentalization, argues that 'the existence of "third world women's" narratives in itself is not evidence of decentering hegemonic histories and subjectivities. It is the way in which they are read, understood and located institutionally which is of paramount importance' (Mohanti 1991, 34). Moreover, it is important to note that Aduna's consumers tend to be white, educated, and affluent – as is the case with most demographics interested in superfood products (Sikka 2019; Menezes, Deliza, Chan and Guinard 2011).

Finally, turning to moving images, back on the 'About Us' page, a video is embedded which features dancing and singing women in a village setting – one of whom is interviewed. She tells a story about how working as a baobab farmer has allowed her to support her family and sidestep corrupt practices that prevented her from maintaining a stable and safe livelihood. The video closes with the #makebaobabfamous hashtag and a call for the public to become involved in making baobab into an economically viable product. The video states: 'If there was a global demand for baobab this existing crop could be worth a billion dollars to rural Africa.' This framing of structural poverty as something that can be tackled, at least in part, through individual acts of consumption is in keeping with neoliberal justifications of consumerism. It is notable that nothing is said about the pay these women receive (what is a 'life-changing sustainable income stream', for example? and are there provisions for sick pay?), any environmental impacts, and who is in control of work processes. This framing infuses neoliberal sentiments with a form of health consciousness that, in keeping with hegemonic good health, seeks to reproduce what we might have experienced in an idealized and mythic past. But, as Aduna assures its consumers, these exotic ingredients are not entirely untouched by modern processes. They are filtered through *Aduna*, a trusted Western company (who it is implied is in charge of processing and shipping – it is actually outsourced), so that consumers can purchase their products with the assurance that the state of wellbeing they seek is socially (and racially) conscious while also being in line with the nutritionist and healthist expectations of Western society (Heldke 2015; Dreher 2018).

The imbrication of health and race as it relates to these visual representations is also reflected in the construction of health as a state of being that exists in and through geographic rootedness. This comes up again in the context of personalized diets – particularly when they are based on ancestral categories that correlate with geographic regions that intuitively map onto race. Following this logic, it is notable that contemporary hegemonic health discourse, unlike in the case of apps and genetic technologies, is made manifest through the fetishization of the Other rooted in colonial constructions of 'the "authentic" and "exotic" Africa' (hooks 2019, 46), and which results in a kind of 'looking' that always 'threaten[s] to dehumanize and colonize' (hooks 2019, 6). Consuming baobab becomes a means by which to connect to an idealized past during which health was emergent and organic. Underlying this is a form of colonial nutritionism that McDonell describes as having the ability to decontextualize individual 'charismatic' nutrients just enough so as to lay claim to authentic and autochthonous health. Health that is simultaneously natural *and* modern, justice-oriented *and* body conscious (Kimura 2013b; McDonell 2015). Consumers thus get the best of all worlds – an ability to feel as though they are resisting neoliberal body norms, registering their anti-racism (via enlightened consumerism), and obtaining results that are aesthetically pleasing and normatively desirable.

Textual references to race on Aduna's website is even more tacit. In fact, race is not mentioned once – anywhere. Instead, Africa, as a continent, functions as a geographic proxy for race – a common rhetorical tactic. This discursive displacement also occurs in the case of genetics, albeit on a more granular level. Here, references are made to 'Africa's' diversity, being 'home to 25 per cent of the world's botanical species, including some of the most nutrient-rich superfoods in the world'. Its landscapes are described as 'rich' and 'natural', and as hiding nutritional secrets, which are 'little known outside of the continent' (Aduna 2021b). Interview excerpts with the women workers highlight their relations with the baobab tree, which one describes as 'like a helpful friend' (Babuya 2021) and another as an 'amazing gift' (Guraseh 2021) that 'has many benefits' (Woebapora 2021). These sentiments are adumbrated in other parts of the interviews along with narratives about the difficulties these women faced in the past. Racialized colonial logics are also visible throughout – particularly as it relates to the revival of 'romantic attitudes toward so-called "primitive peoples" which has a "history … going back at least to Rousseau."' This ethos can be seen in the embrace of an '"imagined" primitiveness' of Africans whose '"authenticity" [is] … opposed to a "decadent" West' (Leigton 1990, 609–10). Health discourses are not immune to this but what is notable about Aduna is that it generally refrains from pathologizing Blackness. And yet, I would argue it still enacts processes of racialization that, despite drawing on performatively positive tropes, remain mired in problematic stereotypes and generalizations.

A few more comments vis-à-vis gender and health are relevant here. Specifically, Aduna's reliance on the image of the older woman in the community – the mother, the caretaker, the healer – from whom trust emanates. This constitutes a formative frame surrounding baobab that is also consistent with hegemonic good health. Remember that one of hegemonic health's primary tenets is that of idealized gendered expectations and norms – ones that are reflective of the 'significance invested in feminine ideals of care' (Cairns, Johnston and Shyon 2010, 592). This speaks to the importance of ensuring that 'a woman conducts herself ... [in ways that are] recognizably womanly' (DeVault 1994, 118). Race bisects gender in potentially troublesome ways here in the case of care work done by Black women as illustrated by cultural tropes recognizable to Western audiences like that of the Black mammy – a maternal and family-oriented woman for whom 'self-sacrifice [was] expected as she performed her domestic duties' under slavery (West 1995, 458). In addition, nationality and citizenship become significant since many of the pictured women self-identify as Black African grandmothers – a demographic that has been interpellated in the past by the media as the continent's carers, educators, and activists, especially during the height of the HIV/AIDS pandemic (Chazan and Kittmer 2016). In each of these interpretive frames, health takes on a heightened role as a duty or responsibility left to women, and in particular Black women, who fit into predetermined, Western-centric, and racialized categories as carers who have knowledge ready for exploitation. Much more can be said about the role of race and gender in the construction of baobab as a health object capable of helping subjects attain the acme of healthfulness they desire. However, in order to ensure other kinds of cuts within this particular assemblage are also discussed, I now turn to new materialism in order to demonstrate the ways in which this health technology, baobab, functions as its own site of agential power vis-à-vis hegemonic good health.

Aduna's Baobab and new materialism

Unlike the other two case studies, which are constituted by digital technologies and genetic services, baobab is its own, self-contained object – one that offers itself as a unique site of agential activity. In this section, I enact two cuts – both of which speak to how hegemonic health and baobab intra-act with one another. They are:

1. Superfoods–baobab–health subculture–health norms; and
2. Tradition–baobab–sustainability–social justice-wellness

Each cut engenders a passage through which elements are 'cut together apart' and produce a 'discontinuous passage [in which] something new [can] emerge' (Barad 2014, 141; see also Barad 2003). While 'the new' is taken up in the final chapter, here I focus on what these cuts tell us about specific manifestations of hegemonic good health wherein each object has its own ontology – one that is diffracted (i.e. not self-contained), and contributes to a health ideology that is reductionist, asocial, normative, and preserves existing power relations (be that corporate, political, or cultural). The first cut is a food-centric one that highlights baobab's role as a powerful actant, a vibrant technology from which health norms are justified on a cultural level. The second focuses on the eco-political in which baobab is imbricated in relations of performed and achieved political change and through an ethic of health and wellness, defined through the lens of productivity, responsibility, and self-regulation, comes to the fore (Pantzar and Ruckenstin 2015). My argument here is that baobab, within our hegemonic good health assemblage, has been enrolled as a nonhuman actant facilitating and justifying its consumption as a technology of health. Demonstrating this through two specific cuts allows for a wider discussion of the myriad elements, forces, and flows that comprise this mediated manifestation of what it means to be in good health.

Cut 1. Superfoods–baobab–health subculture–health norms

This cut places baobab as one part of an ontologically flat (or anti-hierarchical) chain of relations that is founded on a conception of superfoods as forming a socially significant supra-category. Remember that there is no industry or medically accepted definition of superfoods; rather, they are an emergent category of foodstuffs that are seen as especially beneficial for achieving health. Specifically, superfoods are seen as possessing one or more identifiable nutrients that are believed to be healthful (i.e. healthy fats, polyphenols, etc.). Another definition, one that speaks to its historicity, claims that 'Superfoods are plant products that have been used for centuries all around the world as a remedy for illnesses or as ingredients of bills of fare of local tribes' (Ekiert i Dochnal 2015 as cited/translated by Roth and Zawadzki 2018, 106). This places superfoods firmly in the space of non-industrial and 'natural' fare – that is, foods that sits outside of capitalist relations and which have the capacity to address ailments and pathologies brought on by modern society.

Hegemonic good health, despite its tendency to fetishize high technology, plays an important role here since most superfoods undergo some form of processing (into pills/powders), packaging, and discursive de- and re-terrorialization so that they are acceptable to consume in a Western context (Deleuze 2004). While I have defined superfoods already, it bears noting that each superfood ingredient, through its own onto-political forcing and media representation, solidifies superfoods as a relevant category. Discussions of superfood trends (in magazines and online) brought by a surge in interest around a particular food and its nutritional guarantees also can be cyclical. They often follow changes in or refinements to scientific knowledge or a socio-political event that instigates a recalibration of the dominant health assemblage. The hype around quinoa, goji berries, spirulina, and wheatgrass over the past decade are evidence of this, as is the recent rise in sales of superfoods sold as immune boosting, such as turmeric, green tea, and chlorella due to Covid-19.

Baobab, the fruit, emerges from a tree that can grow to enormous proportions and is colloquially referred to as the 'tree of life'. It is comprised of mostly water and only has a three-month 'flowering' season. The first formal bit of Western media coverage extolling baobab's, benefits and its increasing commercial success, can be found in an article titled 'South African villagers tap into trend for "superfood" baobab', featured on *France24* from 2018. The article formulates a narrative similar to that of Aduna's, focusing on grandmothers (who are referred to as 'baobab guardians'), as well as financial security, sustainability, commercial potential, and health (having 'a really good combination of natural vitamins [vitamin C, anti-inflammatory properties], antioxidants, protein and also healing substances which all together makes it an incredible superfood'). Baobab has also been used as an ingredient in an increasing number of consumer products such as cosmetics, vitamins, ice cream, gin, and soda (France24 2018). *The New York Times* also wrote about the fruit in 2018, highlighting baobab's role as 'essential cultural symbols' while decrying the loss of baobab trees due to urbanization and development. Notably, little is said in either article about its potential consumption as a foodstuff in the West. Instead, baobab (and the tree it comes from) is framed as a vibrant material object, one that has its own kind of 'thing power'. It is also portrayed as a multi-functional natural phenomenon that is 'beloved' by the population, functions as 'symbol of the country' (serving as a town hall), and operates as a site for prayer messages, weddings ceremonies, and funeral rites (Searcey 2018).

It is pieces like this that cultivate an interest in superfoods as powerful objects whose intra-actions with Western processes of Orientalism, commodification, and co-optation (particularly as it relates to the environment) provides a basis from which the baobab tree, and later its fruit, comes to take on the characteristics of an artefact whose power is 'actualized through relational bonds' (Diener 2020, 45). The relational reciprocity portrayed in the article is one of allyship and gift giving which, it is hoped, might be transferred onto the Western health assemblage. Another article, by Ferrier in *The Guardian* (2018), speaks to the desire for relational centring through non-human species and gift giving that is not unlike new materialism's conception of 'Zoe [life]- centred egalitarianism', which embraces a 'materialist, secular, grounded and unsentimental response to the opportunistic trans-species commodification of Life that is the logic of advanced capitalism' (Braidotti 2016, 22). The article cites baobab's popularity as grounded in its health endowing properties, its taste, its cultural significance, and the care that goes into its sourcing. It closes with a proverb that speaks to the nomadological force of the tree which reads: 'Knowledge is like a baobab tree; no one person can embrace it' (Ferrier 2018). It would be perhaps overly idealistic to hope for an enfolding of baobab into the Western context in a manner that reflects this powerful affirmative ethic. Unfortunately, thus far, this does not appear to be the case.

Overall, it is this complex of matterings and discourses that baobab brings to hegemonic good health that is most important. Before engaging in a more focused discussion of this part of the cut, a short aside is needed in order to speak to the community and subcultural ties baobab elicits via its intra-action with adjacent cultural forces. To a degree, superfood consumerism has taken on a loosely articulated subcultural valence that ranges from low to high commitment (Sikka 2019). Subcultures, in a formal sense, are defined as practices through which groups attempt to communicate how they 'differ in such things as language, values, religion, diet, and style of life from the larger social world of which they are a part' (Yinger 1960, 626). More mainstream subcultures often acknowledge the larger culture but do so in ways that identify the former as unique. For Dick Hebdige (2012), subcultures take on a more critical edge by being bound up in the expression of and resistance to subordination. For him, contemporary subcultures aim to 'challenge [and disrupt] dominant meanings' (Crosset and Beal 76). However, time and again according to Cagle, subversion occurs in ways that are 'easily copied, dismissed, translated into the context of the omnivorous mainstream' (Cagle 1989, 309).

An understanding of superfood subcultures in a materialist sense can be elicited by the meanings invested in the food objects themselves. These cultural meanings intersect with material objects, whether it is quinoa, goji berries, or baobab, and the bodies that engage with them. I provide an in-depth analysis of this kind of relationality in the following section. For now, it is worth highlighting that food, diet, and health subcultures, inclusive of superfoods, constitute an important site from which to examine how a nonhuman object can act as a materialdiscursive hinge for Western anxieties about health, the environment, mortality, and inequality both as a vessel and as an object with its own agential power. Before speaking to this agency in more detail, it is worth elaborating on the subcultural groupings superfoods like baobab activate.

Primarily, superfood subcultures exist online and, as I argue elsewhere, operate as idealized and idealizing cultural nodes in which neoliberal, regulative, and binarized health and food subjectivities are enacted (Sikka 2019). Superfoods are seen as clean, ethical, and abundant in ways that attract individuals concerned about health, bodily comportment, and the environment. These subcultures often form with the help of claims made by 'moral entrepreneurs' about the significance of a particular superfood or in a more dispersed manner with less pressure to conform (Christopher 2018). They can be organized through superfood meetup groups (www.meetup.com), online communities (Instagram: @superfood.social; facebook: Superfood and Healthy Lifestyle; twitter: #superfood; tiktok: #superfoods), and more committed forms of engagement such as holidays and retreats (e.g. Arizona's Canyon Ranch).

While it would be easy to dismiss these forms of engagement and sociality as consistent with the superficial desires and concerns of the elite, I argue it is important to consider the meaning of these communities to participants. Subcultural formations, inclusive of those that are less insular, can be important sites for meaning making and identity construction. The desire to build relations with other human and nonhumans is an essential part of cultivating a sense of self, and health forms an important part of this – particularly in a society that rewards self-discipline and entrepreneurialism (Petrakaki, Hilberg and Waring 2018). Identifying oneself as a 'health nut', a 'couch potato', or an avid consumer of superfoods brings with it values and objects that have their own discursive and material power. Identifying oneself as a baobab consumer can cultivate a sense of self that is co-constructed with and by the product and meanings associated the fruit itself. This includes those characteristics identified earlier like that of cosmopolitanism, education, affluence, social awareness, and health consciousness. This is important regardless of who the consumers are demographically (at least on this specific point). Thus, if superfood aficionados are finding fulfilment, satisfaction, and benefit from this fruit, in whole or in powdered form, I contend this needs to be taken seriously.

On the other hand, while seemingly enlightened and potentially important for constructing the processual self, it is still the case that these affects and meanings operate in service of hegemonic good health. Additional ways in which this occurs is via baobab's decontextualization and processing such that it become a different object in the West. Baobab is 'lived' differently and 'constituted relationally [in new ways] through [other] entanglements of human and nonhuman bodies, affects, objects and practices' when ingested, for example, in a smoothie after a yoga class (Fullager 2017, 250). This is a different baobab than the one which recognizes, as Tischleder puts it, 'kinship in the other ... (whether "man", critter, tree, stone, phone, trash, or cloud), [and] presupposes telling stories that will not cease bearing the traits of our own embodiment and mindedness in a more-than-human world' (Tischleder 2019, 134).

Perhaps baobab, in its refined and processed form, is simply another object, one that it is constituted by multiple ontologies comprising an ontological heterarchy that reflects different values, forces, and flows depending on the context (Crumley et al. 1995; Harris and Robb 2012). It could thus be thought of as the 'superfood baobab' as opposed to the baobab fruit discussed by the women farmers on Aduna's website or the one chronicled in *The New York Times* article. Finally, before bringing us to the last part of this cut, I wanted to make a quick note about age – an element of intersectional analysis often elided. While traditional subcultures tend to be populated by youth (think music and stylistic movements), superfood health subcultures require some measure of disposable income and self-subjectification that only becomes possible at an older age. Layered on top of economic requirements are pressures associated with retaining youthfulness which baobab consumers tend to be interested in. As Sarah Lamb argues, 'Medicine, the state, ethical regimes, cultural ideals, and personal desires,' inclusive of dietary practices and superfoods, 'intersect in mutually constitutive ways to make the endeavour to eradicate old age seem meaningful, possible, and compelling' (Lamb 2019, 265). A significant amount of research has been done in this area – in particular, examining the pressure to maintain one's youthfulness through cosmetic, dietary, and lifestyle practices (Clarke 2010; Macia and Chevé 2015).

While my focus here is on superfoods specifically, it is worth noting that baobab has increasingly been used in cosmetics as well as in anti-aging face serums, moisturizers, and masks, as noted by recent articles in *InStyle* and *British GQ* – the former of which notes that baobab is a superfruit that acts as a 'soothing, nourishing ingredient' (Lukas 2020; Clark and Bugler 2021). For women, embracing superfoods in pursuit of beauty norms are often justified as a voluntary and potentially empowering exercise of individual choice. This

ethos takes on postfeminist characteristics in its embrace of 'femininity …
subjectification, individualism, choice and empowerment … and an emphasis
upon consumerism and the commodification of difference' (Gill 2007, 148).

Finally, we have, in this cut, one of the most important sluices of analysis
in this book – which is that of baobab and health. While you might ask, have
we not been discussing the entanglements between health and baobab through
this chapter? (the answer is yes), what I would like to focus on here is how
baobab as an object pushes one aspect of hegemonic health that has not been
adequately discussed thus far – namely, its function as a *charismatic* 'health'
ingredient. Food scholar Aya Kimura uses the phrase 'charismatic nutrient' to
describe foodstuffs that 'produce … nutrition as a particular kind of project'
tied to tangible outcomes (Biltekoff, Mudry and Kimura 2014, 39). Baobab's
traditional role as a fruit and tree that performs an important function in
complex ecosystems thus becomes alienated in and by its intromission into
a Western health assemblage. In its natural form, baobab supports a unique
understanding of health – one that is enmeshed in the natural world and
reflective of its material affordances including its ability to retain large amounts
of water (thus acting as a reservoir), its functioning as a mini ecosystem,
providing 'food, water, and shelter for animals [including humans] and insects
of all sizes', its ability to prevent soil erosion, and its role in preserving soil
health (yoursuper.com 2021). Baobab, understood in this way, carries a material
recalcitrance, an entelechy or vital force inscribed within it that is distinctive.
Carrying its own thing-power, the baobab fruit and tree can be thought of
as enacting and sustaining ecological health as part of an indigenous health
assemblage (Lupton 2017b). Donna Haraway describes this as an earth-life (and
health) apparatus that requires we make 'kin sym-chthonically, sym-poetically.
Who and whatever we are, we need to make-with – become-with, compose-
with – the earth-bound' (Haraway 2015, 161). She calls this the Chthulucene.
Baobab's materiality reflects this perspective by working intra-actively with
humans and non-humans in a communal fashion. This is very different from
its manifestation in our contemporary health environment.

In our hegemonic good health regime, baobab's agency is isolated, scientized,
and depoliticized in ways that erase a robust understanding of its (often gendered)
conditions of production, distribution, consumption, and its role and function
in local communities and ecologies. In this way, products like baobab become
another 'instrument of governance that fuels the nutritionism agenda' (Rao 2019,
104). This, of course, is not an inevitable state of affairs. As I explore in the final
chapter, opportunities for resistance do exist – some of which require a de-linking

of the potentialities of the foods and nonhuman actants we instrumentalize for our hegemonic health objectives. One such option, as articulated by feminist materialist scholar Cecilia Åsberg, is to embrace a posthuman ethic of learning so as 'to re-vision, meet up with and inhabit well the continuums of naturecultures' (Åsberg 2013, 6; also see Roy and Subramanian 2016).

One final point before moving on to the second agential cut focuses on the distortion of agency specifically. It requires a quick return to Aya Kimura's (2013) thesis on charismatic nutrients – particularly as it relates to foodstuffs that are valorized due to their properties *after* 'treatment' (read: modern processing) to extract its powerful qualities. Aduna's baobab powder is one such example of this in that its agency and affordances are directed solely towards human ends. While Kimura's critique focuses on the misplaced expectation put on charismatic nutrients to act as magic bullets vis-à-vis under- and mal-nutrition, its materialdiscursive role vis-à-vis superfoods produces similar outcomes. Namely, to function as a *super*food whose potency, as asserted in a recent article for the *Daily Express* (a conservative UK national tabloid newspaper), can help manage blood sugar levels: 'Baobab is rich in fibre which can slow down the rise in blood glucose … It is also high in polyphenols which have been shown to effect the release of sugars from carbohydrates into the blood stream, reducing their conversion into glucose' (Coe as cited by Clark 2017). Yet, as I have demonstrated, baobab has its own history and existence as 'natural' product – one that resists being instrumentalized by Western knowledge claims that puncture its role in daily life. Acknowledging this does not require that it be romanticized or restricted in its use. Rather, it requires demonstrating care for the fact that superfoods often carry a heavy symbolic and material function and thus has its own vibrant material iterations that pushes up against capitalist and colonial imperatives.

Cut 2. De/re/enchanted tradition–baobab–sustainability–social justice-wellness

This next cut takes us deeper into baobab as a meaningful material object with a focus on its movement through circuits of biocultural meaning-making, capitalist exploitation, environmental concerns, and the human-centric desire to 'be well' and 'do well'. Parts of this first element, tradition, has been discussed at some length. What I would like to do here is to trace how baobab's active, vibrant role in the daily life of communities has been threatened while also establishing what this 'does' to human and nonhuman others. I also problematize 'tradition' as a normative, even metaphysical, category that risks attenuating agency and reifying the colonial gaze.

Drawing on the language of enchantment, particularly as it is used by new materialism, baobab can be understood as a sociomaterial object that carries a 'thing-power' which, in light of its enacted and conferred social significance, is excessive and capable of cultivating new forms of causation via its own radical alterity (Deleuze 1994). Bennett refers to this as 'a state of [cultivated] wonder' (Bennett 2016, 3) – wonder that encourages 'ethical generosity' and, according to Fredengren, retains,

> the power ... to reveal alternative assemblages, arrangements and relationships ... it could be deployed to speak to contemporary issues of inter-generational responsibilities (between generations), debates on 'global' justice (in terms of historical inequalities), and our ethics towards, and care for, the human and more-than-human world.

(Fredengren 2016, 483)

This radical alterity is distinctly conative, meaning that it attracts and forms alliances with other human and nonhuman 'things' (Llyod 1990; Spinoza 2002). We can understand this modality of enchantment as fostering a distinctive form of 'dwelling with' – an effect of living in relation with the natural world (Ingold 2002; Perry 2019).

Concretely, as I pointed out earlier, baobab (the tree and fruit: together *and apart*) plays an important role in local rituals; as a source of food (its leaves to thicken, its seeds to consume as a snack, its pulp to eat straightaway or in a drink); in construction (to produce rope); as a water source; and as a means of sustaining soil health (Kaboré et al. 2011). Baobab also contains medicinal properties and has been mixed with water and sugar to treat acute diarrhoea, made into a paste to take care of skin conditions, and used to break fevers for centuries (Sidbe and William 2002; Diop et al. 2005). Baobab can thus be understood as an enchanted object – one that fosters consilience between individuals and communities. Living with baobab in this kind of relation is far removed from the relation of commodification that is dominant in the global north.

We can thus read the insertion of baobab into the diets of the elite in the West both as an indication of intensified dis-enchantment and as proof of a striving for re-enchantment. On the first point, it is significant that the form in which baobab is consumed in the West is as a powder (a point I touched on earlier but deserves further discussion). The production of Aduna's baobab requires that the pulp, fibres, and seeds be pounded into a powdered pulp, which is then put through a sieve to remove any residue. Much of this process is automated and contracted out to third parties. What is important here is the distinction between the baobab consumed in the West for its health properties and its role in the lives of people in Zimbabwe, Madagascar, and South Africa. The question that needs to be asked is: what are the effects of this difference? That is, what is the impact of the transformation of baobab from how it is used in a manner conducive to good relations in the Global South to the commodified way in which it is consumed in the global north?

The operative term here, disenchantment, is in keeping with Weber's critique of modern society which he sees as a product of the exploitation of nature, rationalization of life processes, and embrace of means-ends rationality (Carroll 2011; Weber and Kalberg 2013). Weber's theory was used specifically to critique the bureaucratization of daily life, but can also be applied to the study of the impact of early forms of food processing, mass production, fortification, and safer production practices. These processes were adopted to feed a growing population and are a part of a culture of 'hygiene, health, and food purity [that] permeated early 20th-century' (Bobrow-Strain 2008, 22). This is very different from how we understand 'processing' today which, in most hegemonic health cultures, it is seen as denaturing and disenchanting. Put another way, as an interviewee in a study conducted by Jackson argues, food that undergo this large scale, even biogenetic tinkering and working over "'just doesn't quite feel right and natural'" (Jackson 2010, 160).

This sits uneasily with the competing desire for this powder to re-enchant our disenchanted lifeworlds. To do so would mean it must materially and symbolically transform baobab from an enchanted fruit to a disenchanted powder, and then to an enchanted superfood. As a result, this *super*food would have to do a lot of symbolic heavy lifting. Superfood packaging and marketing has thus taken on some of this discursive work. The question then becomes whether baobab, in its powdered form, has sufficient thing-power to re-enchant and (re)capture 'the innate ability of humans to acquire understanding of their environment beyond intellectual ways of knowing and habitual modes of perception' that the baobab fruit, in its indigenous environment, cultivates daily (van Kraalingen 2019, 15).

This desire does not entail a demand for de-growth or other forms of anarcho-primitivism that would necessitate we embrace a state of nature and/ or reject 'civilization' with all its technologies and institutions. This position is supported by scholars and activists similarly alarmed by climate change, big pharma, rapacious capitalism, mass consumerism, and food precarity (Zerzan

1994; el-Ojeili and Taylor 2020). Many of these scholars focus on civilizational wellness and health in ways that are very different from hegemonic good health. The forms of enchantment scholars like Bennett are calling for are nontheistic and, as I argue in the final chapter, sets some hopeful conditions for cognitive and social change – namely that health can be reconfigured into something that continues to attend to human states of being and doing but is also attentive to nonhuman affinities, to nature, and to transversal ecologies (Braidotti 2011).

Moving from this more abstract and philosophical discussion of enchantment to a more grounded one involving sustainability and social justice requires that we highlight some of the tangible ways in which sustainability intersects with the baobab tree and its fruit. First, is with respect to the affordances of the tree and its operation within a larger ecological assemblage that ensures local environmental resilience. As noted, baobab trees are important sources of food, medicine, and cultural integrity (Lisao, Geldenhuys and Chirwa 2017). It is worth pausing for a moment to highlight three specific ways in which baobab has been used to connect to a model of sustainability that is co-produced through embodied material practices. The first and second relates to the use of the fruit's pulp and leaves as a source of food and medicine, of nourishment and healing. Third is its instantiation as a site of spiritual sustenance. Here, sustainability is understood holistically wherein stewardship and caretaking are seen as elemental and connected to survival.

As a source of nourishment, the body-baobab relation is enacted through actual consumption wherein the leaves are used as a leafy green or to thicken sauces, its flesh eaten as is or added to drinks or milk after being ground up, or its seeds used to extract oils, consume as a snack, or roasted as a replacement for coffee. Baobab's medicinal applications include the use of baobab leaves and seeds to address everyday ailments such as fevers, asthma, allergies, fatigue, dysentery, and diarrhoea (Sidibe 2002).

Sustainability, in this cut, involves being especially mindful of how the baobab tree, its fruit, and its relations with humans are part of an assemblage that intersects with and is co-constituted by other multispecies nonhumans or what Haraway calls 'critters' (Haraway 2018). It thus bears repeating that the baobab tree plays an important role in ecosystem health including as a store of water (it is fire resistant), as a source of food for animals including monkeys, antelopes, and elephants, as a habitat for insects and birds, and in nutrient cycling and pollination (Edkins et al. 2008; Dr. Y 2011; Sabina, Nihmot and Ifechukwu 2020). Finally, sustainability, as a spiritual and community-oriented value, is expressed in the use of the tree as a local place of encounter and as an alter for ceremonies. Its flowers have an aesthetic appeal and, historically, the tree and its fruit and flowers make appearances in mythic stories (like the rabbit and the baobab) and in proverbs, riddles, legends, and jokes: 'For example, it is said the baobab was planted upside down by God as an accident or as punishment for its constant complaining, disobedience, envy, and boastfulness ... by a hyena described as either angry and vengeful ... or stupid and lazy' (Wickens and Lowe 2008; Rashford 2015, 216). Its role as an indicator and actor in the health of a community thus extends from the human and nonhuman to the metaphysical/anti-human.

There are, of course, a whole host of additional material-symbolic ways in which baobab's agency is expressed. As such, before closing this section, a further discussion vis-à-vis the sustainability portion of this cut is needed since it speaks to our understanding of health as well as to the dangers that come with fetishizing the Other. I am referring here to the construction by Aduna and other superfood companies of 'Africa' as a pristine place. This is resonant with colonial desires for a return to pure origins which Hall (1994) warns can result in a kind of romantic nativism that seeks to erase the horrors of colonization and capitalist exploitation. It represents the perennial search for 'some very beautiful splendid era whose existence rehabilitates us both in regard to ourselves, and in regard to others' (Fanon as cited by Loomba 2007, 181). This search for sustainable ecological health reveals cracks in hegemonic iteration. Unfortunately, and because of its binding in and with neoliberal capitalism, the desire for novel forms of health and connection, it has become commodified into consumable products.

Also important is what this fetishization does to our understanding of the agency and the lived realities of those residing in the Global South. For example, vis-à-vis baobab trees, an extraordinary amount of care has been taken by local populations to preserve them as much as possible. This care should not, however, justify the homogenization of the Global South (this time: 'Africa') as a site of monolithic interests, or rely on ahistorical thinking which erases how tightly nations are wound up in global capitalism. Economic priorities, political justifications, and the desire for 'development' are interests that persist everywhere and have also been used by parties in the Global South to justify environmentally unjust actions. Moreover, the burdening of countries that have been sites of unchecked human labour and nonhuman resource extraction to now act as sites and sources of ecological salvation is perverse to say the least. What this does is to place the burden on subaltern human and nonhuman agents and actants to facilitate structural change which, as Alcoff argues, works to reinforce 'racist, imperialist concepts and perhaps also to further silence the lesser-privileged group's own ability to speak and be heard' (Alcoff 2008, 26; also see Kapoor 2004; Fanon 2007).

Finally, on sustainability, the material reality and discursive construction of the harvesting of these fruits for our 'health' in the West/global north is itself a form of exploitation that renders the longevity of these trees and the role they play in local communities less important. It also draws attention to the process by which fruits and trees are bound into global commodity chains and what this does to the environment and the health of local ecosystems. An article in *Nature Plants*, for example, uses radiocarbon dating and tracking to conclude that some of the oldest and largest baobab trees have died or are in in the process of collapse for reasons that cannot be explained by epidemics or a natural death. Climate change is given as one possible reason (Patrut et al. 2018).

Other studies tracking the health of indigenous baobab species have found that their numbers have decreased due to 'unsustainable harvesting, removal as development extends to pristine areas, herbivory, or destruction by fire' (Lisao, Geldenguys and Chirwa 2018; also see Arnold and Pérez 1998). The United Nations Environment Program warns of dangers to baobab trees due to 'logging and slash-and-burn agriculture' as well as 'poverty, migration, climate change and a fragile political situation all combining to push … forest[s] to the edge of destruction' (UNEP 2018). Many of these concerns, it should be noted, can be seen as anticipatory given that baobab trees are categorized on the IUCN Red List of Species as a species of Least Concern (LC). And yet, other researchers have pointed to the reduction of baobab tree populations and their status as protected in Namibia due to 'high demand for baobab products and associated changes in land use' (Dhillon and Gustad 2004; Lisao et al. 2018, 2). Given these concerns, it is important to think about how hegemonic good health fits into this. Recall that hegemonic good health has been efficient in forestalling systemic change by engaging in small material and discursive steps that paper over contradictions (i.e. a return to the natural, supporting the marginalized, etc.). The same thing appears to be occurring with the sustainability of the baobab.

Surprisingly, Aduna itself, in one of its blog posts, responds to the *Nature Plants* article directly as a way to counter concerns about the health of the trees. It is interesting that Aduna chose to address this particular piece since, while it conveys clear concern around the health of baobab trees, that concern is only focused on a selection of older ones. Aduna responds to the article by emphasizing that, currently, the baobab tree population is 'healthy and stable', that researchers are just speculating 'that climate change is a contributory cause', that the trees often collapse but continue growing, and that harvesting the fruit is not only not harmful but is socio-culturally protective (since they bring in money and are thus seen as 'financially' valuable. *Are they not already valuable?*) (Aduna 2021c). Nothing related to the other concerns laid out in the article are addressed.

Finally, as part of this cut, we have the nodes of social justice-wellness. I have added social justice here because, together with wellness, they act as two sides of the same coin. Since I have touched on the commodification of social justice and wellness already, here I focus on health specifically. In this context health is understood capaciously and as part of a larger set of indicators. So as to not tip my hat before the final chapter, in what follows I focus on health as a form of social justice – one that is aimed at ensuring the flourishing of 'communities' health, livelihood, vibrancy and self-determination' (Whyte 2017). While it would be unfair to assume that the testimonies offered by the women harvesting for Aduna are untrue or unreliable, or that they suffer from a kind of false consciousness, it remains the case that the poverty they might find themselves in was not, and is not, inevitable. Rather, it is a product of historical racialized capitalist-colonial exploitation whose 'Relations of dependence were reproduced within this order as the global South remained in a subordinate position to the advanced capitalist countries' (Motta and Gunval Nilsen 2011, 5).

On the other hand, it is also the case that of the superfood companies with high visibility and revenue, Aduna has done much more to ensure information about the company vis-à-vis labour is accessible and that its largely female employees have control over the trees and who they sell to. This is possible because there are no baobab plantations per se. However, currently, harvesting schedules are still dictated to them. Moreover, it is unclear how much they are being compensated, how consistent that compensation is, and whether there are supports built into the relationship. Aduna's recent partnership with the African Union's 'Great Green Wall' tree programme to build/preserve a 8000km wall of baobab trees in the Sahel will, according to CEO Andrew Hunt, 'scale up our baobab supply chain and kick-start the creation of a new billion-dollar baobab industry for rural Africa that can sustain 10 million households' (Devlin 2020). This is similar to a plantation model under which worker autonomy would be lost.

This tree-planting initiative, and the justification given for it, is particularly telling as it reveals a set of discursive gymnastics that complexify this cut. The article in which Hunt gives this quote also details how Aduna has 'championed the baobab as part of the solution to many of the Sahel region's challenges which include desertification *and mass migration* to Europe', thereby demonstrating their own attempt to 'border' as a way to supplement commodified worker inclusion as outlined by Harsha Walia (Devlin 2020, italics added; Walia 2013). The way in which health is drawn into this particular part of the baobab superfood assemblage is as a 'bestselling' product, one that has unique 'health benefits' as well as 'ethical and environmental [read: social justice] credentials' (Walia 2013). Yet health, in much of superfood discourse, is inextricably linked to market logics, consumer interest, consumability, and individual responsibility.

Real health decolonization and justice, of the form that would make Aduna and other superfood companies truly revolutionary, would require the fundamentally re- and de-constructing of our material relations through 'transnationalist, abolitionist, and critical pedagogy movements … ones [that] destabilize, un-balance, and repatriate the very terms and assumptions of some of the most radical efforts to reimaging human power relations' (Tuck and Yang 2012, 28). What this would entail is repatriation, settler colonial restitution, prison abolition, Indigenous sovereignty, and new forms of futurity. Health decolonization is entirely outside the scope of the superfood assemblage since it would require dialogue with 'non-Eurocentric understandings of what constitutes "health," "disorder" and "illness" and for the exploration of the emerging dynamics of ecologies of knowledges and practices of care and healing' (Nounes and Louvison 2020).

Finally, wellness remains an important part of this materialdiscursive cut despite not having been engaged with substantively in this section. This was a deliberate choice and a product of the heaviness of the preceding paragraphs, which take on such topics as capitalist exploitation, expropriation, settler colonialism, and decolonization. Wellness thus feels somewhat trite, a concern of socio-economically well-off elites for whom fine-tuning their expression of hegemonic good health in ways that replace larger concerns with preoccupations around small-scale sustainability, organic production, and personal nutrition is par for the course (Aduna 2021c). It can also be understood as a way in which to make health-work (or wellness-work) part of the pursuit of private wellness goods. Ones that are gendered, ableist, raced, biomedicalized, and discursively and materially tied to outcomes (O'Neill 2020). This conception of health also demands moralized discipline and a form of docile acquiescence such that being or looking 'well', as in slim, young, and vibrant, conveys that you are also a good neoliberal subject (McGillivray 2005; Foucault 2007).

Wellness is also imbricated with hegemonic good health via its connection with embodied engagement wherein instrumentally consuming products that promise health and validation produces its own sense of wellness. Understood in this way, wellness is a cultural practice imbued with power. It is also epistemically healthist in its demand for 'healthy citizenship', its sustained preoccupation with personal health (i.e. a duty to be well), and its nutritionistic fetishization of isolated nutrients (Crawford 1980). As Durocher argues, nutritionism extends healthism and is circumscribed by an understanding of wellness that is regulative and has its own form of 'secular morality' (Kimura 2013a; Durocher 2019). This conception of wellness is also in-keeping with the principles of liberal democracy in which choice and consumption are centred and in which these structures are sustained by 'the maintenance of neoliberal conditions through the rising consumption of commodified wellness [e.g. superfoods], happiness and self-care services' (Datta and Chakraborty 2018, 456).

A more generous, and care-oriented conception of 'wellness' that attends to the desire to experience an embodied vitality within a health assemblage that is co-constituted by a host of intersecting social determinants (poverty, food security, access to care, education, etc.) and extends to one's community and significant others, would require a drastic sociomaterial re-orientation. One that disentangles health from individual products and which sees those products as part of larger socio-economic and material chains that 'explore ... the relationality of becoming that produces agency as dispersed and co-implicated in the intra-actions of the world' (Fullager and Pavlidis 2018, 63; also see Barad 2007). Reconceptualizing wellness as well being (when redefined outside of hegemonic good health) is one way of doing this and can be successful if discursive changes are coupled with material ones.

Taken together, these two cuts are illustrative of the momentary stabilizations of a complex network, a 'cutting together-apart' of agencies and material relations that are constantly in flux (Barad 2007). These settings, for purposes of research and understanding, reflect 'relational achievements', or what Barua describe as networks that are 'fabricated through world-making entanglements of heterogeneous organisms, technologies and bodies' (Barua 2015, 269; also see Barua 2017). These cuts: 1. Superfoods–baobab–health subculture–health norms, and 2. Tradition–baobab–sustainability–social justice–wellness, operate as their own sites of generative world-making in which hegemonic good health, as the dominant health ideology, is solidified, bringing with it new ways of understanding superfoods. In these cuts, we see superfoods as sitting at the juncture between 'natural' and 'processed' and as promising health (youth, beauty, vitality) – achieved through consumption. Also of note is the assertion that consuming baobab will function as a way to recapture a lost sense of connection with the natural world and Others (i.e. through subcultural formations).

These cuts also reveal how hegemonic good health depoliticizes and instrumentalizes health while conferring on baobab a kind of agency filtered through Western knowledge regimes. They also draw attention to baobab's own agential vitality – its socio-historical mattering and functioning *in context* – as well as our attempt to use it to re-vitalize an increasingly disenchanted world. This, I contend, risks setting a permission structure in which hegemonic good health can be maintained alongside claims of social justice – particularly when baobab's discursive framing and material construction fulfils, at least in part, the desire of contemporary modern subjects to do well (environmentally and towards the marginalized) and to be well. The replication of colonial and Eurocentric relations of power and exploitation under capitalism continues to be concerning. Finally, from these cuts we have a positive troubling of the notion of wellness in which hegemonic good health, seen through the lens of baobab/superfood consumption, is revealed to be hollow due to its reliance on nutritionist and healthist norms and values.

In the next section, I construct an auto-ethnographic account of consuming Aduna's baobab powder for two weeks in which I added it daily to foods I already consume as well as using suggestions from Aduna's website. While I discussed my methodological approach earlier, I did want to make a note about auto-ethnography as an STS methodology which, in this case, synthesizes cultural critique with socio-technical constructionism and a theory of knowledge as value laden (Anderson and Sharrock 2015). Auto-ethnography pushes traditional STS scholarship away from practices that rely on data extraction and research that assumes positions of superiority and inferiority as it relates to knowledge production (Ureta 2018). Instead, it places me, as a researcher, in a network of relations that, for these two weeks, includes baobab powder as well as other relations, knowledges, and Others. The insights that emerge are not just personal – rather, 'they are the product of manifold relations between different actors in the network' (Lange 2020, 1). Baobab powder can thus be understood as a technology, a set of relations, a way of seeing the world, an object (worked on through various levels of skill), and an expression of human values (Latour 1990; Heidegger 1977; Fernando 2016). An STS feminist materialist auto-ethnographic examination of technology seeks to reveal, disentangle, critique, 'and … transform the basic assumptions and practices that inform current research in rhetoric of technology as well as extend its range of suitable subject matter' (Koerber 2000, 64). The following sections synthesize insights and critical, embodied observations and knowledge based on my own engagements with Aduna's baobab powder drawing on diary entries, copious note taking, and post-hoc reflections. Writing up and cultivating connections to existing research and to hegemonic good health – as the dominant health discourse – has been especially illuminating.

Auto-ethnography of Baobab

Generally, I myself am a fairly routine and schedule-oriented eater with a penchant for what one might describe as the 'healthy foods' promulgated by hegemonic good health – i.e. fruit and vegetable heavy and very light in what would be considered processed or refined. While not vegan or vegetarian, I eat meat sparingly. I purchased Aduna's baobab powder from Planet Organic, an organic foods company with brick and mortar stores throughout the UK but which also delivers online, for £12.99. Other options included Amazon, from which I was reticent to purchase, and local stores in the city which I had been avoiding going to until my second Covid-19 vaccine. This has meant that one of the things I previously enjoyed doing while food shopping, perusing the aisles for the newest health products (for scholarly purposes of course), was simply not possible.

The next day, the brightly coloured tropical orange, blue, and yellow self-sealing pouch of Aduna's baobab powder arrived. I immediately flipped it over to see whether the package had changed in any way but saw the same statistics and claims that were on the website, including typeface asserting that it is 'high in fibre', a 'rich source of vitamin C', and supportive of 'energy release', 'immune function', and 'skin health'. These claims figure prominently with respect to size and placement. Up top were a few short paragraphs describing baobab as a superfruit emerging from the 'Tree of Life' and text asserting the socially conscious bona fides of the company (e.g. as supportive of rural livelihoods). I took a glance at the nutritional breakdown, mostly out of habit, as well as storage directions and ingredients: 'Organic baobab fruit pulp powder.' I felt a bit of excitement and, later, reflected on how effectively a 'health halo' had been constructed around this product since it had generated in me an impression that it is a healthy product and that its nutritional attributes are likely to be positive. Remember that the health halo effect works when claims of 'one healthy attribute leads consumers to assume that food offers other healthy but unclaimed attributes' (Schuldt 2012, 581). As such, one might assume baobab's vitamin C offerings means that it is a source of other vitamins (which it is not). In fact, I felt a bit disappointed upon seeing that the 10 g serving did not contribute to more than 9.9 per cent of other nutrients including potassium, calcium, and magnesium. Claims of being a 'superfood' in that sense did not quite ring true.

The product itself comes in the form of a fine white powder – I had thought it might be more granular so when I took a little and put it on my tongue it did not dissolve right away. It has a tang to it taste-wise and is mildly sweet. In order to decide how to consume the powder I perused Aduna's recipe section, which was filled with enticing baked goods like raw baobab Easter chocolates, baobab gingerbread with lemon-baobab coconut icing as well as more savoury fare like fonio wraps with chilli baobab-tahini tofu spread as well as sweetcorn, turmeric, and baobab fritters. I found these recipes to be somewhat surprising in that they were not particularly in-keeping with foods one would consider 'healthy' using a hegemonic good health frame. Interestingly, however, each of the recipes did not rely on typical 'red flag' processed foods like white flower, white sugar or butter but, instead, substituted these with items like spelt flour, molasses, and coconut oil. This is in concordance with what was a recognizable technique of classifying food under hegemonic health categories that involve binarizing and coding individual food items as good or bad, pure or impure based on constructed and changing definitions of each category. Mary Douglas, Marcel Mauss, and Sidney Mintz flesh out this dynamic in their work on food, purity, symbolism, and social order (Mauss 2002; Douglas 2003; Mintz and Du Bois).

Not being a particularly 'interested' cook or baker myself, I decided to start by adding two teaspoons of baobab powder to a morning smoothie of milk and frozen fruit as recommended on the package. Specifically, I mixed 1 per cent milk with the powder and half a cup of frozen fruit. For just over the first week, this is how I consumed it. Upon reflection, and in particular thinking about how the smoothie changed my other eating habits in line with a 'clean eating' ethos, I kept returning to Douglas' anthropological and structuralist theories of food and eating vis-à-vis the epistemology of categorization and particularly as it relates to purity, taboos, cleanliness, health, and authenticity. It struck me as significant that the recipes, all of them, did not include any from the site of their harvesting (Senegal, South Africa, Botswana) except for one, the traditional baobab drink. I describe this as form of selective decontextualization such that the materiality of the powder, when coupled with the discursive force of its marketing and packaging (as well as its existence in a cultural conjuncture in which hegemonic good health is ascendent), renders it sufficiently novel and exotic to be enticing insofar as it can be incorporated into recognizable practices and tastes. Other recipes include scones, flapjacks, and a nut roast – all distinctly British foods – with a few more 'ethnic' recipes including houmous, tagine, and baobab falafels. This felt to me as in keeping with the colonial act of 'eating the Other' wherein cultural and economic colonizers see the marginalized as exotic 'Others' to be consumed under conditions that can be controlled. For bell hooks, this results in,

> the commodification of difference [which] promotes paradigms of consumption wherein whatever difference the Other inhabits is eradicated, via exchange, by a consumer cannibalism that not only displaces the Other but denies the significance of that Other's history through a process of decontextualization.
>
> (hooks 1992, 431)

I thought about the process by which this powder came to me as a ready-to-consume substance throughout the two weeks, during which time I returned to postcolonial writing on eating difference, cultural appropriation, and critical diversity studies – especially those writers who spoke to the fact that 'even those with the best intentions can engage in appropriative acts that are damaging' (Miller 2016, 14; also see Cuthbert 1998; Huggan 2002). On more than one occasion this resulted in my feeling guilty for playing into this cycle which then intersected with internal rationalizations on the grounds of 'it's research' and the thought that, at least in some small way, my 'choice', when added to all these other 'choices', could have made someone's life somewhat materially better.

During the first few days I also made notes about the resonances between superfood trends and the low-fat craze of the 80s and early 90s which was then followed by the cultural demonization of carbohydrates (think Atkins and now paleo). I am still averse to consuming sugar outside of fruit and sources I cannot avoid which I believe is at least partially shaped by the anti-sugar ethos of that second phase. This aversion dovetails with becoming more informed about the intersections between sugar and slavery, sugar and racialization, and sugar and colonialism (Sandiford 2000; Gernalzick 2018).

Food choice is also meaningful as it relates to identity, which is something I reflected on regularly, particularly as I tried to grapple with why certain foods have come to take on the symbolic and material value they have. My past research has drawn me to surveys that examine the symbolic meaning of food and perceptions of health which have found that individuals who ate 'healthfully' were seen by others as progressive, likely liberal Democrats, sophisticated, and 'thinner, active ... attractive, likable' (Steim and Nemeroff 1995, 5; also see Sadalla and Burroughs 1981; Stein and Nemeroff 1995; Vartanian, Herman and Polivy 2007). The contestation of the dichtomizing of good food versus bad food persists. It places food in a cultural system in which foods perceived as 'good', like superfoods, confer that goodness onto its purchasers who are seen as exercising self-control, appropriate decision-making, and rational restraint (Askegaard et al. 2014). Being placed in this category, as someone who is a responsible health subject, feels, well, good by reflecting the attainment of a supervalue that manifests an internalization of hegemonic good health norms and is in keeping with public health objectives. The accrual of health capital in the form of nutritional knowledge, the display of appropriate food choice, and ideal bodily comportment is also significant (Kamphuis, Jansen and Mackenback 2015; Bourdieu 2018). I felt this acutely when telling friends and colleagues about what I was doing, mostly on Zoom, but also experienced its absence since working from home (due to Covid-19) meant that the everyday interactions in our faculty kitchen around food was impossible.

Health capital, for me, is important given my actions which include spending time and money on the accoutrements of hegemonic good health behaviours from overpriced yoga pants and fitness classes to smoothie bars and lunchtime energy (salad) bowls. Health capital can be defined as a product of the investment in one's health where 'the payoff' is displayed and performed. This kind of capital accumulation reveals how different bodies are valued vis-à-vis ideal health status. Larsen et al. refer to this as the 'diet body', which he describes as a preoccupation with 'correcting and optimising the body through diet and eating habits'. This fits into a larger constellation of health capital which works to subsidise 'economic, cultural, and social capital and can be deployed [for one's benefit] in diverse positions in different fields and the social space, including in work-life contexts' (Larsen et al. 2020, 2–4). My own embodied experience of this, while attenuated by lockdowns, became internalized and was consistent with the pursuit of cultural health capital and hegemonic good health. Rabinow and Rose refer to this drive as a generalized 'will to health' – one that is 'individualised, voluntary, informed, ethical, preventive' and 'organised around the pursuit of health' (Rabinow and Rose 2001, 3).

Another theme which my reflective writing brought to the surface was the significance of the fact that I was conducting this food auto-ethnography at a particular historical conjuncture (2021). This meant that any possibility of communal interactions, conversations, and sharing on the topics of health, food, and bodies was limited. Also significant was media coverage around underlying health conditions and vulnerabilities that, purportedly, could make you more susceptible to Covid-19 and its pernicious side effects (e.g. long Covid). In regard to the former, I ruminated on several occasions about just how significant food is vis-à-vis community and social health as well as on the distinctive materiality of this superfood (i.e. the ways in which it is intuitively meant to be consumed). I also thought about the implications of its suggested use as an addition to foods that would not traditionally be shared – i.e. in a smoothie, in water, in cereal/porridge, etc. It is notable that the way in which baobab is consumed in situ (i.e. where it is grown) tends to be in dishes and drinks that are meant to be consumed with others – as part of sauces, soups, and stews, for example (Buchmann et al. 2010). Some of Aduna's recipes, however, did open space for the possibility of such sharing despite suggestions on the packaging – thus perhaps indicating the potential for the accrual of another kind of culinary/health/food capital. This was especially the case, I found, as it relates to baked goods. I return to this further on.

Vis-à-vis the second point (health vulnerabilities and superfoods), I noted how anxious I had become around ensuring I had done what I could to keep myself in an ideal state of health in order to avoid the possibility of health complications due to Covid-19. Aduna's claim of boosted 'immune function' on its packaging, and the declarations on its website of heightened access to vitamin C, bacteria gut health, and immunity, felt significant (Aduna 2021d). While my scepticism and knowledge of the supplement industry and its claims kept much of this at bay, it did make me think about how attractive the narrative of consumable health might be to the general public and, in particular, the 'worried well'. The Covid health emergency, particularly when hospital beds and ventilators were in short supply, highlighted how much of a personal responsibility health had become as a result of decades of government budget cuts and austerity. In light of this, I found it striking just how hollow the rhetoric of personal risk management was. On a very personal, perhaps trivial, level, this resulted in the rationing of most health services, including dental ones which meant my dislodged filling had to be repaired, by me, with a kit ordered online (as directed by my dentist) until I could get an appointment – six months later. As Cardona argues,

> The emphasis on policies aimed at economic growth and competitiveness through financial deregulation and privatization, while limiting the size of the government and its social policy agenda, despite robust and repeated evidence of their negative effects on income inequality, and the social determinants of health, illustrate a pervasive commitment to neoliberal ideology.
>
> (Cardona 2020, 5)

This is also in keeping with hegemonic health norms and something I noted almost every day in my diary and notes. It was unnerving that individuals, in a fit of worry and as a result of pressure to conform, would be left with consumer products with questionable health claims in place of a well-funded healthcare system that functions to ensure population-wide mental and physical wellbeing. This was particularly ire-inducing for me as someone who studies the intersections between austerity, racialization, and health outcomes.

Before returning to some further thoughts on race, one other issue related to consuming baobab worth noting briefly is the media and medical discourse surrounding the supposed *causal* link between BMI/obesity and worse Covid-19 outcomes through which increased susceptibility was also racialized (Brody 2021). While some news media also considered the role of subsidized processed foods and cost/lack of access to fresh produce in producing ill health, many tended to home in on calorie-rich snacking, increased alcohol consumption, and the draw of ultra-processed foods. What I found notable on the day I revisited some of these articles was that it came on day 8 of drinking that same smoothie which had made my morning meal exemplary from a health hegemony perspective, but was now something I did not look forward to. This frustration was also connected to the social stigmatization of fatness which intersects with the responsibility to make the 'right' choices and adhere to 'idealized expectations, performances, embodiments, and patterns of consumption'. The fact that fatness qua fatness had been asserted as *causally* connected to the conditions that put one at risk of contracting Covid-19 meant that the body became a site of danger irrespective of the fact that one can be fat and not ill. It also meant that nonconforming bodies would be further stigmatized for not adhering to 'Western standards of health and beauty', for putting oneself and others 'at risk', and for (purportedly) being a burden on the health care system (Byrne 2020; Gordon 2020a; Sikka 2021a). Aduna's baobab powder fits in perfectly with this discourse as it relates to the kind of 'goodness' hegemonic good health envisions and cultivates with consumers seeking help in a (semi)privatized health care system.

Before relaying the nature of a significant change that came after these ruminations, I want to make a few remarks on how class and gender made themselves present in the two weeks I consumed baobab. Class, as it relates to health, diet, inequality, mobility, and class-based-action, is particularly important since, as Counihan puts it, it has often been the case that the elevation of 'choice in diet and self-control ... permits well-off people to decide what poor people should eat and men to determine what women should eat' (Counihan 1992, 55). I noted on several occasions how my class position made it possible for me to purchase baobab in the first instance, but also to have the time, wherewithal, and resources to learn about it. Doing this research had primed my social media algorithms to serve me advertising and content related to superfoods and health across various platforms (Instagram, Facebook, and Pinterest). Were I not in an occupation that encourages (demands?) social media engagement, with access to stable and consistent internet, and my existence as a single cis woman with sufficient time and money to think about these things, it would be unlikely that I would have heard anything about baobab. Yet hegemonic good health would still be in the zeitgeist – as part of the cultural milieu such that an inability to adhere to its strictures would be seen as a moral failing, a dismissal of ethical risk management, and what Overand et al. characterize as the rejection of an important 'healthist' commodity – namely, eating right to convey 'good [class] citizenship' (Ayo 2012; Overend et al. 2020).

Personal, historical, and familial circumstances are also important in this context. For example, I thought about how, as I was growing up, health trends and medical information were ever present in my home despite not having a familial history of cancer, diabetes, or heart disease. Although we were by no means rich (coming from a single income family), apprehensions about health, eating right, and maintaining a slim figure were obligatory and thus foods coded as 'healthy' were always around. As such, in consuming food, I always thought carefully about how food and health are co-constructed – for better and for worse. The class dynamics of hegemonic good health and its relationship to superfood cultures and patterns of consumption came up consistently in my diary entries. At one point (day 9) I starred and placed exclamation points around the comment 'why would anyone pay so much for powders and tablets that don't add anything taste-wise, don't have a discernible health payoff, are consumed in isolation, and are exorbitantly expensive?' Could it be, at least in part, a means by which to assert health capital and class distinction in line with the habitus of a body conscious elite?

Either way, the end result is that individuals unable to make these choices are seen as undisciplined, resistant to regulation, and a risk to the social body politic (Ivancic 2018). Fat bias and stigma often emerge out of this logic alongside ableist policies and norms that are then conflated with class and personal choice rather than being seen as inscribed in the very structures that perpetuate (health) inequality and oppression. Health and body stigma tend to intersect, overlap, and 'sweep together, enabling us to see patterns of prejudice and their horrific outcomes' (Perry 2014; also see Nash 2008b). So much more could be said on this – particularly on how ableism intersects with fat stigma. However, being cognizant of space, I will close this chapter with two final themes that emerged of my auto-ethnographic writing – namely, the subjects of race and health as well as the insights related to health, food, and community that arose after day 8.

'Health is racialised and racializing – and superfoods make this worse!!!' I wrote this sentence around day 4. In thinking about what I meant by this, I began to think carefully and consider the ways in 'race' was being made manifest wherein race is understood not as a biological characteristic or immutable attribute but as a technology of (racial) sorting used to maintain relations of power and subjugation (Gilmore 2007; Delgado and Stefancic 2017). Racialization carries with it related class and body privilege as well as its own form of hegemonic health expectations with respect to racialized groups, including those categorized as Black, brown and Indigenous, who are seen as unable or unwilling to engage in the kinds of health practices that are necessary to be considered a virtuous health subject. Consuming superfoods and engaging in appropriate health practices felt, to me, like a way to push back against racialized expectations – particularly ones that characterize brown bodies as genetically susceptible to diabetes and obesity. These discourses work to further naturalize race as a biological fact (Fullwiley 2008; Coates, Ferber and Brunsma 2017). I wrote about the ways in which the connections made between racialized bodies, ill health, and obesity are asserted as common sense by many in the medical community and media. For instance, I was always told, in no uncertain terms, that weight gain and not adhering to hegemonic good health norms, being South Asian, was particularly 'risky'. Factors such as overwork and stress (related to the immigrant experience), poverty, lack of stable employment, impaired access to fresh food, and limited time and space to move and be active are often ignored. As Mersh and Beck put it, 'Looking for a "purely genetical" explanation for differences in exposure to such factors and ensuing social or health outcomes does not do justice to the undeniable impact of racism and ethnocentrism. Instead, a focus on genes compounds, reinforces, and harmfully justifies racist and ethnocentric tropes' (Mersha and Beck 2020, 3). Despite this, race and health continue to be tightly linked and, for me, diabetes and obesity always seems to loom large. As a result, consuming superfoods like baobab sometimes felt, despite clear knowledge to the contrary, like a bit of harmless risk mitigation and management. This is an important element of hegemonic good health since self-surveillance and healthist practices are often seen as a way to show you are performing your duty as a worthy health subject wherein health is the product of individual choice.

Finally, because of my interest in the relationship between affect, culture, racialization, and health, I made a conscious effort to write about my felt experience of consuming a decontextualized and denatured foodstuff and, in particular, its connection to cultural appropriation. Suffice to say, it did not feel good. In fact, I felt like a little bit of a hypocrite when engaging in acts of boundary crossing that felt inappropriate especially 'when economic livelihoods are at stake' (Chan and Farrer 2021, 5). I have to admit that, for some reason, this cut of 'exotic fruit, processed by capital and marketed through a hegemonic good health lens for an affluent demographic obsessed with performative health' felt particularly distasteful the more I contemplated it.

I will now conclude with a final themes that emerged from these two weeks – specifically, the subject of taste, relations, and community. The framework I used to think about this was that of new materialism which helped me consider what it meant to affect and be affected by baobab powder (specifically to think about its agency *on me*). The observations that reflected this most vividly focused on baobab's taste – which was tart and slightly sweet but a bit chalky and almost indiscernible in a smoothie. It was also not sufficiently soluble to be taken in water. Attempts to source a whole fruit for individual consumption also proved difficult. As such, disappointingly, the pleasure associated with the consumption of *whole* sweet summer fruit at a communal breakfast table or as part of a fruit salad at a barbecue was not possible. I therefore felt a of privation – as if the nutritional gaze had extended so far that it had worked to produce in me characteristics of the nutricentric citizen wherein taste, pleasure, context, and relations enacted by and with food were cast aside, resulting in 'the co-option of nutrition science to extract surplus value and authority relations from food' (Dixon 2009, 322).

For me, the powder was so changed that it conformed to hegemonic good health rather than that of the baobab fruit which, while still part of capitalist circuits of production and consumption, is at least somewhat more open to emergent experiences and capable of forming new generative relations (Barad 2007; Braidotti 2007). I felt and wrote about a lingering sense that the emotion associated with food and health as an embodied state of socio-biological contentment was only rhetorically affirmed by Aduna's baobab powder in which health is understood as molecular, supplemental, risk mitigating, and engineerable (Rose 2001; Wright and Harwood 2012).

I decided to try and rectify this. While I was not able to make changes to my consumption habits entirely, I did decide to try my hand at some baking and to share the finished product with two neighbours (due to isolation and distancing rules this was the safest [legal] option). I thought that perhaps working with the powder directly, consuming it in a pleasurable form and sharing it with others, might engender a new way of relating to it. This approach is in keeping with auto-ethnographic strategies in which narrative, formulated for and with others, is used 'as a source of empowerment and a form of resistance to counter the domination and authority of canonical discourses' (Bochner and Ellis 2003, 749).

I thus chose two recipes from the Aduna website – the spiced orange and baobab Christmas cookies and the gluten-free banana bread with baobab – and made them. They were relatively straightforward recipes with most ingredients readily accessible, although I did have to order coconut oil, coconut sugar and some gluten-free flour. I decided to use the last six days of consuming and reflecting on baobab by eating these treats with coffee or tea in the afternoon. I intentionally made enough to make a small package for my neighbours. In worrying that they may not fit with other baked goods usually served with tea, I also baked some brownies and included them as well. I let both neighbours know what they were for (my study) and they thanked me. A few days later, both complimented me on the brownies but felt that the baobab baked goods were 'a bit dry' for the cookies, 'stodgy' for the banana bread, and, overall, 'tasted a bit like health food'. I felt similarly. The more pleasurable aspects of this exercise resided in the baking process as reflected in the lovely sweet and spicey smells that circulated throughout the house and the contact it established between me and my neighbours.

I also reflected on how far this change in tactic could be interpreted as evidence of baobab's reterritorialization through my attempt to engender conditions within which its meaningfulness could nurtured (Deleuze and Guatarri 1987). This realignment, I had hoped, might instigate localized 'lines of flight' that would re-articulate baobab powder discursively and materially as less of an instrumental nutrient and/or source of commodified 'wokeness' and, instead, as a conduit for enhanced commensality and sharing. Unfortunately, it did not quite turn out the way I had hoped. One reason was that because you could not taste the baobab in the cookies or banana bread, or identify it in a concrete way. Additionally, the baked goods were also coded by my neighbours right away as 'health food' and thus the expectation was not one of affective pleasure or reflective of what Coveney and Bunton call the 'enjoyment of gastronomic riches' (Coveney and Bunton 2003, 165).

Even an expanded understanding of pleasure 'as a form of consciousness-raising; a self-reflexive ... appreciation of materiality as culture' was not forthcoming (Sassatelli and Davolio 2010, 216). Possible reasons for this include the alienated way in which we tend to relate to food (which magically appears on our store shelves or at our doors via online orders), and the superficiality of the few minutes during which I was able to relay to my neighbours the socio-material significance of the fruit (behind a mask and two metres apart). As such, baobab, in this assemblage, retained its supplemental, functional, and hegemonic good health ethos.

My final few days of (returned) smoothie-centred consumption elicited little new, aside from a sense of disappointment and, upon re-reading my entries, a heightened sense of antipathy until the last day on which I found, on the Aduna website, the recipe for the traditional baobab drink. I made it simply by mixing the powder with milk, and sugar and quite enjoyed it. I was able to discern the slight sweet tang of the baobab powder on my tongue and noted a felt sense of refreshment and pleasure that created its own phenomenology of taste. It also elicited a positive bodily sensation as a result of the hot day and slight breeze. As such, in an acknowledgement of how vibrant objects can shape activity, I finished drinking this concoction outside on my patio, slowly, without thinking about what the drink was 'doing' for me but how the contents (healthful? who cares!) made me feel.

Conclusion

In this chapter I have taken up and examined baobab powder using Aduna as case study, first by drawing on political economy of culture and discourse analysis in which I discussed: 1. its imbrication in circuits of capitalist (re)production, and 2. how Aduna as a brand curates and constructs hegemonic good health. Nutritionism, race, racialization, coloniality, and gender (and the intersections between them) were discussed in detail by drawing on a close examination of the Aduna website. Also discussed, using new materialism, were the complex intra-actions within and between two cuts made to this superfood assemblage. Namely: 1. Superfoods–baobab–health subculture–health norms; and 2. Tradition–baobab–sustainability–social justice–wellness. In this section, I focused on the power of the baobab tree as agential object, the role of subcultural formations, the intersections of youth, class, femininity, enchantment and appropriation, and the saliency of social justice and sustainability. The tensions between a desire to *be* well (as a citizen and worker), to *do* well (for others and the environment), and to conform to dominant health norms were unpacked and discussed in detail.

The auto-ethnographic reflections that comprised the final part of this chapter used reflexive and reflective modes of analysis to disclose the affects and effects associated with consuming Aduna's baobab powder for two weeks. Clean eating, colonial Otherness, the sociology of food choice, health capital, fat phobia, Covid-19, and the intersection of race, class and health were examined with an eye towards entangled affect, relational embodied experience, and co-produced agency. Of particular importance were the final stages of the two weeks in which I enacted a 'nomadic intervention' first by re-configuring how and with whom baobab was consumed and then, when that was unsuccessful, consuming it in a way that, at least in part, de-coupled baobab from hegemonic good health (albeit temporarily).

In the next chapter, I apply this basic method to study another technology – one that fits more easily with traditional STS analysis – namely, the personalized dietary advice produced by GenoPalate. Here, hegemonic good health, GB, and PN take on a new power and saliency.

4

Case study two: GenoPalate

In this chapter, I engage in the same kind of formal analysis beginning with an overview and critique drawing on a political economy of culture approach. I focus specifically on the economic and ideological telos of GenoPalate and its product/service. Next, I supplement this critique with discourse analysis to further excavate how the languaging of the company, and the journalistic coverage that surrounds it, constructs knowledge about health. Here, discourse should be understood as 'an integral element of the material social process', one that sees communication as fundamental to socio-political practice (Fairclough 2001, 122). Having set this context, I then use a feminist new materialist lens to examine this discursive-sociopolitical-economic-material-biological assemblage using two material-discursive cuts made in order to bring to the surface the ways in which bodies, technologies, forces, and flows intra-act in both expected and unexpected ways. This approach pushes back against the kinds of binary and solipsistic thinking that have traditionally been 'instruments to the workings of power' (Barad 2014, 170). Finally, I close this chapter with an auto-ethnographic exegesis in which I chronicle and reflect on my experience of procuring my own genetic assessment and follow GenoPalate's dietary guidelines for two weeks. In doing so, I examine how food, science, biology, power, and social expectations form a network of external and internalized forces in which hegemonic good health, PN, and GM play a powerful role. This approach produces a robust experiential accounting which is essential to feminist theorizing in which onto-epistemologies emerge 'from partial experiential descriptions … [wherein] being becomes knowing becomes being' (Skeggs 1997, 20).

This chapter is somewhat unique as it includes a study of discourse and framing that relies on the company's website, some of its promotional materials, *and* my personal report. In order to maintain some consistency and a focus on material engagements, I take up the report in more detail in the auto-ethnographic section. The website thus features most prominently in the sections in which I extend my use of political economy and discourse analysis to examine GenoPalate's ideological assumptions.

Political economy of culture and GenoPalate

Genopalate is a private company headquartered in Milwaukee and specializes in personalized nutrition. It was founded in 2016, primarily with private venture capital (PitchBook 2021). Its founders include Dr Sherry Zhang, a molecular biologist turned obesity specialist, Dr Paul Auer, and Matt Edwards, a nutritionist. As noted, GenoPalate's funding comes primarily from venture capital with its last offering, in 2020, bringing in over $4 million (Owler 2020).

GenoPalate's slogan, 'Eat For Your Genes', is built into its logo and sets up the company's ideological commitments which centre on the belief that 'health' can be attained and obtained through the careful mapping of one's genes. Genetic data is framed as revelatory as it relates to accessing an ideal diet for optimal functioning. This is consistent with a particularly technophilic and functional understanding of hegemonic good health. The company uses proprietary technology and algorithms to determine the contents of their genetic reports but, notably, allows users to submit third party genome maps from which dietary advice can also be extracted. From a political economy of culture perspective, I argue that what GenoPalate represents is a company whose telos is that of profit and extraction wherein biological data is commodified in order to cater to co-produced consumer desires. These desires include that of inhabiting normative bodies and enacting ideal health subjectivities.

While fleshing out the ideological underpinnings of this transformation is important, it is also necessary to spend some time considering how biomedicine and genomic science are enterprises in which much of the basic science was first funded by governments and public institutions before being pulled in different directions by corporations (Rajan 2006). As with pharmaceutical research, these public roots are often forgotten such that new technologies and knowledges are materially and discursively framed as emerging out of entirely commodified spaces. From a political economy of culture perspective, this produces an infrastructure in which the knowledge produced about the human genome is filtered through the profit motive which then gives rise to cultural norms that see health as manipulable, the body as a commodity, and the individual as a health prosumer (Hardey 2019). The health prosumer role, as Lupton argues, enables individuals to have access to the information they pay for as consumers (note that GenoPalate does not give access to raw data), but also reflects their productive work wherein one's biological data is further monetized by genomic companies (i.e. by selling it to a third party). Or, as Mertz puts it, prosumers are 'those who engage in the so-called co-production of end goods and services, by sharing, for example, their knowledge, ideas, or "data" about themselves – in service of potential exploitation and valorisation' (Chertkovskaya, and Loacker 2016).

Another salient point from a political economic perspective is the function of venture capital as a form of funding since,

> Demand for a radically new innovations can only be perceived demand; market surveys and statistics of projected consumption are 'images' or 'visions' (or 'forecasts') of future sales, to be revised as real purchases do or do not take place.
>
> (Green 1991, 62–3)

As such, investors in firms like GenoPalate are betting on the company producing demand for their service – specifically that customers will want access to highly personalized, scientific data coupled with curated recommendations that can be applied in pursuit of hegemonic health goals. Sufficed to say, thus far, these companies have been quite successful.

Finally, it is important to note that what is being produced by GenoPalate is not just a service, but the production, marketization, and sale of a unique form of biocapital which Yoxen describes as an ontological transformation in which 'Life as a productive force' has come to include 'capitalizing upon research in molecular biology … [this is] not simply a way of using living things that can be traced back to the Neolithic origins of fermentation and agriculture [but] … a technology controlled by capital … a specific mode of the appropriation of living nature – literally capitalizing life' (Yoxen 1981, 112). Also important in this context are the neologisms of biocapital, biocapitalism, technobiopower, and biovalue that have evolved to describe the means by which bodies are transformed into data, informatized into 'extended exoselves', and optimized so that collected biodata is made profitable (Birch and Tyfield 2013; Lupton 2017a; Sabina 2018).

These insights extend Foucault's biopolitical concerns with how life has been made available to be manipulated, shaped, and formed to include the ways in which its 'vital potential' (genetic essence) has been taken advantage of (Foucault, Davidson and Burchell 2008; Waldby and Cooper 2008). These 'advantages', to be clear, are consistent with institutional, structural, and capital-centred priorities that have to do with power, profit, and the production of ideal bio-citizens (Chiapetta and Birch 2018). Hegemonic good health fits in well with this formation given its embrace of health behaviours and ideals including regimented fitness and food norms, idealized bodily comportment, and technophilic health practices. It also gives rise to biosocialities that engage with and support this ethos – namely the self-contained individual and their pursuit of a biological self that is normatively 'healthy' and supported by reproductive social networks. There are, however, cracks in these biosocial formations that individuals and groups have begin to exploit wherein the form of engagement made available to users is deployed in novel, more human-centred ways (Heath, Rayna and Taussig 2004).

Initially, I was reticent to send my DNA to GenoPalate even with the option of not allowing the data to be used in the future or for 'research purposes'. I therefore took measures that might muddy the waters a little. For example, I decided to opt out of sharing my information or having my sample stored and bought the kit from a third party (so as to disentangle my name/address from my profile). I also had the package sent to a friend's place, did not affix a return address (upon sending it back), made an attempt to use a pseudonym, and used a VPN server to register so as to further obscure my identity. While not bulletproof, this allayed some of my concerns. I also considered using and adhering to a dummy set of results but felt the auto-ethnography would suffer since the results were not 'mine'. In the end, despite my best efforts, as well the company having provisions to keep one's identity separate from the results (and ensuring users that *identifiable* data would never be shared), my concerns remained. Placing (pushing?) these concerns aside, I finally collected the requisite biological materials and sent them off.

Discourse analysis: The website

GenoPalate's website invites customers to 'optimize and personalize' their 'wellness' by using their genetic health testing kits to help you 'start eating for your genes'. The home page on the day accessed and analysed (1 June 2021) is bright with photos of a range of people handling and cooking food – lots of salads, fruit (coconuts, lemons), and Italian food (pizza, pasta, olive oil, wine) – code for the much lauded Mediterranean diet. This is in-keeping with hegemonic good health's functional nutritionism and fetishization of certain foods (and diets) as especially healthful. For the Mediterranean diet this, rhetorically, consists of the science-based justification of the nutritional benefits of specific foods and the promise that consuming them will lead to, amongst other things, a unique kind 'of sociality, particularly sociable, leisurely eating, which are said to define the Mediterranean versus the North Atlantic' (Meneley 2020, 8). Being able to fuse both together, sociality and health, is key, as are the correlations between 'lifestyle' diseases (heart disease, cancer, obesity), diet, and genetic risk factors. The site's images include an older (white) couple tasting and cooking sauce behind a prominently featured bottle of what looks like red wine and a middle-aged white woman who hands over (or receives?) a large bowl of salad while balancing an individual pizza on her lap. In another image, a 30-something Black man cuts a pizza in half with a bottle of olive oil set beside him. Snapshots of lemons and wound-up pasta are placed next to each of these 'human-centred' photos. It is significant that the men and women depicted in these photos range in age and genders and, notably, are not all white. They are, however, all able-bodied while also conforming to accepted standards of perceived health and beauty as exemplified by hegemonic good health.

Much of the remainder of the website, content wise, is relatively basic and sparse. The website makes clear that theirs is a user-friendly technology with 'Simplified DNA Testing' and four-step process which begins with sending your DNA and ends with the beginning of 'Your Personalized Nutrition Journey' (GenoPalate 2021). Images of a smartphone with data and text next to it form the window through which health advice and results are accessed and which streamlines discovery, understanding, science, and convenience. These frames function as a form of discursive and social practice that speaks to larger relations of power and the production of good health. As Fairclough attests, 'the whole social order of discourse is put together and held together as a hidden effect of power', one which reifies hegemonic good health and focuses on idealized consumer performances and the adoption of health regimes that conform to a Western ideal (Fairclough 2001 46; also see Chouliaraki and Fairclough 1999).

It is important to disentangle claims made by ancestry companies versus those promulgated by GenoPalate and related platforms. Analysis of discourse that surrounds ancestry results tends to include that of belonging, identity, place, tradition, and geography. It also reveals a disjuncture between what is promised, ancestral lineage, and what is provided – a genetic connection to *living* populations for whom data has been gathered. Ancestry tests tend to function in ways that racialize its users and reinscribe race as molecular – which then reproduces a racially designated understanding of population despite all evidence to the contrary (namely that race is not genetic) (Fullwiley 2008; TallBear 2013a; Duster 2015). While ancestry does not feature explicitly in discourse on the website, it remains the case that the inferences and correlations made about diet emerge out of this data laden with racial assumptions. The first discursive frame that can be discerned from my close readings, coding of terms, and examination of how these are tied to relations of power are that of *discovery* and *understanding*. This is underpinned by calls for users to 'Feed Your Curiosity' and 'Make Informed Decisions', as seen in an image of an elderly East Asian woman going through what appears to be a report with her son. The first page of the website implores potential customers to refrain from ignoring their genes and asks if you are 'ready to discover a healthier you' since it is your DNA that 'hold[s] the secrets to your health'. GenoPalate positions itself as a helpful interlocuter capable of unlocking said secrets and providing users with the tools to 'improve your overall health' by devising 'a diet that will keep you happy and healthy for the rest of your life' (GenoPalate 2021).

The cultivation of understanding is essential here and tied to an ethic of consciousness raising wherein providing individuals with information is believed to be sufficient in promoting behavioural change. The 'customer success stories' speak to this belief directly. Here, users wax poetic about their health journeys – how they came to eat better, attain better health, and adopt better habits in light of knowledge about their genes by gaining understanding of, as one customer put it 'what my body requires for nutrients and the best foods for my body. It's given me great insight into exactly what my body needs' (Genopalate 2021). This is an especially neoliberal conception of health – one in which the modern subject is lauded for pursing hegemonic health goals and where individualized (health) technologies of the self comes to stand in for collective and community centred alternatives.

The conjuncture between ancestry and personalized diets adds a novel, even tricky dimension to our understanding of hegemonic good health, PN, and GM as manifest by GenoPalate and its discourses of understanding and discovery. On the one hand, it is important to emphasize that the conclusions about diet embedded in GenoPalate's reports are drawn from a molecular understanding of genes (GM) in which DNA is seen as a powerful, boundary setting set of master molecules we can work with, albeit individually, as health subjects if given appropriate information. GenoPalate's website takes users on a journey of discovery and education promising to 'draft a blueprint for the

nutritional guidelines your DNA dictates', and noting that 'What works for
your sister or neighbour won't necessarily do you any good'. 'Just one genetic
variant', the website contends, 'can make a significant impact in the way your
body metabolizes and absorbs certain nutrients or how you process food …
since all customers are '100% unique'. Instead of spending time interrogating
these claims, I want to focus on their meaning for users and, in particular, the
ways in which these 'texts attempt to position, locate, define, and … enable
and regulate readers and addressees' (Mogashoa 2014, 106). Notably, this
framing does not address the social determinants of health like environmental
racism, health care apartheid, accessibility and affordability of food, everyday
stress, poverty, racialization, misogyny, ableism, etc., that operate as barriers to
attaining 'good health' and in which the 'relationships between social factors
and health' (Braveman and Gottlieb 2014, 20) take centre stage (as do the
health stories of those experiencing cumulative barriers to health based on
their gender, ascribed race, sexuality, ability, etc.) (Warren 2001; Richardon
and Norris 2010; Lopez 2013). Discourse analysis thus reveals how absences
surrounding the prevalence of the discourse of discovery and understanding
can be as revealing as manifest text.

This neoliberal and highly personalized promise of accuracy is tied to claims
about how GenoPalate is able to extrapolate from the 'ancestry' function which
introduces and embeds users into new forms of genetic engagement, belonging,
and community and in which all forms of collective classification are important
(Nelson 2008). Learning that you are connected through DNA to X culture
or descendent from X people has proven to be particularly meaningful. Nash
refers to this as a form of genealogical incorporation, one that 'may produce
an inclusive social imaginary of shared descent but simultaneously deny
ethnic difference and naturalize a genealogical calculus of national belonging'
(Nash 2017, 2). Irrespective of the science, which I discuss below (as well as
the difficulty raised by Indigenous conceptions of belonging which are based
on kinship and relations, not biology (Tallbear 2013b; Walajahi, Wilson and
Hull 2019)), GenoPalate's discursive frames focus explicitly on the discovery
and understanding of the individual and extends the promise that PN and the
molecular understanding of one's genetics (GM) can and will unlock the secrets
of good health.

Before moving on from this point, one other aspect of the role of ancestry
discourse and desire is worth emphasizing. Specifically, how these two tests
(ancestry and diet) function together as onto-epistemological matterings
that circumscribe and fulfil three of the most important aspects of human

becoming – namely, who we are, who we belong to, and who we can become. The options GenoPalate provides, one of uploading one's existing genetic profile or having one done through Genopalate, holds space for the two 'reports' to intra-act discursively and materially to answer these questions.

With respect to larger, community-centric understandings of genetic data, what the above analysis reveals is that the 'who we belong to' question is distorted by overwrought assumptions about what this data can really tell us. It assumes that one would gain representative self-knowledge by learning their origins and roots using genomic data to reconstruct historical identity. This identity, however, has never been fixed, homogonous, or transparent and yet remains embedded in the 'desperate cartograph[ies] of the nation state' (Gilroy 1990, 119), and the 'pure and primordial cultures and races assigned to politically differentiated spaces' (Nash 2008a, 4; also see Abel and Schroeder 2020). At the same time, users are provided with the data needed to realize *individual* health ideals that align with the 'neoliberal tenets of self-discipline, hard work, and discerning consumerism' (Petersen and Lupton 1996, 48–9). This allows users to simultaneously pursue knowledge about who they are and who they could be, which is then tied to the bodies they will ideally be able to inhabit.

This discourse of understanding and discovery also extends to the section of the website that advertises 'success stories' and includes short quotes from users that focus specifically on what GenoPalate did for them. These outcomes align with hegemonic good health but are adumbrated by the promise that 'eating for ones' genes' will help customers break free from constraints (dietary discipline, social coercion, unrealistic standards) once they purchase the correct, personalized, and genetically fine-tuned information:

> Dina, Oneonta, AL: With the info I received on my report, I learned the food items that my body took a liking too! So now, I never fear cutting food out because I just enjoy the ones that fit my body's needs and I eat plenty of them.

> Mary: I have been following GenoPalate for about 8–9 months now and I no longer worry about which foods to buy and eat.

> B.R.: I have told so many people about GenoPalate! I truly appreciate having more concrete information on what my body needs from nutrition.

In each of these disclosures, GenoPalate's customers have concretized the understanding/discovery frame in a manner that places an inordinate amount of emotion and trust in data (Genopalate 2021).

The second discursive frame that came up repeatedly is that of 'science'. This dispositif is connected to our technophilic orientation in which scientific determinism aligns with a belief in the transformative potential of technology to solve social and individual problems. This perspective sees health technologies as instrumental, technocratic, and emerging out of a scientific assemblage that cultivates a technocratic relation to the world rather than one of care, collectivity, and plurality (Arora, Sharma and Stirling 2020). A distinction needs to be made here between technology as a sociomaterial assemblage of entangled tools, machines, artefacts, and materialities; as a set of techniques (inclusive of knowledge, cognitive approaches, and values); and as embedded in organizations/institutions and identities (Collins, Hage and Hull 1986; Latour 2004; Barad 2007; Orlikowski and Scott 2008). In each, science is co-constituted with and by technology while also remaining analytically distinct from it. Science, and scientific determinism, is used to describe an onto-epistemological worldview that sees itself as neutral, objective, predictive, and capable of pushing humanity towards progressive ends (Popper and Barley 2012). It is taken up by scholars of STS, such as the late Bruno Latour, who describes contemporary forms of determinism as living in networks of people, organizations, facts, and machines that have a '*vis intetia* of their own' (Latour 1987, 133).

Faith in biotechnology, agribusiness, pharmaceuticals, and genetic engineering to solve health problems is endemic in this kind of deterministic thinking and is expressed throughout the GenoPalate website – the first few lines of which touts its use of the 'the latest genomic nutrition science [to] … optimize your health'. Also made clear, in its 'Our Science' section, is that its techniques have been tested using 'carefully vetted, evidence-based research from high-impact clinical trials, as well as population studies'. Further on, GenoPalate begins using recognizable but authoritative lexical lingo around DNA testing and health. This includes 'drafting a [personalized] blueprint' (PN) which reflects how 'your body metabolizes and absorbs certain nutrients or how you process food' since 'Your genetic code and science-based nutrition are the foundations to devising a diet that will keep you happy and healthy for the rest of your life'. From this framing, GenoPalate promises that health will emerge out of a meeting of genetic markers and 'evidence based research correlating your genetic variants with nutrition that's shown positive health outcomes'. However, in a neoliberalizing sleight of hand, GenoPalate also, in its 'Our Science' sections of the website, asserts that they 'don't dictate your diet' but 'simply present you with a plethora of insights customized for your genotype'. Acting on this becomes the responsibility of individuals who have been furnished with the information needed to become an ideal health subject (Genopalate 2021).

There is, however, a discernible disjuncture visible in this framing of 'conventional' medical science. For example, in the 'personal stories' section, contributors note how the information gleaned from GenoPalate helped them feel more confident in their discussions with health professionals and even helped them diagnose conditions before their physicians (e.g. lactose sensitivities). One noted that some of the information even 'ran counter to what I [the consumer] had been told by mainstream nutrition authorities' (GenoPalate 2021). This represents an interesting turn since it situates GenoPalate as both a cutting-edge technology based on the latest health science, as well as being different from the mainstream. This allows the company to interpellate a wider community of interested health consumers. Specifically, those who align closely with mainstream science as well as those whose sociopolitical beliefs, for whatever reason, resist establishment opinions (Earp 2015; Rekker 2021).

It is important to underline that the seemingly objective and self-actualizing, good health-based results GenoPalate promises does not address other ways in which the medical and health science community has failed certain groups for whom scepticism might be warranted. This includes women, racialized minorities, the disabled, those who identify as fat, and individuals who exist at the intersections. Fat stigma, structural and interpersonal racism, cis male-centred medicine, and a history of medical malpractice and criminality adds to this (Lawrence 2000; Phelan et al. 2015; Baptiste 2020). While absent from this frame, it is important to consider precisely how this gap operates to solidify GenoPalate's demographic, which may not include these groups explicitly (which is itself an important insight), or could, in time, function as an aspirational health technology – one in which hegemonic good health, as a normalizing and idealizing health regime, applies just enough socializing pressure so that previously marginalized groups are made to 'take responsibility for their own health by using labels and other nutrition-related bio-pedagogical practices [e.g. GenoPalate] to train and discipline their bodies' (Silchenko and Askegaard 2020, 15). This, however, is not certain – particularly since inclusion in a neoliberal health regime does not represent the kind of prosocial political practice most critical STS scholars have in mind. Taken together, it remains the case that this framing of science and technology as objective, dispositive, causal, and a priori 'good' is consistent with hegemonic good health and thus embeds GenoPalate within hegemonic health discourse.

It is GenoPalate's focus on science, discovery, and understanding that forms the most important planks of its discursive health assemblage which then operates to solidify its role within a political economic milieu based on monetization and neoliberal capitalism. There is, however, one final frame which adds to this and is worth noting because of the way in which it reflects modern socio-economic pressures: that of convenience. I was struck, when sorting through the frames collected from the website, by the number of times ease of use and convenience featured in how the technology and its processes were described.

Concretely, this language appears most prominently in pre-selected customer comments, such as A.B. who describes their experience as 'quick, easy and informative …', stating, 'The layout of the report was great as it's straightforward and comprehensive'. Similarly, Mary makes note of how easy it had made her shopping while Andy describes his plan as 'easy to understand' and the process as 'easy to execute'.

This ethos of convenience extends to GenoPalate's 'DNA-Approved' personalized recipe service, which blends genetic specificity (GM) with personalization (PN) for the busy urban professional. Aside from the brief acknowledgement of customer preferences and a promise that the food will be 'both nutritious and delicious', these recipes fit within the frame of ease of use and execution. Wider discussions of taste and pleasure are circumvented by focusing on nutrition-centred and functional goals. It is also significant that it is assumed that these meals will be consumed alone. This draws eating and its imbrication with health further away from a relation of commensality (the act of eating together) in which 'the material and affective elements of cooking and eating together' are seen to 'nurture collective spaces of encounter' and towards one of isolated, goal-oriented, and objectivist consumption (Marovelli 2019, 190).

Vitamins based on one's genetic profile are also available to be purchased and are advertised as offering a convenient way in which to get your body the absorbable nutrients it needs – ones that are 'bio-available', 'flexible', and 'cost effective'. This political economic integration provides GenoPalate with further ways in which to make a profit, despite the fact that the science behind these supplements is highly suspect (Otero, Pechlaner and Gürcan 2014).

On the whole, what CDA has allowed me to do is to extend the cultural analysis of the political economic critique and, in doing so, create a socio-economic basis from which to initiate a closer study of the forms of materiality GenoPalate and the networks surrounding it incite and excite. Having done the test myself, and having followed the resulting recommendations for two weeks, the next step is to decide how to 'cut' this assemblage in order to draw out important insights and observations vis-à-vis GenoPalate as a socio-technical object.

GenoPalate and new materialism

Cuts:

1. GenoPalate – 'the science'–race–gender–disability–intersections
2. GenoPalate – commodification–privacy–(self)surveillance

These two cuts reflect priorities found in STS, my own analysis, as well as the operation of hegemonic good health, PN, and GM where all are seen as constituting powerful discursive and material forces in our understanding of health. Both are taken up below:

1. GenoPalate – 'the science'–race–gender–disability–intersections

Much can be said critically about the science that underpins GenoPalate's product/service. Its claim, to begin with, is that its methods are 'vetted [using], evidence based research from high-impact clinical trials, as well as population studies, which are then used to "draft a blueprint" for nutritional guidelines based on "27 nutritional traits" extracted from one's DNA' (GenoPalate 2021). GenoPalate has a downloadable document which goes into the science of the DNA test in more detail (beginning with a primer on DNA) and, importantly, explains that their technology relies on the mapping of specific genetic variants, or single-nucleotide polymorphisms (SNPs), that impact how diet translates into 'health' for individual people. The following quote lays this out in more detail:

> Studies examining the connection between a person's genes and their environment show that there are variables in different individuals' bodily systems when it comes to nutrient requirements. These requirements largely depend on an individual's genetic variants, as each person's individual genetic makeup directly affects the metabolizing of nutrients, their transport throughout the body, and how their body removes waste and toxins.

> For instance, someone carrying the MTHFR 677T allele – one of at least two alternative forms of a gene that occurs due to a mutation found at the same place on a chromosome – will need more vitamin B and folate in their diet to keep their homocysteine levels low. The MTHFR gene provides instructions for making an enzyme that plays a role in processing amino acids, which are the building blocks of proteins. Researchers have linked lower MTHFR enzyme activity and higher homocysteine levels to poor cardiovascular health.
>
> (GenoPalate 2021)

Variations in genes that influence caffeine metabolism, carbohydrate processing, vitamin uptake, fat intake, etc., are given as examples. It is also made clear what the limitations of this kind of testing are, including the inability to definitely diagnosing disease or allergies, while also critiquing scholarship that claims that nutrigenomic science does not work as expected.

What is of most significance here are the sociomaterial matterings that emerge out of the forces connected to the test's underlying presuppositions. These presuppositions are founded on the assumption that there is a kind of transparency associated with our genes. The causality asserted from this is of particular concern since while there is some acknowledgement of factors impacting health outside of DNA (including 'emotional, social, economic, and environmental factors'), it is made abundantly clear that GM, as an ideology and material force, has an outsized impact on health. The assumption is that if this hidden knowledge is made transparent, hegemonic good health ideals, inclusive of 'idealized expectations, embodiments, and patterns of consumption' as well as 'Western standards of health and wellbeing', can be achieved. The 'entire movement of eating for your genes', they state, is 'a solution that has provided many with increasingly positive outcomes. We dive deeper to unlock all the secrets once and for all' (GenoPalate 2021).

It is important to spend some time discussing how functional this model of health is and how it 'feeds certain human sensibilities only: rationality, reduction, and objectivity'. Even this is not done particularly well since a robust approach would also take up and grapple with significant environmental factors (Mudry 2009, 3). Environmental stressors like pollution; daily stresses linked to poverty, economic precarity, racism, misogyny, ableism; and epigenetic factors, RNA messages, hormones, and body chemistry (microbiome) are just a few of the myriad forces that have been left out (Swan 2012; Anderson et al. 2018; Roberts and McWade 2021). It is also the case that most diseases have a number of genes involved in their activation even where a case for soft determination can be made – something GenoPalate does not address (Ulder 2019). This, as Riordan and Nadeau contend, is to say nothing about "so-called "modifier genes" that modulate the phenotypic manifestation of target genes in an epistatic manner' (Riordan and Nadeau 2017, 177). As such, it is crucial, in understanding this health assemblage, that we also think carefully about how GenoPalate's articulation of the science, specifically its non (or attenuated)-relational ontology, limits more heterogenous understandings of the biomaterial and environmental interdependencies that co-construct health.

Moreover, the form of worlding GenoPalate enacts through their tests and reports perpetuates a hegemonic biosociality, one that remains somatic and corporeal and thus encourages acting on the self (Rose 2007; Clarke et al. 2010; Gurrieri, Brace-Govan and Previte 2014). This understanding of health is nutritionistic, healthist, and highly individualized but promises agency, happiness, and health through self-knowledge. One would think that this kind of technophilic determinism, GB, and technoscientizing of life might curtail agency and encourage a kind of fatalism wherein DNA is seen as health destiny. However, as the success of companies like GenoPalate and the rise of neoliberal health responsibilization and risk management make clear, attaining better bodies through self-improvement is still seen as salient and necessary.

One striking lacuna on the website is the absence of diet talk or even normative body talk. Body types, slimness, beauty, and attractiveness are not mentioned at all. Invitations to use the test to 'celebrate your body', 'indulge in … gene friendly foods', 'inspire the healthiest you', and 'eat better for a healthier life' is the language used in its place (GenoPalate 2021). This, I contend, is intentional and reflective of the expectation of a higher-level internalization of hegemonic good health and desire for PN coupled with the diffusion of a social norm in which the *explicit* discussion of body ideals (i.e. the pursuit of thinness) is now considered to be culturally unacceptable. This, in part, is the result of changes to how we talk about health and bodies in which aesthetics, as least performatively, have taken a backseat to wellness. However, I maintain that this masks a discursive sleight of hand in which hegemonic good health is overlaid with a veneer of progressive body positivity (it's about health, not how you look!) wherein, despite the elevation of wellbeing, a slim, fit body remains the desired outcome (Bartky 1990; Lazuka 2020). As such, instead of an explicit discussion of how our self-worth is all too often connected to our appearance, we have the prevalence of\discourses of self-care, 'healthy habits', and an understanding of wellness that draws on postfeminist and neoliberal ideals.

This reflects similar movements that extoll body liberation but mimic diet culture by focusing on self-transformation (Morris 2019). Choosing to engage in normative health practices becomes a way in which to perform hegemonic good health in acceptable ways – ones that are 'infinitesimal[y]' detailed and "meticulous[ly] control the operations of the body," by simultaneously cultivating its capacities and optimizing its compliance with convergent health and beauty norms' (Sanders 2017, 17). Remember that postfeminism maintains that traditional feminist concerns are no longer pressing and, instead, advocates for the elevation of choice, personal responsibility, meritocratic striving, and entrepreneurship wherein body/healthwork is framed as 'fun' (Gill 2016; Toffoletti, Thorpe, and Francombe-Webb 2018; O'Neill 2020). This idea of 'fun' is in keeping with GenoPalate's aesthetic with happy users sharing how they 'loved the whole experience', 'enjoy[ed] certain details', and were 'surprised (in a good way)', which is then connected to a presentation of health that is hegemonic in substance but de-aestheticized so as to feel less stigmatising (GenoPalate 2021). While I have focused on women in much of this cut, it is also the case that a very similar form of framing also applies to men's health labour but filtered through the lens of strength and ideal masculinity (Garfield, Isacco and Rogers 2008).

It is important to keep in mind that, overall, ideal masculinity and femininity tend to be coded as white, young, Western, and able-bodied by default. Thus, race, and ethnicity are strategically elided with no overt discussion of either in the primary sections of GenoPalate's website. The only places in which race emerges is implicitly in the way ancestry tests inform dietary prescriptions (which assumes racial categorization) and in GenoPalate's blog in which several of the articles do mention race and ethnicity explicitly.

The most significant way in which race is reflected in these tests is on the assumption that race is, at least in part, reflected in one's DNA as a factor deeper than phenotype. This understanding permeates genetic ancestry testing as well as nutrigenomic PN. While it is unclear precisely what kind of testing and sampling GenoPalate relies on (it is proprietary), its reports and place in the industry means it is likely to be a microarray method in which admixed populations, constituted by a 'mosaic of segments inherited from their [also admixed] ancestors' (Fu, Welsh, deVillena and McMillan 2012), have their genetic variations mapped out which is then compared to the company's (often limited) reference population. Here, allele frequency is key but not particularly revealing since genetic patterning will vary due to genetic drift, demographics, and selection. In any case, it is clear that race, as a method of differential categorization, does not correspond to genetically distinct human types but continues to be relied upon (Kittles and Weiss 2003)!

I maintain that the science GenoPalate relies on, in terms of what it claims to tell us, is lacking in both context and information. All ancestry testing methods nutrigenomic prescriptions rely on are founded on,

mtDNA and Y-DNA [and SNP focused] tests [that] compare a consumer's genetic sample to a selective proprietary sample database and analyze a small percentage of a test-taker's DNA; and provide probabilistic outcomes) and historical dynamics (e.g., racial and ethnic identities are sociocultural phenomena and the unpredictability of human migration patterns suggest that contemporary social groups cannot be easily correlated with earlier ones), the associations inferred through genetic genealogy are necessarily provisional.

(Nelson 2016, 237)

Greely then puts the lie to the promise of scientific certainty as it relates to the genealogical claims associated with personalized nutrition:

the real science of genetic genealogy is riddled with qualifications and limitations; it deals with varying degrees of probability and not with anything close to certainty. It looks at precise questions, precisely defined, like a direct paternal or maternal line. Genetic genealogy skips the caveats and in doing so promotes a false perception of science; it invokes science's power without accepting its limits.

(Greely 2008, 231)

This places the claims made by GenoPalate under the microscope and further problematizes its assertions about the representativeness of its data sets, the robustness of its sampling techniques, and its conception of 'purity' (TallBear 2014; Duster 2015). Dietary assumptions and prescriptions extrapolated from these findings are tainted by similar shortcomings – ones that are techno-scientific as well as socio-political/cultural. To be clear, the critique here is that instead of seeing race for what it is, a constructed technology of enacted and differential sorting (based on perceived phenotypical difference), it comes to reflect a pernicious form of biological determinism. As such, much of DNA ancestry-based testing does not tell us what we want or think it does (Fields and Fields 2014; Gillborn and Ladson-Billings 2020); namely, who we are, where we belong, and how we might live long, healthy lives. Health risks and nutritional deficiencies have also become racialized since admixture-based testing, as Fullwiley contends, reifies beliefs in racial difference and ignores the most important factors that determine health – namely, environmental pollution/stress, access to healthcare, availability and affordability of food, spaces to move, community belonging, financial security, education etc. (Fullwiley 2015; Braveman, Egerter and William 2011). GenoPalate's approach, however, fits well within our hegemonic good health assemblage in which technophilic determinism is key.

On the level of representation, race presents itself in this cut in a few other ways – the most obvious of which is visually in the diverse images of people used on its website. This reflects changing norms around visibility and inclusion and the realization, on the part of corporations, that their customer base extends well beyond white men and women. The politics of racial inclusion, however, gets tricky when it is seen as performative and thus ignorant of ways in which race functions materially. Namely, as a technology of 'mattering, given that racialized-gendered bodies *come to matter*, i.e. they manifest materially-performatively and discursively' (Pulsifer 2019, 8). As such, we need to think carefully about how race functions in this cut on the level of visibility and how this can be addressed pedagogically.

Turning to GenoPalate's blog, there are a number of instances in which race and/or ethnicity (where the latter acts as a stand-in for race), is taken up directly and towards which an explicit connection is made between race, genes, and health. This includes an article which states that 'certain races and ethnicities are also at an increased risk [of diabetes] (African Americans, Hispanic/Latino Americans, American Indians, Pacific Islanders, and some Asian Americans)' (GenoPalate, 10 November 2020). Also of note is a brief mention of race in the context of nutrition and supplementation in which one's ascribed race, it is argued, 'can impact our overall nutritional status' (GenoPalate, 8 May 2020). Ethnicity, which often acts as a proxy for race, is also discussed in the context of insulin resistance as well as in an article about blood pressure, which states that risk for 'high blood pressure can increase based on your age and your race or ethnicity' (GenoPalate, 10 November 2020; also see GenoPalate 2019). Taken together, this language brings into focus and solidifies the belief that there is a genetic component to race which, to be clear, is patently false. A recent publically available article in *National Geographic* titled 'Why Race Is Not a Thing, According to Genetics', makes this clear:

> when we look at the full genomes from people all over the world, those differences [skin, morphological features, hair texture] represent a tiny fraction of the differences between people. There is, for instance, more genetic diversity *within* Africa than in the rest of the world put together. If you take someone from Ethiopia and someone from the Sudan, they are more likely to be *more* genetically different from each other than either one of those people is to anyone else on the planet!
>
> (Worrall 2017)

Overall, what the racialized and racializing diffractive force the GenoPalate test brings to the fore illuminates the ways in which agential cuts reveal relations of power that reflect 'the movements between meanings and matter, word and world, interrogating and re-defining boundaries ... in "the between" where knowledge and being meet' (Barad 1996: 185). Race thus becomes a discursive-material force within this assemblage and a powerful agent within this cut – one that is reinscribed through technology and concretized in social settings with its own set of divisions, institutions, history, and power relations.

Turning to the last elements of this cut, gender and dis/ability, absence rather than presence is the formative force. While I discuss gender in a significant amount of detail in my auto-ethnography, what I want to underline here is how gender as a constructed discursive-material identity position is presented vis-à-vis PN and GM. In general, gender is addressed sparingly by GenoPalate with a few mentions of it in a discussion of calorie intake and nutritional needs, as a factor in tailoring a customized diet, and in accounting for differences in BMI and waistline limits. The images of women in the 'stories' section consist of mostly white women of different ages – all of whom have normative bodies. Overwhelmingly, women have borne the brunt of hegemonic good health's rigorous body expectations which include weight as well as the cognitive burden of constructing nutricentric diets for one's whole family. Thinness is thus seen as a material indicator of hegemonic good health and as a manifestation of ideal femininity in visible form (Bordo 2018). With GenoPalate, this ethos of ideal bodily comportment is aligned with a vision of the a perfect body – what Quinn and Crocker call a 'body for success' (Quinn and Crocker 1999). Whiteness and thinness are co-constituted and concretized using a genetic lens in which Black and brown women's bodies are seen as unruly, unhealthy, and uncontrollable (Strings 2019). Genetically based diet plans also have the potential to buttress postfeminist understandings of empowerment, choice, and rights in ways that repackage old restrictions as liberation (Morris 2019a). Women are still pressurized to be thin, fit, and attractive biocitizens using the appropriate amount of carefully calibrated, control and release (Greenhalgh 2015). GB diet plans thus act as an instrument, a material force enacting gendered behaviour but in ways that appear chosen. This is how GenoPalate exerts agential force since its very claim to PN – i.e. to producing individualized, biogenetically tailored programmes – can both scratch one's consumerist itch (by purchasing health rather than examining structures that give rise to ill-health), and make a blanket claim of humanness over race, gender, class, sexuality, dis/ability, etc. Because GenoPalate and other PN services offer a microscopic level of personalization, they can also claim racial and gender specificity and/or personal specificity based on consumer demographics.

On the level of representation, while it is the case that the images used by GenoPalate are slightly more representative with respect to race and gender, they are not at all with respect to disability or bodily comportment. The website, inclusive of the blog, makes no mention of disability at all. What this absence brings to the surface, as part of this cut, is the double erasure of disabled bodies: first, in the context of hegemonic good health, of which GenoPalate is a part and in which ideal health is explicitly able-bodied – what McRuer (2010) calls 'compulsory able-bodiedness', and second in the history of genetic science in which the physical and existential erasure of disabled bodies became a formative part of science under the umbrella of eugenics (Michell and Snyder 2003; Scully 2018).

New genetic technologies oriented to screening and/or editing one's child's genetic makeup so as to 'science out' disabilities (through techniques like pre-natal diagnosis (PND), non-invasive prenatal testing (NIPT), and CRISPR (Clustered Regularly Interspaced Short Palindromic Repeats)), form a constellation of new technologies that bioethicists and others worry risks re-embedding the social engineering ethos of much of the nineteenth and twentieth centuries. During this time, ableism and colonialism intersected with racism leading to the institutionalization and surveillance of targeted populations, forced sterilization to prevent reproduction, and, in the case of the Third Reich, actual extermination (Kenneth and Garver 1991; Stern 2016). The deep connection between the study of genetics and heredity reflects attempts, as Francis Galton (1883) put it, to 'study and advocate for "well-born" children, emphasize heredity, and exert a powerful impact on social policies' (Galton 1883). It also forms an authoritative and seemingly 'scientific' discourse that continues to seek to 'correct', 'improve', and transmogrify perceived human limitations. Contemporary liberal iterations of eugenics are more in keeping with current forms of genetic testing in which informed (parental) choice, agency, and quality of life-based justifications form a hegemonic discourse with very real material consequences for how disabled citizens are valued (Agar 1998).

Nothing explicit in GenoPalate's literature points to or broaches disability as a material identity. However, as with race, it remains the case that the science on which its relies has historically been exploitative and dehumanizing. If we think about science as value-laden we also have to consider how past interests and motivations continue to colour present objectives – particularly as it relates to a desire for a social order in line with objectives like economic productivity, human perfectibility (i.e. the Quantified Self), a burgeoning life science industry, and an individualized conception of health (Evans and Moreno 2015). Ancestry testing, which informs GenoPalate's dietary prescriptions, is part of this socio-historical assemblage and thus contains remnants of genetic determinism. This is where GenoPalate's agential power is made manifest – namely, as a technology whose hegemonic conception of health is filtered through the language of scientific neutrality and responsibility. Genetic information and individual choice thus become the means by which to avoid objectionable states of being.

Additionally, no depiction or reference is made to fat bodies, thus reproducing the connection between fatness and Otherness. Schlauderaff refers to this as a mediated process of 'reifying the normate' such that individuals are expected to fall 'in line with normative societal beliefs and expectations' consistent with 'stories' that 're-create the normate and connect these healthy, middle-class and family-value laden lives with the product' (Schlauderaff 2018, 11; also see Beckmann 2005). It is important, however, to make a distinction between fat bodies and disabled bodies which do not always overlap (and are distinguished in law, i.e. the American Disabilities Act (ADA)). However, I have recently been persuaded by the work of Anna Mollow on this subject in which she makes a compelling case for disability studies and fat studies to collaborate on producing a 'setpoint epistemology', which consists of a combination of 'feminist setpoint' and 'crip sitpoint', and which speaks directly to the existence of 'fat-disability cross-identifications' (Mollow 2015). One of the ways in which this resonant is through Mollow's assertion that the characterization of fatness and disability as 'risks' overlooks the fact that they are both physical traits not behaviours to be mitigated. It is from behanviourist logic that harmful stereotypes and stigma emerge such that fatness and disability are pathologized. Space, however, must be made for differentiating between the experiences of fat, able-bodied individuals and their fat, disabled counterparts for whom experiences can be vastly different. None of this nuance is discernible as it relates to this cut or GenoPalate and, instead, is indicative of the intentional absence of non-normative bodies in hegemonic good health discourse.

One final element worth discussing here is how hegemonic good health, for both those who identify as fat and/or disabled (and fat-disabled) takes on the rhetoric of self-improvement. GenoPalate offers a way in which to achieve an improved state of being through a science-based dietary regime that it claims will help you transform into the ideal human subject. While weight loss is not mentioned as a goal in most of the forward-facing literature, it makes an appearance in the blog with a customer named Patrick, who discusses his 150-pound weight loss, and Andy, who relays his past struggles in managing a stable weight (until GenoPalate) (GenoPalate 2021). The remainder of the entries are highly health and wellness oriented and pushes users to change so as to become healthy and well (an indicator of which is a smaller body). A disabled user would likely be drawn in on similar lines – potentially as reflecting the 'supercrip', someone whose disability is 'overcome' through hard work, perseverance, and grit (Shapiro 1994; Schalk 2016).

It is significant that nonbinary and gender nonconforming bodies and identities are also absent in the company literature. However, their material absence, as with all other identity positions in this cut, can and often do intersect – whether it is in terms of the experiences of the racialized disabled body, the fat nonbinary body or any other permutation of overlapping affective, semiotic, and material identities. By and large, however, what is clear about these absent-present representations is how they are co-constructed with and by lingering conceptions of health in which felt and representational bodies are seen as unworthy of acknowledgment and yet consistently interpellated by health discourses that render their bodies and experiences as Other.

2. GenoPalate – commodification–privacy–(self)surveillance

This second cut takes on a more diffractive lens in which GenoPalate's input, output, and unfolding intra-active relationships draws attention to the sociomaterial aspects of privacy, commodification, and self-surveillance. I begin with a discussion of commodification, followed by privacy and (self) surveillance which, I maintain, are co-constituted.

The 'commodification' component of this cut is associated first with the logic needed to see one's DNA as a commodifiable product – one that is rich with biovalue and market potential. Again, this value added comes from repurposing ancestry tests for other objectives including law enforcement, medical research, and drug development. It also lends itself to the commodification of one's autobiography or what Roberts and Mackenzie refer to as autobiology, a fetishized commodity that seems stable but is actually socially constructed (Roberts and Mackenzie 2019). This kind of GM conceives of health as consistent with a biomedical and capitalist reproductive logic in which bodies are filtered through specific biopolitical health regimes in order to attain the right kind of bio-material subjectivity. One that allows for maximum productivity and, because of its centring of health, aligns with neoliberal conceptions of individual responsibility. If provided with the right information, the logic goes, individuals will act upon said information in order to achieve a visibly 'healthful' state. Issues of cost, knowledge, affordability, and time investment are consistently ignored.

Hegemonic good health, through this lens, becomes a sociomaterial burden which, since its attainment is by default inscribed on the body, can lead to stigma and lost opportunities – particularly when the default is white, cis, slim, and able-bodied. An accompanying tendency toward commodification extends the nutritional gaze to the molecular level as a way to 'control the body's inner geography', such that health becomes an imperative driven by an audit mentality (Scrinis 2013, 167). Braidotti refers to this as the commodification of our generative vitality – one that is in line with a biogenetic form of capitalism that is post-anthropological, but definitely not posthuman (Braidotti 2013b).

What is most interesting about this kind of commodification is that it is based on a scientific project that is itself thoroughly imbricated in structures of profit making where companies like GenoPalate sell a service and packing user data for third-party exploitation (i.e. for the purpose of marketing and biogenetic profiling – both medical and non). Vis-à-vis ancestry this process is also rooted in a desire to connect with community, to feel a sense of belonging and shared history – all of which are promised but often not realized since they require time and cultivation rather than simple ascription.

The intromission of hegemonic conceptions of good health is also perpetuated by the media, consumer culture, work culture, and governments who work to denature these basic desires by turning health into an imperative that is individualized and bureaucratized. They, as Giesler and Veresiu argue, work to hail social beings into neoliberal 'free, autonomous, rational, and entrepreneurial subjects who draw on individual market choices to invest in their own human capital' – something I have discussed and critiqued extensively (Giesler and Veresiu 2014, 841–2).

The connection of these tests with personalized biogenetic vitamins and genetically tailored recipes expands this circuit of commodification by tying this ethos of self-improvement to the 'dietary-genomic-functional/ superfood industrial complex'. It also 'create[s] purchasable solutions to the problem it generates' in the sense that a system of extensive exploitation and commodification, which contributed to the conditions of ill-health, is now seeking to solve this through the sale of superfluous tests and specialized diets (Guthman and DuPuis 2006, 441). The materiality of this form of social (re)production is felt in and by the body, and is discursively justified through the promise of self-knowledge. This biologically quantified body, as I discuss below, has its rights to privacy undermined and is forced to submit to a regime of surveillance in order to create the conditions of an ideal health subjectivity in ways that add to the vital economy.

On the subjects of privacy and self-surveillance, it is important to begin with what GenoPalate says explicitly in its privacy policy which, in a short paragraph linked to the terms of service, assures potential customers that their data is robustly encrypted and that they 'will never sell, lease or share your data without your explicit consent' (GenoPalate 2021). The text of the policy, however, is significantly more complex. The gist is that a host of personal information will be collected in the course of using the product, answering questionnaires (so as to 'provide Services more customisable to you' (GenoPalate 2021)), and accessing the results. Of particular interest is the fact that a third party does the genetic testing and that IP information and cookies are automatically collected. My own attempts to skirt around these rules so as to avoid as much collection and collation of personal data as possible is illustrative of how difficult it can be to remain anonymous (if that is what is desired). Because GenoPalate requires the collection of genetic data, the sale of that potentially lucrative information is a concern as are moves to collaborate with law enforcement (Hosman 2015; Winston 2017). Garner places these concerns into three categories: 1. knowledge harms, such as inaccurate, troubling, or incomplete information; 2. autonomy and trust-based harms, which encompass concerns about consent and control of information by others (the state and police included); and 3. harms related to data misuse, as in a data breach or lost personal information (Garner and Kim 2018). The intromission of concerns about individual autonomy and integrity, like those articulated by Garner, are an outcome of intra-relationships with related human and non-human actants. This perspective is meant to draw attention to the manifestation of public harms wherein privacy is seen through the lens of materiality, multiplicity, relationality, and distributed agency.

Surveillance qua surveillance extends this cut and concerns about privacy to focus in on physical spaces including workplace surveillance in which quality health care coverage has increasingly been substituted by individualized, technified, and hegemonic good health programmes. While there are a few cases of workplaces mandating genetic tests for a variety of reasons, my interest lies more in the trajectory of health-oriented surveillance in the workplace which will inevitably create a permission structure for even more dietary-health-oriented surveillance going forward (Brandt-Rauf and Brandt Rauf 2004; Chapman et al. 2020)

Here, privacy and 'regular' surveillance are co-constituted wherein the monitoring and sharing of ostensibly private information is of primary concern. In some cases, the surveillance of bodies by the state as a form of risk management is necessary as it relates to the provision of services or, as we have come to learn, to monitor pandemics. However, it takes on a different valence when it is in the service of hegemonic good health-based objectives. This includes more invasive forms of normative health intervention (i.e. public health initiatives), as it relates to, for example, monitoring hunger, and malnutrition (as well as cancer, heart disease, and diabetes) (Stoto 2005; Griffin 2012). The state-directed misuse of compiled genetic data (including through ancestry tests) to track down individuals accused of breaking the law is likely the most conspicuous outcome of genetic surveillance.

Workplaces, over the past decade, have accelerated their use of health and wellness programmes which employees are encouraged to enrol in (many of which are connected to and with insurance companies), and engage in personalized health practices. This includes things like nutritional monitoring and counselling, yoga and meditation, the use of health trackers, discounted gym memberships etc. It is important to note that these programs persist despite evidence that challenge their efficacy (Ehley 2014; Anderson 2016). Currently, in the US, legislation is in place allowing companies to consider the genetic information of the employees determining insurance premiums on a voluntary basis – often accompanied by inducements and pressure (Wolfe 2018). This form of biogenetic and health surveillance is often presented as altruistic – part of the workplace's desire to have a happy, healthy workforce. Inevitably, however, this approach functions as a replacement for robust primary health care coverage by redirecting attention to the pleasure of metrics (QS), workplace competition (gamification), and therapeutic self-care (Lupton 2017a).

Self-surveillance, as mode of hegemonic good health-led self-subjectification, elicits boundary drawing and the reification of the self as a circumscribed subject tasked with monitoring their own health status and proving, to their employers, their desire to be healthy. This can be seen as evidence of a 'will to health' enacted through a dual surveillance regime – first of the company on the individual, and second, on the worker who is encouraged to surveil themselves. Pizzorno describes the latter form of surveillance as a self-initiated set of actions aimed at limiting 'its [the body's] own recalcitrance, resistant unpredictability, and … obtaining its own docility' (Pizzorno 1992: 207). This perspective is grounded in Foucault's (1980a; 2018) framework and has been elaborated on by scholars like Rose (2001; 2007), Lupton (2016b; 2012a) and others as a way to understand bodies and how health care has been turned into individualistic self-care (Ruckenstein and Schull 2017). Since I have taken up this point elsewhere, I will simply underline that, consistent with hegemonic good health, one of the central tenets of Western health discourse is that the health subject must use their agency to self-surveil so that they 'become an active partner in the drive for health, accepting their responsibility for securing their own well-being' (Rose 2001, 5). Oftentimes a central objective of this process is to actualize the employer's agenda of using their employee's own mediated surveillance practices to engender individual monitoring – what Crawshaw calls 'governing at a distance' (Crawshaw 2012).

This is a particularly insidious way in which to exercise power since it uses the rhetoric of choice (to sign up or not) but in a context that is highly pressurized and incentivized. The ultimate goal is to produce a 'pixelated person of precision medicine', one that is disciplined, empowered, and equipped with the knowledge needed to act on the self in pursuit of employer-friendly hegemonic health subjectivities and embodiments (Greenfeld 2016). Because companies like GenoPalate have been already been brought into the workplace (e.g. DNA FIT, Caligenix) it is clear that this is likely the next step for this company as well (McDonald et al. 2020). In 2019, Founder and CEO Sherry Zhang was interviewed by Ease Academy, during which she pitched the company as perfectly placed to become part of the workplace-wellness nexis so as to produce, 'A more intelligently empowered workplace', one that harnesses biogenetic healthy eating to 'help the workplace become a stronger force as a whole' (Harris 2019).

This amalgamation of postmodern forms of privacy intrusion, surveillance, self-surveillance, dataveillance, and other forms of looking and seeing is given a new kind of significance through genetification, datafication, neoliberal responsibilization, and the moral regulation of health. This cut stands in stark contrast to the other option: namely, the provisioning of a capacious, embodied, and responsive public health system coupled with forms of collectivity that attends to the structures and institutions that give rise to health inequalities in the first place. A new materialist understanding of ethical responsibility would frame privacy not only as the control of private information, but also as a form of respect and care wherein data is shared for purposes that serve the common good. Privacy and surveillance would need to be stripped of all coercion and subjectification and, instead, be operationalized to support 'Relational connections, affective forces, digital and bodily affordances and agential capacities' that enact positive and pro-social 'action, knowledge and responses' (Lupton 2020a, 394). This approach reflects a mutable and distributed sense of agency as well as an embodied cartographic ways of feeling/seeing/being in the world – one that engenders 'myriad temporalities and spatialities and myriad intra-active entities-in-assemblages – including the more-than-human, other-than-human, inhuman, and human-as-humans' (Haraway 2016b, 160).

When taken together, these two cuts: 1. GenoPalate – 'the science'–race–gender–disability–intersections and 2. GenoPalate – commodification–privacy–(self)surveillance, raise important concerns around the world-making role of science (taking GenoPalate as our case study), the intersections between science and how race is concretized, how gender norms are 'made/done', and how dis/ability is enacted. The second cut's focus on the synergies between commodification, privacy, and (self)surveillance brings to the fore a more capacious understanding of the 'dietary-genomic-functional/superfood industrial complex' and the ways in which this complex produces effects and affects that are exploitative. Rethinking the politics of the gaze, the reduction of bodies to their biovalue, the monetization of personal information, and the functioning of biopolitical surveillance brings into view obstacles and, potentially, opportunities for change.

Auto-ethnography: GenoPalate

As mentioned earlier, the process and experience of becoming part of this research as it relates to signing up for the GenoPalate test was personally fraught. I am still unsure as to how successful my attempts at obscuring my personal information were. In any event, after receiving the report my objective was to eat in a manner consistent with their recommendations for two weeks. I considered, but ultimately decided against, the monitoring of detailed weight and health statistics (blood pressure, cholesterol, etc.) for purpose of comparison due to my feeling that it would perpetuate hegemonic-related body norms as well as fat stigma and diet culture. My approach, instead, was to focus on my lived and felt experience during this process and to do so by producing reflexive and 'recursive feedback loops between explicit articulation, conscious thought, and embodied sensorimotor knowledge' (Hayles 2006, 135).

This form of posthuman auto-ethnography pushes up against and challenges human-centric approaches and, instead, frames me (the subject) as plural, 'decentered, nomadic, multiple, incomplete, complex … tentacular' and always intra-acting with other actants inclusive of technologies, food, environments, and relations (Warfield 2019, 148). As such, I begin with a brief overview of the report supplemented by some of my most salient, reconstructed reflections before delving deeper into my experiences during the two weeks and the material and discursive effects and affects it ignited.

After ordering and receiving the testing kit, I swabbed the inside of my cheek, packaged it up, sent it back and received the results shortly thereafter. The report itself was sent in an accessible pdf document (also available on the app – which

I did not download). It contained a lot of scientific lingo – stating that the test had investigated just under 40 'well-categorized' genetic biomarkers connected to variations that could impact my metabolic health when consuming particular foods. The key takeaways, ostensibly connected to specific genes (GP-F006, GP-F007, etc.), were that I would benefit from eating a low-carb, low-saturated fat, anti-inflammatory diet, and that I needed to increase my intake of vitamins B12 and D as well as polyunsaturated fats. Also recommended was avoiding caffeine. The report has sections titled carbohydrates, fats, vitamins, minerals, dietary type, substances, and performance before in addition to a concrete diet plan. In the carbohydrate section, for example, the report states that having GP-C003 activated (which it appears I do) indicates that I should lower my carbohydrate intake in order to increase HDL cholesterol levels. Overall, the recommendations in the various sections struck me as quite quotidian and not particularly surprising having been told, for example, that refined carbohydrates and saturated fats, and inflammatory foods should generally be avoided.

The section I was struck by in particular was number 7, performance, in which it was stated that I had GP-P001 (Survival Gene 1). Having this variation, the report notes, makes me predisposed to having a reduced ability to lose weight due to an 'evolutionary advantage' such that I am 'more likely to survive times of famine and food shortage'. This sounded to me suspiciously like the 'thrifty gene' hypothesis which was used, falsely, to support the assertion that Indigenous peoples are genetically predisposed to diabetes. It has also been applied to South Asian communities despite solid evidence refuting this (Southam et al. 2009; Duster 2015). This hypothesis has been critiqued for reify racial difference, ignore environmental factors (including access to fresh food), and employ an ahistorical understanding of when and how diabetes developed. As such, I found this interpretation of 'Survival Gene 1' to be odd and warrant further probing. My biggest concern, and something I took note of (and starred), was how purportedly 'objective' scientific evidence was being used to perpetuate narratives about genetic predisposition that, while not explicitly invoking race, is historically rooted in explanations of ill health that are racialized (Ford and Airhihenbuwa 2010). It also is steeped in a history of science in which these same racial categories were hierarchized into 'advanced' and 'primitive;' 'superior' and 'inferior'. This is what makes the thrifty gene hypothesis and its popularity less about science and health and more, as Fee argues, 'a story about "racial" identity' (Fee 2006, 2992).

The final recommendation in the report of note was that I should follow an anti-inflammatory, low carbohydrate diet – one that did not exclude food groups entirely (and thus would not lead to 'cravings'), but that consisted of a 'balance of grains, lean proteins (especially seafood) and plenty of fruits and vegetables … monosaturated and polyunsaturated fats …', and saturated fats 'in moderation'. Watching sugars and portion sizes was recommended as well. Specifically, this meant a maximum caloric intake of 1950 calories (approximately 680 from fat or 75 g). This was then broken down between the three types of fat and a total carbohydrate intake of 170 g, 145 g protein, 30 g of dietary fibre, and no more than 70 g of sugar. A BMI was given and an entire RDA table broken down into categories like Immunity, Nervous System & Brain, and Metabolic Health with vitamin and mineral goals listed underneath. Overall, this document reflects the healthism and nutritionism discussed previously, one that sees the moralization of one's striving towards health as a supervalue and the functional reification of nutrients as the most important characteristic of food. The focus on BMI, another roundly criticized marker, is incorporated without context despite robust research critiquing it as methodologically inappropriate (it was supposed to be applied to populations, not individuals), reductive (it is a crude metric that does not consider muscle mass, fitness level, fat distribution, etc.), and pathologizing (Griffin 2012; Wright and Harwood 2012; Warin 2015). I have always thought of BMI as a perfect exemplar of biopower in action – one that homes in on how power is reproduced in bodies through discourses, technologies, and institutions that work to control them.

Having been given all this information, I was left slightly frustrated and unsure about what to do next. My first instinct was to go online, take out a calculator and start crunching numbers. Although I did have a list of optimal foods and a way to track everything through the app, I felt pressure to purchase the diet plan since this would make things much easier (which is likely intentional). Instead, I took all this information to a nutritionist friend of mine who worked up a basic dietary plan based on the recommendations broken up into three meals and two snacks and which matched, to the extent possible, the benchmarks set out in the report. To keep it simple, breakfasts consisted of fruit smoothies and egg whites with some cheese, lunches of a salad with beans/lentils and an olive oil vinaigrette, and dinners a lean protein or fish (salmon/halibut) and vegetables with some grain (usually brown rice). Snacks were often fruit and nuts.

Suffice to say, the diet was restrictive. From my notes and entries restriction is the first theme that figured prominently and these feelings of restriction intensified throughout the two weeks. I felt quite sad/depressed/resigned about these limits – expressed first in a 'is this all I get?' sentiment, but also in how intensely and insidiously panoptic it felt. Before unpacking this further, it is important to point out that this 'experiment' was undertaken during lockdown which made it much easier to stick to. Were I teaching, going out, eating out, seeing friends, etc., it would have been significantly more difficult.

With respect to the first dimension of this theme, throughout the two weeks I wrote consistently about the loss of and desire for the pleasures associated with consuming spicy, salty, and sweet food. Not in the sense of so-called 'junk food' or 'fast food' or 'comfort food,' but food with interesting flavours to be consumed spaces in which I did not have to think about micronutrients and fat percentages. This feeling was amplified since the meal plan was also repetitive, uninspired, and meant to be consumed in isolation (this likely would have been the case even if I had been able to move around the city freely and safely). While I generally liked all the foods I ate, after about five days the repetitiveness really kicked in and after eight days I really longed for more flavour. This was the case despite being drawn to routine and structure in my everyday life as reflected in work and generally in my health/food behaviours.

'Pleasure', I wrote on day 8, 'is such an important and affective part of our relationship to food, our bodies, and our connection with others'. Food is a socio-culturally significant object that can be personally resonant and historically important. However, pleasure vis-à-vis food has also been cast as sinful, hedonic, and expressive of damaged agency as discussed in the previous chapter and by those advocating for the exercise of willpower, discipline, and control (Dean 2018). Yet, at times, I did feel a kind of self-satisfaction, even pleasure, upon completing a day intact – i.e. having followed all of the 'rules' demonstrating that I was a 'good' hegemonic health subject. This feeling was amplified if I had exercised and made even stronger if that workout had been especially difficult. Being labelled a 'good' and 'moral' health subject as it relates to food and fitness in this context is not unlike the accounts I had read of QS adherents for whom self-discipline, goal seeking, and achievement are powerful drivers of strict health behaviours (i.e. behaviours that are taught, internalized, and deeply held) (Gimpel, Nißen and Görlitz 2013). This feeling of pleasure is also tied to dietary ethical self-governance and an ethic of 'salcvation, creating a beautiful life, a culture of enterprise, or an active citizenry' (Catlaw and Sandberg 2018, 12). The creation of this ideal life and maximal happiness through control is one that appeals to me and which GenoPalate promises in the sense that it is connected, discursively and materially, to the guarantee of self-improvement backed up by personalized genetic science (PN and GB).

However, the type of pleasure I desired but lacked during these two weeks was a form that comes of out of relations of commensality, of eating and sharing with others – something I could not do due to Covid-19 but would also have been unlikely to as a result of the constraints of the diet. 'Pleasure and food' formed another theme in my notes – particularly as it relates to the careful balancing act GenoPalate demanded wherein pleasure experienced through the classical Greek lens of decadence and indulgence – particularly when experienced with others – was replaced by an Epicurean integration of pleasure with ethics. One which is philosophically hedonic and includes 'tranquillity of mind and health of body ... living wisely ... [and the] reasoned balancing of choices' (Hedegaard and Hémar-Nicolas 2020, 160–1). The Protestant ethic of self-denial, temperance, and renunciation of bodily pleasures is also embedded in hegemonic good health and it felt, to me, that this was a central pillar of GenoPalate's ethos except for its promise of pleasure in health 'to come'. Pleasure therefore comes from working within the program, by 'explore[ing] what it means to get your body the nutrients it really needs'. GenoPalate promises to 'help you make specific, nourishing choices; crush your healthy lifestyle goals; and steer yourself down the right path' with meals that are 'appetizing and easy' if, of course, you are able to afford their personalized recipes. The recipes themselves, of which six images are given for free, include recognizable foods such as an omelette, a niçoise salad, a shrimp stir-fry, cereal with fruit, and a vegetable stir-fry (GenoPalate 2021).

I wrote extensively on a number of days about the historical moralizing of particular foods (e.g. spicy, salty, sweet foods) as sinful due to its proximity to Otherness as well as to sex, excess, and indulgence. Abstaining from foods coded as 'bad' is thus re-articulated as a pleasurable act, one that promises future satisfaction in the form of health, longevity, weight loss, and ethical righteousness. Pleasure in the form of bodily affect, taste, emotion, and desire was excised entirely from the GenoPalate healthscape. This framing reifies the health/pleasure, reason/desire, control/excess dichotomy that constitutes hegemonic good health wherein the phenomenology of the lived body is suppressed in favour of the left side of these binaries (Vogel and Mol 2014). It also homes in on individual choice as the locus through which health is enacted.

Access to health care, an anti-racist environment, fresh and affordable food, a stable income, safe surroundings, education, etc. (the social determinants of health) are elided by GenoPalate in favour of health understood as individually appropriated through rational choice (Greco 1993, 357; also see Gkiouleka et al. 2018 and Ravindran 2017 on social determinants of health). I tried several times to write about the experience of eating the food on the menu – i.e. the salmon (which I usually love), the fresh fruit, the colourful vegetables, the walnuts and pecans. Having an everyday diet that is made up of most of these foods anyways, it did not require onerous adjustments. I slowly came to the conclusion that my growing resentment with the diet and frustration with its limitations had to do with the lack of choice, of the banishment of some foods, and the reduction of meals to a functional, asocial, and instrumental activity. Scholarship in food studies from this perspective broadens the aperture through which food is understood by centring context, aesthetics, taste, sourcing and history. Discussions of terroir, palate, taste, symbolism, and sensory pleasure (an Epicurean perspective), can be contrasted with more visceral pleasures that encompass taste but tend to be centred on the body and include impulsive and hedonic desires – say, for example, a chocolate bar that is devoured quickly (Hoyer and Stokburger Sauer 2012; Bodunrin and Stone 2019).

Massimo Leone's scholarship on food reflects another way in which to think about this higher-level relationship between food, pleasure, and life. He writes that people are 'hungry not only for delicious dishes, but also for what they embody: an immediate, engrossing, and simultaneous confirmation of existential presence. I eat, ergo I exist. I feel the pleasure of ingestion, ergo I am alive' (Leone 2016, 183). Suffice to say nothing about my two weeks came close to this kind of pleasure, whether Epicurean, visceral, or existential.

The pleasure of sociality, as noted previously, was absent from these two weeks by necessity (due to Covid-19) but again this meal plan was not conducive to convivial sharing. GenoPalate's hegemonic good health regimes (personalized 'for you' – PN and justified by science – GM), was individualized in ways that did not encourage or assume a significant role for commonsality defined as the revitalization of social bonds and 'fraternal agape' that occurs over shared meals (Simmel 1998). As Masson, Bubendorff, and Fraise put it, food practices are how we organize society, reproduce social bonds, build group cohesion, develop taste, create purpose, and think collectively (Masson Bubendorff and Fraise 2018; Smith and Harvey 2021).

One final aspect of note is the significance of consuming 'culturally appropriate food' as discussed by Finn (2017). I personally missed eating Indian food – any 'ethnic' food really. Due to Covid-19 restrictions I had been unable to visit family for over a year and missed my mother's cooking immensely. This, I wrote, made the food of my childhood something I desired especially since it provides, for me, an emotional anchor while also reflecting my 'nostalgic longing for the familiar' (Mannur 2007, 11). While this nostalgia is fragmented (since the past can never be re-captured), it also acts as a way to feel connected to family. This is to say nothing of the visceral pleasures I associate with consuming Indian spices – cumin and garam masala in particular – especially when cooked with vegetables and/or lentils and beans – all of which I had bodily, pre-noetic cravings for. This form of affective engagement is reflected in the relational intensities and sensations that food enacts within us and is absent from GenoPalate. Affect, in this context, is not only about 'personal' feelings; it also reflects the emotions enacted between human and nonhuman actants and through relational bonds (Rice 2008). Pleasure and affect, with respect to food, felt, for me, as overwhelmed by expert knowledge, which was then folded into the body and used to 'colonize … physicality to homogenous, monocultural, white [and heteronormative] conceptions of the "fit, slim body"' (Azzarito 2012, 184).

This brings me to some thoughts on the inverse of pleasure, of the feelings of guilt and shame I felt which acted as an internalized warning system of consequences to come. While much of my motivation for sticking to this regime was that it was time limited and necessary for research, I did reflect on a deeply held desire to: 1. hold feelings of guilt at bay and 2. do well and inhabit a desirable health subjectivity. With respect to guilt, on day 9 I gave in after a long day of marking and meetings and put in for a delivery of dosas (lentil and rice crepes with potato stuffing), sambar (lentils), and gulab jamun (syrupy dumplings, for dessert – something I had been craving for days). I ate it much faster than I would have on any other occasion, and likely enjoyed it a little less, which I believe is consistent with the restriction/binge cycle that results from most diets (Bordo 2004; Calogero and Thompson 2010). The guilt and regret felt afterwards was tied, for me, to feelings of failure and of a disrupted good health subjectivity (Lupton 2012b).

This guilt was also gendered and racialized wherein the pressure to maintain an ideal body is hidden under discourses of health, reason, and self-mastery while ill health is seen as a problem of biology (race) and genetic predispositions exacerbated by bad choices. I was reminded of Amelia Morris' book, *The Politics of Weight: Feminist Dichotomies of Power in Dieting* (2019) and Sabrina Strings' (2019) *Fearing the Black Body: The Racial Origins of Fat Phobia*, in which (Strings) examines the process by which Blackness is made co-extensive with fatness, unruly bodies, ill health, lust, greed, and danger. Being fit and able-bodied, irrespective of race, 'become[s] the markers of class and citizenship, further justifying the discrimination of those who do not meet the prescriptive paradigms of embodiment' (Usiekniewicz 2016, 21). In this sense, GenoPalate and services like it can claim to be race-neutral but genetically specific since its use of genetic information relies on epistemologies that still assume racial difference, whether directly or by proxy.

While it is true that some more 'ethnic' food could have been made to fit the diet's parameters, it would most definitely have required an afternoon of intense planning were I to use my own 'recipes' (which lack precise measurements), or time spent looking for recipes that have existing nutritional breakdowns (followed by some tinkering with the ingredients to meet GenoPalate's rules). This felt to me like too much 'cognitive nutritionist labour' which requires the mental enactment of nutritionism in the form of work that would then be used to police my own behaviour. Although I do not have children, I also reflected on the fact that expectations around this work (the work of 'health') is often replicated for one's children and tasked to women for whom the production of an ideal, 'healthy', successful child becomes an indicator of maternal self-worth. As Wright, Maher, and Turner argue, maternal foodwork and healthwork 'includes prevailing expectations of mothering and care, and circulating discourses of responsibility, especially in relation to the direct care of children and diet' (Wright, Maher and Turner 2015; 425; also see McNaugton 2011). When thinking about this, I wrote that were PN and GB, in pursuit of hegemonic health, popularized to include children (a likely prospect), it would become yet another task adding to women's work and responsibilities.

Turning back to guilt for a moment, I also, on two occasions, drank coffee – something I do ritually and take immense pleasure from at the moment of consumption; only to feel a sense of guilt soon thereafter. However, I also ruminated on the fact that I did not feel guilty in the same way that I did about consuming the dosas. After some thought as to why, I came to the conclusion that this likely was because of its 'nutritional nullity'. Specifically, coffee has no caloric trace – it is divorced from weight gain, fatness, and often used as a means by which to avoid consuming food. It reminded me of two mantras often heard in pro-ana (anorexia) online communities I had come across: 'Coffee, smokes and cold Diet Cokes that's what pretty girls are made of' and 'Chemicals over calories for me thanks' (Schott 2015, 13). This ethos is important in light of GenoPalate's warning that because of biomarker GP-S001, I would 'Benefit from Avoiding Caffeine'.

Another leitmotif expressed in and through my reflections was related to the effect of the myriad forms of panoptic power expressed by the internalized dietary gaze and through which a particular kind of femininity was enacted (Bartky 2002; Warfield 2019). This form of power encouraged conformity and was made manifest though the desire for a small, sculpted, and 'worked on' figure (which this diet plan ultimately encourages through implicit and explicit discussions of weight loss). This, for me, felt particularly in keeping with gendered health and beauty norms and as connected to the scientific-technopatriarchal gaze. As Bartky puts it, in 'contemporary patriarchal culture, a panoptical male connoisseur resides within the consciousness of most women: they stand perpetually before his gaze and under his judgment' (Bartky 2013, 454; also see 2015). I also noted how patriarchy is supported by postfeminist beauty discourse, hegemonic good health norms, and faith in GM.

The final theme which emerged from my written contemplations and audio notes (which I began to rely on more and more), had to do with its psychological impact. I thought carefully about how the techno-scientific process of GM converged with a (marketed?) demand for PN and the growing 'dietary-genomic-functional/superfood industrial complex' such that hegemonic good health had become the dominant health ideology. This felt intractable. The agency of the various human and non-human actants within this assemblage had produced a set of circumstances in which I, as an individual human actor, was constantly adjusting my behaviour and agency to fit. Mentally, this manifested in what I increasingly began to feel was an unhealthy obsession with food – when I would eat, what I would eat, etc. This 'orthorexic behaviour', as Chrisler puts it, occurs when individuals with a strong health orientation adopt a 'obsessive-compulsive approach to the practice of health behaviours, especially those related to nutrition intake' (Chrisler 2018, 39). Having my own history with disordered eating meant that this raised a whole host of red flags. Suffice to say, I was happy when the experiment was over.

This is not, however, to deny that pleasure in self-knowledge, control, and improvement cannot also be an outcome of receiving actionable information. I take this up in more detail in the next chapter on self-tracking wherein compliance is rewarded and, for some, gratifying. This, however, was not my experience and despite adhering to most of its rules, in the end I felt frustrated with no discernible improvement in health or wellbeing broadly defined.

Taken together, this chapter has endeavoured to provide a critical and reflexive analysis of GenoPalate as an exemplar of hegemonic good health drawing on PN and GM. Using a political economy of culture and discourse analysis to home in on the company's structural and ideological commitments, what was revealed were allegiances to profit, ideal biopolitical citizenship, self-discovery, normative bodily comportment, authentic ancestry, and a mythos of belonging refracted by science and individual choice. Applying new materialism to examine this assemblage in productive ways resulted in two cuts: 1. GenoPalate – 'the science'–race–gender–disability–intersections, and 2. GenoPalate – commodification–privacy–(self)surveillance. This section addressed issues of assumed genetic causality as it relates to health (biogenetic destiny), the duty to health, postfeminism, 'chosen' health work, racialized wellbeing, thin femininity, objective science, and the erasure of disabled, fat, and other non-normative, nonbinary bodies. The second cut brought to the fore concerns around privacy, biocommodification, the growth of the 'dietary-genomic-functional/superfood industrial complex', as well as the entrenchment of surveillance qua surveillance as well as self-surveillance in pursuit of an ideal self. The auto-ethnography, in which I took on the task of living in accordance with GenoPalate's logics for two weeks, revealed a number of insights that connected experiential knowledge with 'bits and pieces' of my personal narrative, and my relation to Others (in this case with technologies, food, knowledge, norms) (hooks 1988, 159). This process revealed modes of relationality between me (the knower) and known with respect to my own changing ontology of health. Through my note taking and critical reflections, what was became apparent were concerns around racial identity, weight centricity, the psychology of restriction, the significance of pleasure, and the pursuit of a constructed 'ideal life' though diet. Also discussed was my experience with the stigmatization of certain foods (as 'bad'), the denial of commensality, the erasure of 'culturally appropriate food', and the experience of guilt.

This chapter has taken the reader on a journey in which GenoPalate emerges as a technical manifestation of hegemonic good health, GM, and PN. Drawing on a multi-modal approach, by integrating a political economy of culture, discourse analysis, new materialism, and auto-ethnography, I have elucidated several important insights as it relates to the entanglement of humans, nonhumans, technologies institutions, structures, and emerging health knowledge.

5

Case study three: GetFit

As mentioned previously, I wanted to choose a health tracker for this case study that met specific criteria including that it be 'free', user friendly, accessible, somewhat niche, up and coming (vis-à-vis revenue, downloads), and not American but with an Anglo presence. The latter point is intended to offset the American-centricity of the of Aduna and GenoPalate thereby bringing a more global dimension to the 'dietary-genomic-functional (super)food industrial complex'. One of the limitations of this approach, however, is that clear, consistent information about some companies is difficult to obtain. From what I can glean from public information, GetFit Apps was founded in 2017 and is part of Total Appyfurious, a larger parent company with revenue of over $3 million (although their Apple app store profile lists 'App Prodakshn, OOO' as the provider). They describe themselves as a mobile app company whose focus is on harnessing A.I. to develop health and fitness apps (SensorTower 2021). The company's US headquarters is in Great Neck, New York, but, according to their LinkedIn page, the company has 70 employees (doctors, trainers, developers, marketers, etc.) located in Minsk, Belarus, and thus they identify as a Belarussian company (LinkedIn 2021). Its CEO and co-founder, Alexei Kuvels, is a developer and entrepreneur who has been working in the app development industry for over a decade. GetFit is highly rated on the Apple app store (4.2 as reflected by 2500 ratings) and has been downloaded over 15 million times in 100+ countries. Other apps they offer include a walking tracker, a focused diet and meal planner, a meditation and sleep app, and a yoga app (SensorTower 2021). GetFit is recommended alongside other recognizable trackers like Fitbit, MyFitnessPal, and Noom. Despite being a smaller company, I contend that GetFit Apps has the same political economic objectives as its counterparts – ones that are founded on a commodified notion of health and wellbeing.

I begin this chapter by probing this ethos in detail (drawing on a political economy of culture approach), followed by engaging in a discursive analysis of the company's promotional literature (website, LinkedIn, App Store description etc.).

I then discuss and unpack the significance of two agential cuts through which a performative and emergent analyses of the sociomaterial affects of this technology can be discerned. These effects and affects are tied to hegemonic good health in specific ways – namely through the embrace of an understanding of health that is idealized and idealizing with respect to health-oriented expectations, performances, embodiments, and patterns of consumption. This conceptualization of health is 'dominated by gendered and raced technophilic knowledge regimes' and, as such, 'reproduce[s] regimented and coercive western standards of health and wellbeing'. Finally, I provide an in-depth and iterative autho-ethnographic account of my use of the app for a period of two weeks, during which time I adhered closely to its suggestions around fitness and movement and to its dietary guidelines (although I focused less on the latter).

As reflected on in the chapter on political economy, it is clear that GetFit, as a corporate actor, has a specific set of objectives similar to that of GenoPalate or Aduna. Namely, to translate hegemonic good health capital, activities, and services into profits. There are a number of ways in which this takes places including the isolation and commodification of data, the elevation of measurement, the monetization of behavioural change, and the economic capture of movement. It is important to point out that in this section there is some slippage between political economy, which tends to be more about structures, exploitation, markets, and profits, and a biopolitical analysis, which focuses on discourse and power. While distinct in several ways, I contend they are co-constituted in this case since many of the political economic objectives laid out require biopolitical subjectification (i.e. in the context of productivity and the internalization of hegemonic health norms) to function.

To begin with, the objective of health apps like GetFit is two-fold. First, to collect, package, and sell user data thereby producing newer forms of biovalue for the company and, second, to provide a service that is ostensibly oriented to help users 'get healthy' but which, when probed further, raises more questions about what this means in practice. I contend that GetFit's interpretation of health is firmly ensconced in the hegemonic good health perspective and is aimed at harnessing desire in ways that produce a compliant 'healthy' subject. This subject, to be clear, is biological and cultural and inscribed with and by capitalist productive capacities. It also reproduces cultural expectations around bodily comportment as well as physicality, gender, race, class, dis/ability, and sexuality.

What is important in the context of data collection is that the data amassed and used to extract profit is distinctive. In other domains, it is the product of labour that matters – something Fuchs (2014) discusses in relation to programmers and creators but can also be applied to users. In this case, it is the entry of data around meals, coupled with the cognitive labour required to remember and then configure the device for monitoring (and then physically exert oneself in accordance with the app's parameters for exercise), that functions as uncompensated labour. Often described as immaterial or digital labour, this instantiation of work takes the form of consistant exercising, inputting, and sharing which is then filtered through a digital infrastructure that generates millions by 'convinc[ing] users that it is leisure, not labour'. This is then justified 'through []the erosion of the distinction between work and play' (Till 2014, 449). It also creates what has come to be known as the modern prosumer, someone who both produces and consumes content and whose subjectivity is actively placed in alignment with these processes and positioned as open to being exploited by informational capital (Fuchs 2011; Mosco 2014). This process speaks to a larger movement towards quantification and measurement consistent with QS as well as a set of practices oriented towards risk mitigation, self-optimization, and control in support of a 'data-driven health revolution' – one that benefits the larger capitalist order much more than individual actors (Didžiokaitė, Saukko and Greiffenhagen 2018, 9; also see Lupton 2014b).

Surveillance forms another important part of this political economic formation, particularly as it relates to how surveillance capitalism generates a locus through which personal data is generated, collected, packaged, and sold for profit. Zuboff's analysis of this kind of datafication and dataveillance is important in that it speaks directly to the rise of a new model of 'information capitalism [that] aims to predict and modify human behaviour as a means to produce revenue and market control' (Zuboff 2015, 75). The strategic cultivation of normative hegemonic good health behaviours using this data (and selling products that promise its fulfilment) forms an important part of this logic. On a systemic level, apps like GetFit operate as capitalism's answer to a gutted health care system, one whose 'failure to serve the needs of second-modernity individuals' has created conditions under which 'we now access health data and advice from our phones while these pocket computers aggressively access us' (Zuboff 2019, 237). One of the most interesting forms of neoliberal surveillance in the context of health and fitness apps is how they have been used to cultivate mineable forms of community sharing, confession, competition, and support – what Lupton calls a 'sharing economy' (Lupton 2021). Notably, GetFit does not have an integrated community function (although it does have a Facebook and Instagram page) and, in any event, I felt that participation in this kind of network for two weeks was insufficient to really get a sense of its dynamics.

On a meta-level, health and fitness as a sector represent part of a larger system of apps, technologies, systems, and institutions that are control-oriented in a manner unique to digital communication. The majority of these apps benefit private industry, are power-asserting, and have become normalized and accepted (hegemonic) over time (Frith and Özkul 2019). Apps like GetFit, according to Mansell, should be seen as reminders 'of the significance of power relations in the changing technological and institutional environment in which information is produced, circulated and applied' (Mansell 2017, 3). The idea of control-oriented technologies is an old one going back to Heidegger, Marcuse, Ellul, Borgmann, and Ihde, who all made important contributions to the philosophy of technology by unpacking the epistemological and ontological underpinnings of our technoscientific society – ones that give rise to structures of control that are profitable but which ignore the larger contextual and social dimensions of health.

A final note on the political, economic, and cultural functioning of GetFit can be seen in the compelling accounts of how fitness trackers capture, construct, and translate movement in ways that are subject forming, and because of this, economically lucrative. Williamson (2015) articulates how trackers interpellate the body in ways that ensure it is always working and open to be intervened upon and optimized. This post-Fordist technique is used to collect large amounts of data, measure and quantify it, and use it for other (i.e. marketing) purposes. Even when this information is anonymized, it is quite simple to cross reference and identify users. This data includes location, heart rate, sleep patterns, blood pressure (all which are useful for employers and insurance companies), as well as dietary preferences and products purchased which are then sold to advertisers (McCarthy 2013; Papageorgiou et al. 2018).

While I chose a health app that did not constantly monitor my vital signs, I did integrate some of that somatic tracking to get a sense of this kind of surveillance. Specifically, I borrowed Apple Watch and relied on the app's monitor to calculate my resting heart rate (which was then used to calculate my caloric intake) using my index finger which was placed over my iPhone's camera lens for 60 seconds. The impact of this function, and ones like, it is that they treat movement as something to be tracked, disciplined and used to 'orient the self even more acutely towards disciplinary technologies (which are periodic and decisive), potentially bringing the norms of discipline closer to the psyche and body' (Davies 2019, 522). These forcings' core objective is to collect data but also, as this quote illustrates, to encourage the profitable internalization of hegemonic good health norms – ones that align themselves with the cultivation of ideal and productive health subjects. It is to these health norms that now I turn and examine in more detail, thus extending the political economy of culture's ability to address the reproduction of hegemonic good health.

Discourse analysis: GetFit

My analysis of the frames and themes GetFit uses to discursively construct a meaningful dispositif around its app focuses on its home website, its app home pages (on the App Store and Google Play, respectively), as well as its developer description on CNET – a noted technology and consumer review website. Analysis of the app itself, and its language, is examined in more detail below. In sorting, assessing, and deconstructing the ideological themes, values, and interests around health what became evident is how connected they are. The taken-for-granted beliefs around ideal bodies, patterns of consumption, normativity, routine, and individual striving are especially pronounced. My application of CDA here, to reiterate, is inductive and iterative, which means that the data collection and analysis conducted occurred at the same time and involved the collection and sorting of notes and themes into categories supplemented by my own critical analysis (Cukier et al. 2009; Johnson 2014). Issues of power, domination, inequality, hegemony, racism, and misogyny are particularly important in this kind of work in that they reflect how,

> practices, events and texts arise out of and are ideologically shaped by relations of power and struggles over power; and ... how the opacity of these relationships between discourse and society is itself a factor securing power and hegemony.
>
> (Fairclough 1993, 135)

In contrast to GenoPalate and Aduna, there was not a lot of company-produced promotional material to work with and this is not inconsistent with other trackers who seem to opt for a streamlined and minimalist aesthetic. Beginning with its website, GetFit conspicuously uses an austere presentation style with monochromatic backgrounds that change to highlight each of their products. A smartphone is placed on the right with short descriptions that change so as to display each app as the screen transitions.

The first significant theme is that of personalization, which is reflected in GenoPalate's use of PN and GM. GetFit promises a 'personalized workout plan built on your ECG and tailored around your health', which is supported by 'unique AI algorithms' and a 'personalized diet plan' complete with a barcode scanner and junk-food meter (GetFit 2021). GetFit's newest app, RocketBody AI, promises to tailor its workouts to the user's heart rate. It would appear the company's interpretation of A.I. is that of smart adaptation in which recovery and intensity expectations change based on ECG readings. As in its other apps, GetFit also homes in on the values of uniqueness, tailored needs, and adaptation. As discussed previously, personalization is a central component of the hegemonic good health assemblage made concrete by the rise of PN. With respect to discourse, this plays out through a desire to be seen as a discrete agent and product of self-produced action in line with the objectives of a neoliberal society.

GetFit's services and products attend to these needs in ways that fit into the Durkheimian (2005) conception of the 'cult of the individual', but in a manner that is filtered through late stage/digital capitalism. In its 1-page, 20-line product description of GetFit in the App Store, personalization takes centre stage and is brought up three times in just one bullet point: 'Personalized and masterclass programs. Achieve your goals through short personalized daily bodyweight workouts designed by certified GetFit fitness trainers and tailored to you' (GetFit App Store 2021). What is unique about this iteration of personalization is the way in which it functions alongside individual action to produce a discursive juggernaut in two moves. First, by making individuals take responsibility for their own health which takes the pressure off of stressed public health systems. Health then becomes a product of individual choice, not of structural inequality. The second move works by presenting personalization in a way that naturalizes the individual as the sole means by which to 'succeed' and where success is defined through 'self-entrepreneurship and the obsessive acquisition of resources to achieve success in a competitive system' (Pendenza and Lamattina 2019, 100). Health thus becomes another form of capital, one that is inscribed on the svelte, normative body.

Other important themes in GetFit's self-representation include that of simplicity, speed, and ease of use. For instance, its diet counter is described as having an 'all in one functionality', its workouts as requiring 'No Gym' and 'No Equipment' allowing users, in 'just 42 minutes a day' to get healthy 'without challenging your busy schedule'. Next is the discursive relationship between speed/acceleration, simplicity, and health. The presumption in the preceding statements is that we live hectic lives in a fast-paced world in which eating 'right' and exercising is difficult. This narrative places blame on the individual while offering a solution that meets the needs of neoliberal capitalism (i.e. a productive worker) and the objectives of hegemonic good health. The speed and simplicity associated with the app is part of an economy of click purchases, two-hour delivery, instantaneous communication, just in time manufacturing, and platformization in which health is made to fit into a system of what Mark Fisher calls 'capitalist realism' (Fisher 2009; also see Chen and Sun 2020). GetFit fits seamlessly into this assemblage by constructing a symbolic and discursive image of itself and its users as hard working, entrepreneurial, and always on the move. Their 42-minute fitness contract is particularly emblematic of this logic. Overall, GetFit, and programs like it, are put forward as capable of offering quick results, without the need for a lot of forethought (or investment), as easy to use, and as equipped with quick answers to individualized health problems. These solutions, however, fail to address the social determinants of health and, in doing so, reproduce hegemonic conceptions of good health.

The final rhetorical theme GetFit uses to buttress hegemonic good health is that of 'scientific precision in pursuit of efficiency'. GetFit's website highlights its use of AI, which it claims 'efficiently analyzes your heart rate data and automatically adapts your workout plan in response', by drawing on algorithms that produce 'workouts based on scientific research', and 'projections of your physical readiness'. According to their App Store overview, GetFit aims to produce 'Time-efficient workouts with no equipment', so that 'With these bodyweight workouts, you'll get the most out of your time, no matter how short it is' (GetFit 2021; GetFit App Store 2021). Similarly, their Google Play profile assures users that the app will help them to 'fit a body workout into your busy schedule', – one that requires no equipment' or a gym, but allows you to 'burn calories in a way you never knew you could' (GetFit App Google Play 2021).

First, it is important to point out just how in-keeping this fidelity to efficiency and precision is to the neoliberal order – primarily by extending productivity through abstraction. This approach, according to Meller and Schilling, is body pedagogical in that it enframes the body in ways that give preference to the efficient body over the experiential body (Meller and Schilling 2010). Self-objectification is an important part of this process and the app, at least rhetorically, constructs an image of the self that fits into contemporary expectations around being a responsible (i.e. productive) citizen. Datta and Chakraborty term this the desire to be 'neoliberal fit' – which is very much in line with the principles of the Quantified Self in which metrics are married to an ethic of efficiency (Datta and Chakraborty 2018). Rest, in this context, is seen as necessary for furthering productivity.

The means by which the language, images, and rhetoric used by GetFit becomes persuasive lies in the fact that it is deployed in a context in which efficient systems and maximum human potential are seen as pro forma. As such, productivity and efficiency act as master socio-material signifiers – ones that drive the economy, work, government, and individuals towards maximal optimization. The app promises to accelerate, tighten, and ease users into a precision-oriented lifestyle wherein the self's co-constituted vital capacities are directed towards disciplined and disciplining activities (Bennett et al. 2010). GetFit's promise of 'results' in 42 minutes, without equipment, allowing users to 'get the most out of your time', is important in its elevation of the modern busy lifestyle – one that teaches us to engage in instrumental self-care, get fit, and affirm hegemonic good health (GetFit App Store 2021).

This discursive construction of good health operates as a form of socio-ideological practice, one that 'when viewed tacitly from within the Western neoliberal hegemony, seem[s] to be neutral and commonsensical' but, when examined closely, acts in service of particular interests (Ayers 2005, 529). The cultivation of this form of 'metric culture' is oriented to the realization of freedom minus government and, when combined with the frames of personalization/simplicity/ease of use, produces a network of inter-related dispositifs that materially shape how we understand health and how we go about pursuing it.

New materialism

1. GetFit App – Energy and Bodies–Body-World Relations–Data-Trust
2. GetFit App – Fatness and Health–Access–Dis/ability–Gender?/Race?

The two cuts I have chosen to focus on in this chapter 'hold together' sociomaterial forcings and enactments that revolve around bodies, trust and energy, and subjectivity and selfhood. In this first section, I discuss the Get-Fit app in relation to energy and bodies as well as body-world relations which are co-constituted in and through the app. Notably, GetFit relies on metaphors of machinic efficiency and assumptions about energy balance – both of which have been taken from economics and applied to weight loss and body manipulation. Here, weight loss is *a*, if not *the*, goal, with GetFit, in their CNET profile, describing possible goals the app can help users achieve. It asks: 'Want to lose belly fat and get six pack abs for the summer?' 'In search of effective bikini body workout for women?' and asserts: 'Get the best workout plan designed to help you lose weight, get fit or strong, and even gain weight!' (CNET 2021). In the setup process, GetFit asks about goals, current weight, and uses an energy-deficit model to calculate caloric range and exercise estimates.

This forms a central part of hegemonic good health and is reflected in the fetishization of technophilic knowledge regimes. What is so interesting about this part of the first cut is Get-Fit's assumptions about how the body works. In terms of body-world relations, it is troublingly reliant on the notion of energy balance that sees bodies as machines – ones that consume and burn energy like factories or a car. As such, it is the calorie, for GetFit, that is used to measure what is consumed and burned. Through the app, users are given an ECG-determined estimation.

As with Aduna and GenoPalate, GetFit also treats health like an individual problem while ignoring the other determinants that co-produce health (Griffin 2012). Moreover, exercise as a form of output and labour, and which is also tied to the ideology of energy balance, also hews to hegemonic good health orthodoxy.

Historically, the focus on energy balance emerged out of nutritional experiments and research tied to factory workers and the amount of sustenance they needed to engage in arduous physical labour. Charlotte Biltekoff (2013) traces this lineage in her book, *Eating Right in America: The Cultural Politics of Food and Health*, in which she outlines the history of nutrition as a form of moral citizenship that is scientifically testable, tied to ethical moderation, and enmeshed in concerns about waste, wartime frugality, national policies, and ideal productivity. Apps like GetFit draw on the same logic – specifically that an energy deficit can be produced bringing users to the magical 3500 calories (equalling one pound of fat) level generated through a combination of 'healthy' eating and intensive, time-efficient, exercise.

Using a relational and new materialist lens, what becomes clear is how disconnected this logic is from the body as a sociomaterial force, a mattering that is an embodied effect of other agents including institutions, values, naturecultures, objects, and nonhuman actants. Braidotti calls this the enfleshed Deluzean subject, one that is a product of 'a folding-in of external influences and a simultaneous unfolding outwards of affects' (Braidotti 2000, 159). This is a critical point in that it draws attention to how the body, and 'subjectivity', is cultivated, marked, and yet unstable from the start.

This explains why the caloric-energy deficit model is so highly contested and should be viewed with scepticism. In keeping with the decentred notion of embodied subjectivity, what becomes clear is that this model tells us little about, for example, the complexity of metabolism, the impact of sleep, of eating rhythms, and of just how resistant the body is to weight reduction (Thomas et al. 2013; Bacon and Aphramor 2014):

it [also] tells little about how the body determines when and how such energy is stored, mobilized, or utilized or how food affects the regulation of these processes. Many factors – including molecules in food or lack thereof – can impact food-related physiological processes and behavior, including fat storage.

(Biltekoff et al. 2014, 225)

This is to say nothing of the erroneous assumption that body size is a perfect indicator of one's health status. In fact, body size tells us little about the amount someone eats and/or how much they exercise. In drawing this analysis away from food and onto movement, I also would like to focus the reader's attention to the way in which food choice has been moralized and connected to class. News stories and TV shows featuring 'poor' families purchasing and consuming large amounts of processed food, for example, act as a form of boundary making wherein 'ideal whiteness' is made malleable such that 'obesity, as a central trait of inappropriate whiteness', comes to 'carr[y] reduced racial privilege'. Fat, racialized bodies, on the other hand, are seen as *a priori* inferior, unruly, and 'in excess of white standards of physicality and propriety' (Sanders 2019, 6; also see Farrell 2011). Eating well thus becomes an act of *racial* boundary making and is intimately tied the logics of the modern agential subject, wherein the (white) self is seen as the most capable of adhering to the carefully balanced consumption and energy goals of hegemonic good health.

A similar argument about the complexity of food, fat, health, and energy can be made with respect to exercise and how the body processes energy: efficiently? effectively? to its maximum potential? GetFit states that it uses AI to determine heart rate metrics and estimate calories burned with precision. As stated in the previous section, goal-oriented effectiveness and efficiency are central to GetFit's ethos wherein 'temporal characteristics are closely studied with short (5min) and long (24hr) ECG records made within each test. Such testing methods include time and frequency domain testing and analysis of nonlinear chaotic oscillations of the cardio rhythm' (GetFit 2021). The app sets out daily calorie burn goals as well as number of steps, muscle status, and workouts, with a progress report tied to workouts and minutes engaged in physical activity. This approach to exercise and movement is of particular import to this cut in that it seeks to reduce complex bodily systems, forces, and flows to charts, metrics, and measurements which serve as a proxies for health. As Till argues, 'digital tracking devices are having a considerable impact upon how exercise is understood … because of their ability to objectify and standardise the activities and capacities of heterogeneous bodies in such a fashion that value can be extracted' (Till 2014, 447).

This kind of quantification, much like in the QS movement, elides other forms of bodily knowledge and formalizes an understanding of movement as bodywork wherein exercise becomes part of an 'attempt to redefine or reshape the body and its appearance to more closely comply with health and beauty standards' (MacNevin 2003, 271). Fitness labour and bodywork, defined in this way, is goal-oriented and 'geared to shaping the body and physical control' (Coffey 2019, 73). What results is a new body ontology – one that is made up of seemly neutral data but actually oriented towards a very particular form of health subjectivity.

Conversely, I argue that we should think of exercise as way in which to engage with the world and others through movement. These bodily engagements can be joyful, difficult, strenuous, gentle, engaging, worlding, and affirmative. Moreover, movement need not be a purely functional activity but also ethical and relational. The active body engaged in movement would then be seen less as an energy-efficient machine, striving for deficit, than as an unfolding actant performing and intra-acting with materialcultural matterings in ways that are diffractive and affirmative (Barad 2007; Hultman and Lenz Taguchi 2010). Moving for the enjoyment of the lived body in a manner that is 'specific, concrete, subjective, and corporeal' and reflects 'experiences and feeling states (the "phenomena" element)' are left out of the dominant account entirely (Allen-Collinson 2010). There is a plethora of research examining and documenting embodied exercise experiences that do not rely on reductive healthicization. For example, scholars like Fullager (2018) examine how embodied movement is correlated with depression recovery, and how different forms of physical activity (running, mountaineering, (team) sports) enact productive entanglements that goes beyond the energy balance model (Allen-Collinson, Crust, and Swann 2018; Thorpe and Clark 2020). However, it should be noted that these assemblages can change drastically when sports become functionalized. Also of importance is research demonstrating that users can find tracking pleasurable when the device acts as form of play, through the gamification of exercise, for example, or through the instigation of self-reflection and knowledge production (Gimpel, Nißen, and Görlitz 2013; Lupton 2019).

The data and trust component of this cut is important in a double sense. First, we have trust as it relates to privacy and control over information. There has been a surfeit of fantastic investigative work and academic research carried out revealing the mechanisms and scale at which data is shared with interested third parties by health trackers (Almuhimedi et al. 2015; Zimmer et al. 2020; Klosowski 2021). This includes transmitting sensitive data (e.g. location), tracking internet traffic, using insecure protocols, not complying with privacy protocols, and directing large amounts of data to tracking companies, advertisers, and analytics (Gioacchino et al. 2021). A 2019 *Wall Street Journal* story named GetFit, along with other trackers, as companies that are currently sharing user data with Facebook without permission (Schechner and Secada 2019). The risk of said data being shared with employers, particularly when they are used as part of employee evaluation, is especially acute insofar as it 'enable[s] big data-driven interests such as employers and organizations to encroach on and penetrate into work, consumption and leisure' (Calvard 2019, 265). Insurance companies are another organization for whom this data is useful – particularly as it has been used to approve or deny coverage and monitor health status (Troiano 2017). It is important to underline that while recording steps taken and calories burned might seem innocuous, when combined with other data it can reveal a great deal about a person's preferences, habits, and behaviours. Consider the interests of law enforcement and how valuable this data could be in constructing a narrative of criminality in a manner that appears objective but is highly biased and racialized (Levinson-Waldman 2018; Benjamin 2019; Garcia and de Roock 2021).

Interestingly, while most users of digital apps like fitness trackers claim to value privacy, their behaviour often reveals the opposite. This has come to be known as the 'privacy paradox', in which a higher threshold for information sharing, one more robust than that what might be willingly consented to, is maintained in action. This misplaced trust is troubling yet understandable given the complexity of privacy policies, lack of knowledge about how discrete bits of information can be used, and social norms (like that of superfluous sharing) (Williams, Nurse, and Creese 2016; Gerber, Gerber and Colamer 2018). Moreover, the tracking industry is adept at exploiting this uncertainty by banking 'on this double insecurity: the customers they imagine, unsure whether to trust their own senses, desires and intuitions as they make mundane yet vital choices' (Schüll 2016, 9).

It is also significant vis-à-vis data, trust, and the privacy paradox that fitness trackers like can GetFit facilitate a kind of estrangement from the everyday by collecting data about the self that is then used to produce a 'data double' – a reassembled, digitized self that is decorporeal, algorithmic, and 'calculative' (Pink and Fors 2017). Here, trust is attenuated, almost invisibilized through estrangement from the digital self (i.e. it is not the 'real me'). However, with respect to hegemonic health subjectivities, reassembled digital selves experienced through apps tend to be used to amplify discipline, moralize a duty to be well and, operate as a resource for further self-optimization (QS) (Rich 2014; Ruckenstin 2014). Data, in this context, is experienced through a lens of impartiality and detachment wherein the body speaks through technology to produce a 1:1 representation that is shorn of the messiness of feeling, embodiment, and emotion. The GetFit app draws on this health ontology with its daily progress reports which include projections, training statistics, productivity levels, and milestones. Together, they produce a 'continually re-enacted and reconfigured' digital self – one that can be used to transform the fleshy self but does not have to (Lupton 2015, 107).

Trust, as a result, is especially fraught and includes faith in the veracity of the data double – of its fidelity to the self, where those bodies are stored, who can re-materialize them, and for what purpose. With respect to health and fitness data, this can include the organizations discussed above – employers, advertisers, law enforcement, insurance companies – who use this data to police, surveil, and exploit. As I make clear further on, however, there are cracks in this ontology which can be prized open in order to make space for resistance and transformation. As Kozel argues, 'Bodies are not [only] dissolved into the digital and rendered easier to control, protect and preserve, in fact their materiality only becomes more complex' (Kozel 2017, 111).

Taken together, this cut has drawn attention to the ways in which energy, bodies, body-world relations, and a data surfeit–trust deficit doublet work to entrench hegemonic good health and undercut just and pro-social health outcomes. Machinic efficiency, energy deficits, weight loss, quantification vis-à-vis movement, and the surfeit of data and lack of trust thus form the planks of our health economy.

2. GetFit App – Fatness and Health–Access–Dis/ability–Gender?/Race?

This second cut subtends from the first one and begins with a deeper analysis of fatness and health. As noted previously, there is, both on the GetFit app and its promotional material/webpage, a clear orientation towards weight loss *framed as an act of health*. Its developer description for CNET, for example, includes the statement: 'lose weight, get in shape or even gain weight?' (wherein the 'even' does a lot of work in framing gaining weight as an outlier). Potential objectives include the ability to 'lose belly fat and get six pack abs for the summer' by using their 'effective bikini body workout' (CNET 2021). The app itself, during the setup process, offers the following options: 'lose weight (get in your dream shape), stay in shape (get a toned and leaner body), get strong (bulk up and build muscle).' It also advertises workouts tailored to 'problem areas' (arms/breast, abs/core/back, butt/legs). Primary workout options include astronaut, hourglass figure ('uncover your curves and bring them to light. Hello slim waist, shapely hips and well-toned butt'), bikini ready ('get a swimsuit-worthy abs, sleeker arms, thighs, and butt with this ultimate program designed to help you slip on a bikini with confidence'), post pregnancy ('Yeah, baby! Get your strength, shape, and balance back with the program designed to ease you back into workout mode after giving birth'), and mom and baby ('the main goal for you here is to get your body back in shape and have fun with your child'). There are reminders to log one's weight, water consumption, food intake, and exercise where health, throughout, remains tied to pervasive anti-fatness.

While this may not appear to be a particularly novel insight, i.e. that a mainstream fitness app would be oriented towards hegemonic good health and PN health norms, what requires further probing is the underlying anti-fat and ableist bias it reflects. Remember that 'fit' subjectivities are framed as achievable through the energy deficit model – which relies on the quantifiability of food intake and energy expenditure. Undergirding all of this is the taken-for-granted assumption that fatness is *causally* linked to illness and thinness to health, happiness, beauty, and earned citizenship. It is important to emphasize just how hegemonic this assumption is. Lebesco (2010) chronicles the history of the medicalization of fatness, tracing it to the notion of sin, Protestant self-control, and a desire to discipline the marginalized (the poor, women, the racialized, the 'sexually deviant', the disabled). This understanding intersects with moves to enact difference and apportion blame on the individual for ill health (also see Strings 2019). Azzarito examines the rise of the homogenous body ('fit' and white) as part of neoliberal globalization and as a pedagogical tool aimed at colonizing 'physicality to homogenous, monocultural, white conceptions of the "fit, slim body"' (Azzarito 2008, 184).

It is important to emphasize here that I, like many others, consider fat phobia to be a reflection of deep-seated social fears about bodies out of control and hold that fatness has not been proven to be *causally* connected to ill health. On top of this is the fact that energy deficit diets are rarely successful, that cycles of weight gain and loss can be damaging, and that fat stigma in the medical community accounts for a significant amount of hesitancy in getting medical attention (due to negative interactions wherein weight becomes the focus of appointments irrespective of the medical complaint) (Campos 2004; Guthman 2011 and 2013; Gordon 2020a).

What is ignored in this framing of health is an understanding of the lived experience of the fat body – specifically how it is embodied and inhabited. GetFit's focus on the projection of an ideal body, one that is 'slim', 'shapely', 'well-toned', is then connected with a body that is well, lively/energetic, happy, and accepted. The fat body is constructed by Getfit through its absence since all visible images on its website and app are of toned, youthful, and attractive men and women featuring close-ups of bodies and body parts that are in line with the normative ideal. Embodying these kinds of bodies is the penultimate ideal since it is believed this will help cultivate an empowered, accepted, successful and healthy life. Relations, forces, and flows with others (human and non) are left out of this narrative entirely since this particular understanding of 'care for the self' requires the cultivation of a 'docile body' – that permits relentless surveillance (Longhurst 2012).

In the case of Anduna and GenoPalate, the pursuit of hegemonic health tends to stress only 'the repressive moments in the construction of the slender body, contra the enabling function of the dieting process'. Positive outcomes include a sense of power, of confidence, and self-acceptance (Heyes 2006, 136). Returning to the cut, the absent fat body is seen as the contra-, the anti- to the ideal body. This leaves unaddressed any understanding of larger bodies as worthy, powerful, and desirable. Materialist and affective work in this area has a lot to offer since it sees the body as relational and as 'produced in affective relation with others'. It also highlights the importance of feeling comfortable in one's body through movement but is critical of programmes that encourage solitary forms of exercise (Hynnä and Kyrölä 2019, 2; also see Saw 2006; Pausé, Wykes and Murray 2016). Understanding bodies in this way – through what might be characterized as the queer fat body, the fat racialized body, and/or the fat disabled body – acts as means through which to rewrite fatness by:

> turning away from the moralizing and impossible work of realizing a happy future and by turning toward a politic that affirms both embodied difference and acknowledges the ever-changing nature of embodied experience.
>
> (Tidgwell et al. 2018)

This quote transitions us nicely into the next element of this cut – one that focuses on GetFit and its relation to access/accessibility and disability. Each and every element of the app – including its configuration, the exercises it recommends, the images it utilizes to draw consumers in, the relations of identification and aspiration – assumes or depicts able-bodiedness. The women and men are all young and face no discernible impediments to engaging in the kinds of movement the app demands. One of the most prominent images that illustrates this is on the GetFit website, on its page encouraging users to sign up for their 42 club (42 = the minutes spent in each session). Next to a description of the programme is an image of a muscular man and svelte but well-toned woman stretching together in yoga-like poses with the woman wearing a crop top and the man, no shirt at all. In fact, all of the images on the app and website are of 'fit' men and women either standing or engaging in some form of staged movement. The erasure of disabled bodies from basic representation is in keeping with the neglect of nonnormative bodyminds and the perception of disability, as per the medical model, as something to be overcome. This compulsory able-bodiedness means that GetFit acts as a health gatekeeper wherein users must be 100 per cent able-bodied to participate (Butler and Parr 2005; McRuer 2010). While not requiring a lot of impact, the exercises take for granted that users can squat, plank, lunge, crunch, and lift with no assistance, use dumbbells for added resistance (optional), and have a certain level of 'fitness'. Moreover, all exercises are presented as isolated endeavours requiring vision (note that there is some audio direction).

The problem with this 'ableist project' is that it assumes an abled imaginary, one that 'relies upon the existence of a hitherto unacknowledged imagined shared community of able-bodied/minded people ... held together by a common ableist homosocial world view that asserts the preferability and compulsoriness of the norms of ableism' (Campbell 2008). It does not, for this reason, allow for a more capacious understanding of exercise and movement – one that refrains from deifying the 'supercrip' (i.e. the driven disabled person who is able to adapt, strive, and attain hegemonic good health), or a conception of health, fitness, and movement that is non-normative, adaptive, and emergent. Such an approach would trouble the abled/disabled binary and do so in ways that account for the specificity of disabled entanglements – specifically ones that encourage alternative exercise assemblages. While there are options out there, e.g. the Cerebral Palsy Foundation's fitness app, even those have been found to be wanting in terms of options and capabilities. The intersection of disability and fat subjectivity provide some interesting ways forward, including initiatives that push for a non-medicalized reimagination of bodily difference (Shakespeare 2008).

The one aspect of accessibility GetFits gets right is reflected in what it requires of the user – or, more precisely, what it does not require. Specifically, it does not demand any travel, equipment, or subscriptions (minus some optional in-app purchases). Having a smartphone and some room are all that is needed which, while not by any means available to all, makes it much more accessible than other programmes.

The final element of this cut revolves around gender and race. I placed question marks beside both in order to think about them as troubled and overlapping as it relates to GetFit, exercise, movement, and hegemonic good health. Representationally, the GetFit website features women prominently, which is not surprising since a large portion of the fitness app industry targets women. For my iteration of the app, because I entered my gender as female (note that only two options were given), the images featured were mostly women – 'fit', young, attractive women specifically. On the website, any men featured are also in shape and embody hegemonic good health norms. Overall, the kind of femininity portrayed by GetFit depicts women as youthful, strong, self-possessed, hard-working, and attractive. These representations work through and with digital infrastructures to cultivate 'gender norms, patterns, and power relations [that] are bound in and among the increasingly indistinguishable sociotechnical relations that entangle our offline and online lives' (Fullager, Parry and Johnson 2019, 227).

'The 'Post-Pregnancy Program' and 'Mom and Baby Program' sections of the app feature women who have 'bounced back' from pregnancy and now inhabit fit and trim bodies showing no visible indications of childbirth. The former features a perfectly coiffed woman in a sports bra – while the latter uses an image of a woman in a crop top holding her baby with text stating that this programme will allow users to 'get into shape and have fun with your child'. This understanding of femininity is intimately tied to reproduction in two ways: the first is with respect to the mere fact of its existence (which reproduces a form of biologism that sees women's bodies as tied to childbirth), while the second has to do with the way in which reproduction must occur in the 'right' ways – ones in which women are 'quickly reabsorbed in the capitalist regime she has already inconvenienced by reproducing' (Cunningham 2002). This is also tied to the anatopolitics of the body and population in the which the 'responsible woman' ensures the vital capacity of society through the application, internationalization, and performance of hegemonic good health (for themselves *and their children*) (Rabinow and Rose 2006). This, of course, is not inevitable. Alternative ways in which to think about health and reproduction might, for example, include conceptions of reproductive ecologies in which 'every life is dependent upon a whole range of openings to other lives' (Hird 2007, 4), and in which ethics and responsibility extend beyond the skin (Neimanis 2014).

GetFit's enactment of gender is also consistent with the kind of 'lean-in', postfeminist ethic that fuses neoliberal responsibilization with the assumption that feminism, having achieved its goal of equality, can now take its place in the choice economy (Gill and Scharff 2013; Cairns and Johnston 2015; Toffoletti, Thorpe and Francombe-Web 2018). This economy sees self-mastery, surveillance, and bodywork as fun and empowering, enabling what Bordo refers to as the correct, postfeminist 'management' of desire (Bordo 2004, 187). This is where the accessibility, flexibility, and affordability of the app rubs up against the realities of women's contemporary lives in which childcare, family care, home care, work, and the pressures of hegemonic good health converge so as to make even a confined, quick, isolated, and homebound exercise routine difficult to do. Exercise thus becomes detached from care for the self and elides embodied and 'affective engagements through which things comes to matter' (Murphy 2015, 721), It, instead, operates fully in line with quantified, numerical, and functional health practices. This kind of lean-in, 'have-it-all' ethos is consistent with QS, healthism, and an understanding of gender inequality as comprised of discrete acts women can challenge, meritocratically, on their own. Gill describes this kind of feminism as 'complicit with not critical of capitalism, and of other systems of (classed, racialized and transnational) injustice' (Gill 2016, 7; also see Gill 2017). GetFit and hegemonic good health authorizes and reinscribes this enactment of gender in ways that risk intensifying patriarchal relations of power. However, as I relate in the auto-ethnographic section, this does not mean that this assemblage is impermeable or that digital forms of embodied health identities that reflect gender performance and enactment cannot resist and exceed this cut.

While my focus here is on the constructed and material enactments of gender vis-à-vis femininity, rather than masculinity, I think it is important to broaden this cut slightly to think about how, whether, and to what extent there is *any* intromission of destabilizing engagements with respect to gender. The only image I could identify is one used on the app for the 'Office Workout' in which a (white) woman is depicted. While she has a normative body, she also has short, mohawk-styled hair that is buzzed on the side – which is quite unlike all of the other women in the app. While it would likely be a step too far to infer any gender bending here, it is reflective of a more butch aesthetic, one that might have a lesbian-subtext – something that Danae Clark (1995) writes about in *Commodity Lesbianism*.

With respect to race and racialization, the most obvious way in which race becomes visible is in relation to the images used by GetFit. Significantly, all images on the website and app are white or white passing with one only woman, the face of the 'Astronaut Workout Program', who appears to be Black. She has her natural hair and is fully covered in an astronaut's outfit. The lack of representations of racialized minorities is, of course, not a particularly novel insight but one which acts as an important indicator of social priorities, preferences, and hierarchies. It also reflects and concretizes the exclusionary nature of hegemonic good health communities, particularly online, which tend to be white and affluent.

GetFit also, reflecting its QS oriented and body normative ethos, places health responsibility onto the individual in ways that elide the racialized hierarchies that constitute the social determinants of health with marginalized communities bearing the brunt of environmental racism (Aldon and Agyeman 2011). In relation to exercise and movement, minority raced communities in most nations are more likely to live in areas that have low air quality, less green space, and might be considered 'unsafe' by traditional crime metrics. Racialized communities are also more likely to experience high levels of stress, long hours/ overwork, low pay, and multiple familial responsibilities (Dudd-Butera, Beaman and Brash 2020). Finding time, space, and the opportunity to engage in the practices of the 'worried well' tends to cleave along racial lines in ways that serve a purpose – namely as technologies of division that have the effect of reproducing racial (and other) hierarchies. Racialized groups are also often underrepresented in online health communities whether as users of health apps, or adherents of health trends or alternative health movements (Bender et al. 2014). This, however, is beginning to change, as in the case of Black veganism (Harper 2009), progressive health movements, and the development of social justice-oriented health technologies. A prime example of the latter is GrpFit, a social platform for Black users to gain support and access information about Black health as well as general health and fitness tips (complete with fitness challenges). Also of note is the NYRR (New York Road Runners) racing app which invites users (in New York City) to get fit and learn about running from runners in the Black community (NYRR 2021). The telos of both of these apps, however, remains tied to weight loss, fit bodies, and individual responsibility with the driving force of GrpFit, according to the founder, being that of the 'shocking ... health stats for our community ... for example, 76 per cent of Blacks are either overweight or obese ...' (GrPFit 2021). Despite this small move towards representation, it remains the case that most of the influential and lucrative digital health spaces and apps remain highly exclusionary and rooted in the same hegemonic ideologies I have critiqued throughout this book (Alkon and McCullen 2011). As such, I argue that apps like GetFit form racialized *digital* closed spaces – ones that mimic the exclusionary spaces of farmers markets, organic grocers, QS, and mHealth. While there are no clear metrics on GetFit's users, it is likely that its demographic breakdown will replicate that of smartphone users, internet access, and uptake of other digital health technologies (Anderson-Lewis et al. 2018). However, it is also important to point out that this is beginning to change with recent scholarship showing increased use of health apps and participation in online health movements amongst marginalized groups as well as moves towards inclusion and representation (both online and off) (McMahon et al. 2022; Lyle, Wachter and Sarkar 2021). And yet, in many instances the explanation for this rise tends to be less about new forms of engagement and openness, but as a way to deal with a lack of access to affordable health care in these communities (Anderson-Lewis et al. 2018; Statista 2019).

On the other hand, as I discuss below, it is also important to think about how the simple inclusion of racialized groups in digital tracking can have pernicious outcomes.

This is particularly problematic when the addition of racialized communities into elite health spaces on the level of use and representation (i.e. not in design) functions as a form of enforced health subjectification. While this most often reflects one's co-optation into dominant health pedagogies, it can also function to produce avenues for novel forms of workplace surveillance wherein who gets surveilled, for what, and how often is racialized and reflective of hegemonic notions of who represents an ideal worker (male, white, young, heterosexual, able-bodied, and English-speaking). Evidence of this goes all the way back to Henry Ford's system of workplace and home health monitoring in which employees, including immigrants and Black workers (who often bore the brunt of this), were docked pay for being insufficiently 'healthy' (Dryud 2015). While GetFit does not appear to have established any corporate synergies (i.e. corporate wellness programs) many similar trackers have. According to Giddens, Ledner, and Gonzales, as of 2017, nearly 2,000 companies have integrated some form fitness tracking into their corporate policy using either smart phone-based apps or devices (e.g. Fitbit, Garmin, Jawbone) (Giddens, Ledner, and Gonzales 2016).

Taken together, what becomes clear is that intersections of race, technology, surveillance, and health norms introduce processes that re-inscribe, rather than resist, racial ideology. This includes the ways in which racialized bodies are disproportionately policed and coded as Other through technology. This can occur when collected data is used for carceral purposes and by workplaces to surveil and penalize employees they see as insufficiently inhabiting hegemonic good health subjectivities. Being able to justify this as 'fair' and the data collected as 'objective' ignores the fact that technologies, inclusive of algorithms, are social artefacts through and through. As Safiya Noble agues, 'they [algorithms] oversimplify complex phenomena. They obscure any struggle over understanding, and they can mask history' (Noble 2018, 116). The underlying health problems of racialized communities, who do suffer from higher rates of diabetes, high blood pressure, and asthma, thus become their responsibility. Rather than addressing the structural causes of those conditions through a living wage, clean environment, and access to health care that is free at point of access, racialized employees are given an app (which is much cheaper) and told to internalize the 'health gaze' of the ever-present employer (Owen, Carmona and Pomeroy 2020).

Leaks, policing, skewed (raced) risk construction (of health risks and/ or criminal recidivism) in an era of big data works to identify patterns and make claims that *appear* neutral (based on data), but in practice replicate hegemonic power and knowledge assemblages (Hannah-Moffat 2013; Okidegbe 2019). Additionally, these technologies amplify and intensify what McMillan Cottom refers to as 'predatory inclusion' – a kind of inclusion that sees in the marginalized the possibility for profit which explains why apps like GetFit will often include a token, non-threatening minority body to make it appear more inclusive as a company. This kind of inclusion works by 'including marginalized consumer-citizens into ostensibly democratizing mobility schemes on extractive terms' (McMillan Cottom 2020, 443). Thinking about these apps through the lens of digital racial capitalism helps to explain how the desire to belong is made profitable while also keeping hierarchies in place.

Finally, there is one more, rather unexpected manifestation of race in this cut worth unpacking. Specifically, there is an underlying ethnic ambiguity with some of the women featured which then feeds into a conversation about colourism. It is important to note that racial inclusion is broadly consistent with trends in contemporary advertising and public relations in which more capacious representation has come to be seen as necessary, but also potentially alienating. Using racial ambiguity to skirt this line is significant in that it allows companies like GetFit 'to do the discursive work of managing difference in ways that come across as safe, relatable' by presenting 'a "naturalized" version of the foreigner, one who embodies attributes of diversity but is ready to consume like an American' (Shankar 2013, 164). The fetishization of this kind of ambiguity and/or diversity, as Carter (2018) puts it, are de rigeur and part of a new aesthetic he calls mixploitation. Another way to think about this is through the aesthetic of racelessness wherein the image produced is that of an 'urban, multicultural, and presumably postracial world in which the ... [men and women] perform cultural border crossing with ease' (Beltrán 2013, 76). It is notable that the Black woman has light skin which is in keeping with the colourism or 'skin semantics' of much of contemporary advertising and reflective of the rise of the 'Instagram look' that many of the woman featured reflect (Evans and Davies 2011). Fuertes describes this aesthetic perfectly:

> The flag emojis may be trying to say, 'Look at how beautiful diversity is!' but the look is eerily uniform: full lips, tiny Disney princess noses, catlike eyes, caramel skin, and painfully hourglass figures. This homogenized mass of the ethnically ambiguous 'Instagram baddie', as it's now been coined, could, in different lights, be of Latin, Black, Arab, or Asian extraction in a way that is just as unattainable and exclusionary as the leggy blonde bombshell of the 1990s.
>
> (Fuertes 2018)

The agential intromission of race and gender in the final part of this cut is important in how they intra-act with technical infrastructures, technologies (GetFit), ideologies, institutions, and norms to reproduce hegemonic good health. The subjects of accessibility and disability round out this second cut and work with the first's focus on the relation between energy, diet, weight and bodies, body-world relations, and the ethics of data and trust which allows for a robust consideration of how the app works with dominant discourses and political economic structures to solidify hegemonic good health. This new materialist approach brings to the fore *relations* as a unit of analysis and materialdiscursive intra-actions between contingent forces and forcings as forming the basis of understanding. In the next section, I engage in an auto-ethnographic exegesis in which I use GetFit and become part of the assemblage, what Ray characterizes as being 'entangled within the assemblages of study' for two weeks (Ray 2019 94). In doing so, I add to this already rich account of GetFit as a hegemonic good health technology from yet another vantage point.

Auto-ethnography: GetFit

It is important to emphasize that the form of auto-ethnographic analysis I have and continue to engage in here is not solipsistic or bounded by and through the individual body. Rather, it is posthuman and post-phenomenological wherein any sense of isolated subjectivity emerges out of entanglements with human and nonhuman actants bounded by diffractive relations. Diffraction, as opposed to reflexivity, sees knowing 'as part of the material process of the world's becoming' in which thought is understood to be 'an unfolding, performative, intra-active relationship that involves humans, nonhumans, discourse, time and space' (Thorpe 2020, 2). The auto-ethnographic account I seek to capture is affective and corporeal while also being relational and co-constituted (Taylor 2017; Warfield 2019).

Consistent with chronology of this book, GetFit was the final two-week exercise I completed. After a month of participating in these 'experiments', and what I felt was a draining previous one, I was looking forward to engaging with a technology that was less food-centred, although I did try to log my intake and stay within the caloric bounds of GetFit's meal plan, usually 1650–1800 calories. I paid less attention to the macronutrient breakdown but adhered to their 'low processed' ethos. I also tried a few of their recipes which, overall, were not bad. In setting up the app, I chose the classic meal plan, rather than high protein or paleo options, and the 'hourglass figure' fitness programme which called for 10,000 tracked steps per day and, for five days a week, a 42-minute planned workout with options for additional 'targeted exercises'. There was something viscerally 'cringe-inducing', for me, in choosing the 'hourglass figure' exercise plan but I decided it was necessary as an explicit manifestation of what the app promised.

I then answered a number of questions about when I would like to work out, how often, and other lifestyle-related queries – ostensibly so the app could tailor its offerings around my daily life. GetFit mapped my progress with daily and cumulative projections and statistics including 'active calories', 'water intake', 'training effect' (aerobic and anaerobic, based on heart data), productivity levels (broken down by stress versus productivity – also measured by heart rate), and, finally, weight loss progress. I intentionally inputted my current *and* goal weights as the same so as to avoid any proclivity to make this about weight loss.

The first element I wrote about with some consistency was the app's promise of providing a novel experience, a 'health journey' which obviated some of the pressure, intentional or not, to think of it as a discrete and bounded diet. Discourses around health programmes have, over the last decade, drifted away from traditional diet talk and towards notions of 'lifestyle change', 'individual transformation', and 'changes for life'. Talk of 'a healthy body, mind, and spirit' and the cultivation of a 'healthy mindset' (by GetFit), spoke, for me, to a sense of temporal boundless and bodily integrity rooted in a slightly more capacious understanding of health (GetFit Apps 2021). As such, while my project was temporally bounded, I did find it somewhat heartening that the app refrained from a rhetoric of short-term punishment to reach specific body goals. And yet, as the days went by, it became clear that this wellness framing had slowly been displaced such that the rhetoric of lifestyle transformation was made to do pretty much the same hegemonic health work. That is, GetFit remained reliant on the equation of a slim body with health, morality, and status, coupled with the elevation of particular ways of eating (in line with 'diet culture') (Harrison 2019). The recent rebranding of Weight Watchers as WW International Inc., for example – which I return to – is also indicative of this trend since it is a company that operates on and through an ideology of healthism wherein individual responsibility and moralizing health practices are elevated in daily life but placed behind a more palatable and less alienating 'wellness curtain'. I felt this acutely when it came to the food which was pitched as pleasurable and satisfying while also being 'smarter', 'flexible' (for busy lives) and 'results-oriented' (GetFit Apps: Diet & Meal Planner 2021).

Overall, I have to admit I adhered less closely to the dietary guidelines as time went on – mostly because my focus here was on exercise, but also due to the specificity and non-repetition of the recipes given. Observing them would have required a lot of planning, cooking time, and the purchasing of ingredients that would likely be wasted after one use (many were difficult to source due to the limits posed by Covid-19). Moreover, while the app did allow users to specify food allergies and preferences, no matter what permutation you tried (I attempted several), most of the recipes were Western/Mediterranean oriented, sometimes with a hint of spice (i.e. curry powder – an entirely Western invention). Items like a caprese salad, avocado toast, arugula and cherry tomato salad, creamy shrimp pasta, and ratatouille with goat cheese were as 'exotic' as it got. I was struck, however, by GetFit's decision to rely on recipes that required more high-end and pricey ingredients which I noted spoke directly to its targeted demographic – namely, consumers with relatively high levels of health, cultural, and economic capital (which then translate into markers of class). These elite foodways can 'marginalise those who are perceived to "lack" the economic, cultural and social capital to engage in "healthy" … foodways' while also monitoring those with the means and time to adhere to these norms as closely as possible (Parsons 2016: 3). This orientation also has the potential to alienate racialized users searching for different food options, ones that are in line with their cultural values, tastes, and norms. The all-important food–pleasure–tradition–desire nexus, as such, is discounted from the outset (Slocum and Saldanha 2016).

Of all the requirements around consumption and movement over my six-week experiment, the exercise programme was the most enjoyable – with some caveats. As someone who likes to move, challenge, and exert myself, having participated in difficult 'cross-fit adjacent' group classes for years, these sessions were not particular alien or disruptive to my usual workout routine in terms of time, intensity, and frequency. Having purchased a new elliptical trainer during the first lockdown, I felt comfortable engaging in at-home exercise, despite traditionally preferring group classes and a busy gym. The social dimension of fitness is something I missed. Even when not engaging in group classes, there is something satisfying about taking time out of your day to tune out and engage in an activity in an environment with others doing the same thing. As Andersson and Andreasson put it, group fitness can work as sites of commonsality in which 'Interactions with befriended fitness enthusiasts seemingly enables successful interactional ritual chains, which, in turn, generate belonging and socio-emotional connectedness' (Andersson and Andreasson 2021, 118). Classes do this by generating an insider relationality derived from shared experience (i.e. a really intense workout).

I will note, however, that some of the classes that I have been involved with in the past, i.e. Bar Method, Soulcycle, Bikram's Yoga, can encourage unhealthy forms of attachment, commitment, and insular forms of solidarity. This ethos is not a part of GetFit – largely as a result of its underdeveloped social community. The underlying ethic of belonging to a larger grouping of imagined others also seeking to improve and transform is compelling. However, it can also give rise to a misplaced sense of heightened individual autonomy and choice exercised outside of social forces, expectations, and norms. I felt this to be the case on several occasions wherein a sense of self-contained discipline and commitment worked to produce a self-generated 'health halo' – one that, if directed outward, I worried might result in the stigmatization and judgement of nonnormative others. Upon reflection, I also noted that it could be the case that the commitments elicited by the app might be even more pernicious in a biopolitical sense for users who engage with it but lack the sociality that a group might elicit. This kind of power, as Scott contends, 'is most effective when it secures the willing compliance of subjects to be governed' such that it is often seen 'in [one's] ... own interests to comply with regimes' (Scott 2011, 240).

The workouts themselves offered choice, but I tended to stick to the 42-minute 'workout of the day' with, on occasion, a 7-minute cardio session or one of their 'muscle isolation' routines. The longer workouts were all quite similar to one another and did require some equipment (dumbbells – which I had), They consisted of low-impact, strength-oriented sets of things like lunges, squats, raises, push-ups, etc., narrated by a cheery female voice accompanying a video of a slim, young, white woman leading the exercises. With sufficient weight (dumbbells) and intensity, I found the workouts to be challenging but not uncomfortable. I made several entries and voice notes about affect, what it felt like on a fleshy, visceral level to engage in this kind of exercise. This auto-ethnographic technique involves forming narratives that are 'evocative and "alive"' so as to 'unearth concrete "forms of life" and otherwise hard-to-capture affective embodiments' (Bødker and Chamberlain, 2). For me, this included paying attention to my limits (e.g. knee pain connected to past engagements with sport), experiences of vitality during exercise (e.g. after numerous push-ups or squats), a relational entanglement between myself and the equipment (wherein the latter is seen as agential and dynamic), and the pleasurable excess of intensity experienced after completing a workout (Ticineto Clough 2009; Massumi 2015; Thorpe 2020). New materialist approaches to auto-ethnography pay close attention to the material processes of lively matter and the embodiedness of material discursive phenomenon (Fullager 2017). Tracing my own embodied feelings became a site for interrogating both old and new affective relations. To the extent possible, I tried to capture (in text) the aliveness of my body, how it reacted, and what it could do – almost on a pre-noetic level. Despite the 'contrivedness' of the app and my reasoned scepticism of the health assemblage it perpetuates, for the two weeks I engaged with GetFit I found the exercises to be pleasurable. Reacting to changing speeds and tempos, pushing twitching muscle fibres to the point of exhaustion, executing that last rep, and getting in a good sweat felt great! Being rewarded with a heart rate reading that was high – and a 'job well done' from the app – added to this sense of accomplishment. My experience closely reflected Parviainen and Aromaa's insights on how 'the agency of the lived body' can act 'as a source of knowledge in physical activity' so as to foster self-awareness and the subsumption of motor skills into kinaesthetic bodily movements (Parviainen and Aromaa 2017, 477). This accounting for affect and feeling (as opposed to emotion which is more structured (the display of feeling)), is an important element of auto-ethnographic sociology, and represents a perspective that is, unsurprisingly, lacking in hegemonic good health.

Yet, it was also obvious to me how this pleasurable affect was simultaneously being turned into capital by the app which was manipulating my biomediated body in so far as 'preindividual affective capacities have been made central to the passage from formal subsumption to the real subsumption of "life itself" into capital', and 'the accumulation of capital has shifted to the domain of affect' (Clough 2008, 17). A large part of auto-ethnography involves engaging with these disjunctures. In this case, it required reconciling hegemonic good health-related pleasures with the very real knowledge that at least some of these feelings are a product of neoliberal subjectification, dominant health norms, media influence, socialization, and the 'dietary-genomic-functional (super) food industrial complex'. I also considered how cultural practices around the body, 'the way it moves, is represented, has meanings assigned to it,' is imbued with power (Silk and Andrews 2011, 6). For example, I felt uncomfortable vis-à-vis the assumptions around what constitutes 'normal' movement and ability embedded in the sessions. The intersection of ableism and fat erasure in and by the app was notable in that it further entrenched hegemonic good health centrism and assumed an understanding of the self as autonomous, powerful, competitive, and able-bodied. Additionally, it is also the case that intentionally hypermediated 'exercise' has increasingly been criticized as inauthentic, contrived, elitist, and divorced from 'everyday life' (Shuda and Feito 2017). Back to basics exercising (i.e. cross fit and other forms of 'functional exercise'), on the other hand, have become popular as a way to counteract this. GetFit's workouts, I found, successfully balanced function with selective meta-level belonging.

For me, another set of themes emerged around the gendering of exercise and the app's focus on strength. Although there were short cardio videos available, it was striking that the exercises for women did not fall into and reinscribe the strength/weights/male vs. cardio/female binary. This site of gender differentiation is rooted in assumptions and fears about women's bodies becoming too big, bulky, and/or, masculine. In the gym, this translates into women disproportionately using cardio machines and participating in group aerobics and fitness classes while men stay in areas with weights, working in pursuit of the very bodies women are warned off of (Salvatore and Maracek 2010).

In engaging in these strength-centric programmes I found myself feeling anxious about the lack of cardio – of sweat-inducing, calorie-burning cardiovascular exercise. While committing to sticking solely to the exercise programmes on the app I did, on three occasions, add a half-hour cardio session on my home elliptical trainer. My thinking went back and forth between 'am I doing this because I genuinely enjoy the movement and challenge posed by cardiovascular exercise', or, had I internalized hegemonic good health so completely that it had become difficult to challenge these norms? I concluded that it was most likely the latter. It made me think about the politics of elliptical trainers which are designed not to mimic everyday movement (as opposed to a treadmill, stairclimber, or stationary bike), but to produce movements that heighten calorie burning. Despite reports that these machines often overestimate calories burned and intensity levels, they are popular for their claims of efficiency – something women, inclusive of myself, have internalized for decades as important. This is in-keeping with the energy deficit model discussed above and also speaks to the gendering of exercise. The constructed correlation between women, exercise, and weight loss, as Coen Rosenberg, and Davidson argue, works to delimit 'the boundaries of femininity in [and outside of] the gym' in ways that are 'narrow and rigidly policed' (Coen, Rosenberg and Davidson 2018, 33). I felt this acutely and repeatedly noted that this draw to cardio persisted despite full awareness of the likely explanation.

Returning briefly to the subject of affect and embodiment, I noted above that the exercises in GetFit's programme were largely strength focused except for a few short cardio options. While performing them, I could envision and viscerally feel myself engaging muscles that I would use in everyday contexts to lift, push, pull, move, etc. Over the two weeks I did the programme, I had three days of post-workout muscle soreness – something I took pleasure in as an indication of hard work – another component of hegemonic good health and a gendered health subjectivity I was aware of but internalized nonetheless.

In going over my notes about the somatics of exercise and how movements made me feel on the corporeal level (as a bodily phenomenon), I reflected carefully on how this form of embodiment was biosocial (i.e. not a priori but relational) and mediated. I also considered how *the digital* intersected with and shaped the kinds of affective experiences I was having. Initially, the devices (my phone and watch) felt like accessories but slowly became part of my immediate lifeworld such that this state of monitoring became automatic and felt natural. Checking my heart rate, steps, eating record, and calories burned became par for the course and almost automatic thereby solidifying a self-initiated, but now almost intuitive, clinical gaze co-produced with and through technology (Fox 2017). The gamified and engaging visuals, future-oriented patterns, constant updates, and push notifications spoke to and impressed upon me the agency of the technologies and health assemblage. What they 'do' and the kinds of relations and practices they encourage became paramount (Knorr-Cetina 1997; Latour 2005; Barad 2007). For me, this included being surprised by how I related to the data produced by GetFit as at once a representation of me and as 'useful' information about me. The production of this kind of a 'data double', according to Elmer, means that the body observed by technology is abstracted and then 'reassembled in different settings through a series of data flows. The result is a decorporealized body, a "data-double" of pure virtuality' (Elmer 2003, 611). While compelling, I found this explanation to be somewhat restrictive. My abstracted data-double, in making me knowable, is *supposed to* affect new health practices and behaviours using newly produced knowledge. Instead, what I became interested in were the cracks in this representation which came up when the app became glitchy or made wildly incorrect estimations. This reminded me of the technology's fallibility (i.e. that it is not a 1:1 representation of 'me' data-fied) and made me think about how I might resist these abstractions and the rhetoric of perfectibility and optimization. Resistance, on a personal level, consisted of altering exercises I did not like and, for one day, just not engaging with app to which I received what were supposed to be encouraging (but felt shaming?) push notifications.

With respect to technological agency, I wish I had the technical ability, and access, to GetFit's actual algorithmic code. While it is clear that GetFit is programmed to collect, sort, and place data into patterns for commercial purposes, as well as to inculcate biopedagogical norms, I was left wondering what else is being assumed and built into the technical infrastructure about gender, race, dis/ability, and sexuality that go deeper than what can be discerned on the level of use and observation. Finding this out, however, was all but impossible. What I was left with, and which is still important, is some clarity about the ways in which GetFit is intimately involved in what Williamson calls 'constant algorithmic diagnostics of patterns of human life' which 'use[s] the insights gained from those data to derive new models, classifications and theories of both individual and social behaviours' (Williamson 2016, 404; also see Benjamin 2019). These aspects of control and, subtending from it, self-subjectification is important but do not answer the questions I had about race, gender, sexuality, and dis/ability as it relates to algorithmic design.

On the level of gender, what was evident was that the assumptions built into the GetFit app were expressed through the entrenchment of the male/female binary. I found this to be rather presumptuous and constraining for an app that purported to be flexible and dynamic. This gender normativity is consistent with that of larger society but can become pernicious when it perpetuates assumptions about women as interested in health in so far as it fulfils hegemonic good health objectives. This coded normativity is amplified as the algorithm assumes this is desired/accepted through the app's repeated use. I reflected on the fact that this would likely end up re-inscribing and perpetuating the gender binary, complete with distorted conceptions of women's desires around movement and health embodiment. It would also, as Takahashi contends, 'harm the user experience of women, because who would feel comfortable when you are ignored, misunderstood and objectified?' (Takahashi 2019, 6; also see Kirkpartrick 2016; Constanza-Chock 2018).

I generally avoided playing with the parameters of the app in order to maintain a focus on experiential rather than comparative relations but, on the final day, I switched over to see what the 'male' version of the app looked like. I did this to further probe the app's built-in assumptions (its agency) given the lack of access to its codes. A cursory look found differences in the types of workouts as the most conspicuous. The categories were all strength centred, with titles like 'Fat Destroyer', and, 'Power & Strength', as were the exercises which used dumbbells or some sort of weight more frequently (and with no pregnancy or childcare discourse of course). There is a significant amount of existing research on masculinity and exercise relevant in this context which I am unable to go into here (Kennedy 2000; Nash 2018).

My thoughts around racialization, ethnicity and the ways in which the app exerted forms of sociomaterial power that shaped how I understand race and health were not particularly forthcoming either (again due to the opacity of the algorithms). From what I observed, there was a lack of diverse representation, the use of fashionable ethnic ambiguity, and pricey Western food choices (which intersects with race). Class was also embedded, expressed, and reinscribed through assumptions about the time and energy needed to engage in these forms of hegemonic good health practice, the space to do so, and the ability to access/afford the equipment (a smartphone, watch, and stable internet) (Garcia 2016; Madden et al. 2017; Tushnet 2018; Turner Lee 2018). Additionally, built-in norms about ability and bodily capacity, I noted, enforced certain forms of embodiment at the expense of others. Overall, if we consider each of these subject positions as a matrix of overlapping oppressions, rather than as discrete and distinct, what becomes clear is that the codes of this app work to reify and enforce particular kinds of subjectivity (Hill Collins 1991; Crenshaw 1990). A racialized, fat, and disabled woman, for example, might experience a form of intersectional disempowerment that would not only alienate them from hegemonic good health as the dominant health paradigm, but also imprint upon them the label of a failed, uncooperative, blameworthy health subject. This idealized health citizen, remember, is gendered and racialized since hegemonic good health itself developed out of a racist, patriarchal, and capitalist social order. As Cifor and Garcia state, for all users but particularly the marginalized,

> understanding one's body through universalized commensurable data points flattens the depth and complexity of gendered personal health, relationships, behaviors, and experiences by relegating them to easily measurable and shareable physiological parameters and symptoms. As a result, the simplification of health experiences contributes to a masculinist normalization that positions

ideal citizens as those that take self-responsibility and privileges healthist views
of the self that overlook gender and other [class, race, sexuality] socio-cultural
and economic determinants of health and wellness.

(Cifor and Garcia 2020, 2)

One final note on the observations I made about the agency of the app had to
do with agency denied. Thus far, I have discussed how these devices have been
programmed to act in ways that: 1. encourage forms of behaviour, patterns of
thought, and self-reflective practices that are consistent with hegemonic good
health; 2. hail subjects differently based on their identity positions; and 3. while
programmed to exert biopolitical control, are also entangled with other human
and nonhuman actants and thus cannot not be thought of as totalizing. I take up
the subject of resistance more fully in the final chapter.

Returning to the themes that came up during the course of the two
weeks, another formative experience I had, to do with cultivation of desire.
Specifically, a desire for a 'fit body' became more and more pressing and
tended to be reflected within and through the lone superfit, young, white
woman demonstrating the exercises. My desire was not just to reach to her
level of 'health', but to be able to execute the exercises at the same level (push
ups in particular). This form of competition felt natural, like a biological
predisposition, but also uncomfortable in that it meant that health was being
defined as a zero-sum game, as a property, and as a form of (health) capital
to be accumulated and used to convey status. It is this form of competition
that apps with robust online communities deploy by sharing metrics alongside
personal narratives (e.g. failures and triumphs) to extract newer forms of data
and encourage engagement. GetFit has options to share user progress and
concerns on their Facebook and Instagram pages but the level of engagement is
relatively low when compared to technologies like FitBit or even MyFitnessPal
which have large user communities. There is, however, interesting scholarship
documenting how the communities that arise out of app-centred health
experiences can be helpful and function as a source of connection and a means
by which to make sense of information and experiences (Fiore-Gartland
and Neff 2015). Lupton discusses how these forms of participation can even
inculcate 'notions of participatory democracy, citizenship and community ...
what I call "self-tracking citizenship"' on the part of its users (Lupton 2016c,
112). While I did not participate in these forms of communal intra-action, it is
important to highlight how new forms of sociality and solidarity can emerge
out of technical configurations that might not be designed for this purpose.

I also considered how the model exercises were highly standardized and objectified so that bodies that have different capacities, ranges (i.e. disabled bodies), and abilities were discounted. This, I argue, is purposeful and done so that bodies are homogenized and, as in the case of a myriad of digital activities, reliable value can be extracted (Till 2014). Exercise was also, like superfoods, medicalized in that they were transformed into technologies of health self-subjectification, a practice of the self that is reflected in and through fears around obesity and the rise of risk consciousness (Parker 2020). I found this to be intensely moralizing and a way to exercise control that was framed as self-initiated, but increasingly felt imposed. This is in keeping with contemporary postfeminist sensibilities that portray choice as occurring in a vacuum such that my 'choice' to pursue hegemonic good health and normative body projects/bodywork is framed as empowering and fun because it is 'chosen'. Also of note is the internalization of risk mitigation tied to the health imperative (Riley, Evans, and Robson 2018).

In line with postfeminism, and with respect to my own experience, I thought about how all this fits into understandings of the women featured in the videos and the woman voicing the enthusiastic and motivational voiceover. Both, I wrote, were performing a kind of 'digital aesthetic labour'. This required labour in the form of their own carefully observed food and fitness regimes (to maintain the hegemonic good health aesthetic) as well as the multiple takes from various angles that would be needed to get the video 'just right'. This labour, as Toffoletti, Thorpe and Francombe-Webb put it, is largely hidden and rooted in the entanglement between desire, pleasure, and empowerment on the one hand, and mastery, regulation, and surveillance on the other. As a result, the business of cultivating a hegemonic-body becomes 'enabled by the transformation imperative, through which transformation is constructed as empowering by offering self-mastery, health, a moral position and associated citizenship, and hope/expectations of a good life' (Toffoletti, Thorpe and Francombe-Webb 2018, 213). Since engaging with the app, I have become more and more interested in the various forms this health labour takes, how it operates in a digital environment, and how the app itself could be thought of as doing its own kind of work. Namely, as an agential cultural intermediary selling expert, authoritative, and tailored knowledge to an audience primed for this kind of information.

The fact that all of the women acting as instructors or demonstrators are white was noted with respect to how health, fitness, efficiency, and desirability are coded as white characteristics. The social coding of non-white bodies as Other, unruly, irresponsible, unhealthy, and fat, while not an explicit part of the app, creates the conditions under which the absence of undesirable Black and brown bodies goes without notice (Crawshaw 2020). This line of thought also made me think about how my own labour was being used such that the app, through its tracking of my patterns and choices on a day-to-day basis, was using gamification and engagement, coupled with a socially desirable goal – a fit body, 'to promote an entrepreneurial selfhood as the ideological frame that informs the strategy through which labour value is extracted without payment' (Till 2014, 446). Except that, in my case, I had gone one step further and actually paid to get access to more videos! Exercise, in this sense, facilitated the objectification of my labour and became something I could use for my own purposes (to see what I have 'achieved') and then turn over as a commodity for free.

Through this auto-ethnographic study of GetFit, I have added an experiential and embodied dimension to the political economic, discursive, and materialist analyses that precede it. In doing so, I have attempted to layer on an affective voice to these cuts and frames by demonstrating how mediated interaction with a digital app introduced a haptic, multisensory form of relational knowledge – one in which 'the body acts to enframe digital information …' which is to say "its own affectively experienced sensation of coming into contact with the digital' (Hansen 2004, 13). Through this analysis, I have taken up and attended to several experiential modalities including a 'health journey', foodways, the pleasure of movement, the commodification of my (free) health labour, and how gender (femininity), and race, class, and dis/ability are encoded in and through the app to shape co-produced health subjectivities. Also of note are my affective experience of anxiety, datafication, desire, labour, and alternative forms of agency.

Conclusion

This final case study has allowed me to articulate a fulsome and multi-dimensional account of GetFit as a socio-technical artefact that, like Aduna and GenoPalate, is indicative of a hegemonic good health oriented technology that works to perpetuate dominant health norms. As in the previous two chapters, I have drawn on political economy, discourse analysis, new materialism, and auto-ethnography to assemble and execute a critical examination of GetFit. In doing, so, I have discussed the political economic production of biovalue, surveillance, and control; the discursive deployment of the frames of personalization, simplicity and speed, and efficiency; the intra-acting exigencies of energy, bodies, trust, fatness, dis/ability, gender, and race; and the cultivation of an account of my embodied experience with the app drawing on the themes of the 'health journey', movement, biomediation, access and ability, and the gendering of exercise. In the final chapters, I turn to some alternatives and explore what we can do going forward.

6

Alternatives

The picture I have painted in the preceding chapters, with hegemonic good health, GB, PN, and the 'dietary-genomic-functional/superfood industrial complex' at its core, is not particularly encouraging. I have laid out a structural, discursive, material, and embodied account of a health/wellness juggernaut – one which is normative, self-subjectifying, gendered, racializing, classed, highly idealized, individualizing, technophilic, and consumerist/capitalist. Yet, there are alternatives – ones that are aimed at challenging and disrupting the existing order and exploiting cracks within the existing system. In this chapter, I introduce and unpack some of these options. I begin with a reflective and theoretically grounded examination of Aduna, GenoPalate, and GetFit vis-à-vis the non-normative possibilities they offer (i.e. as sites of resistance and social re-articulation) followed by a discussion of two existing conceptions of health that, I contend, push back against hegemonic health – specifically, health justice and equity, as well as fat health justice.

STS and technofeminism: Can we fix this?

Apropos of technology, and in particular health technologies, we need to think carefully about the need to repurpose and rearticulate existing technologies for prosocial ends as well as the creation of new devices and artefacts that attend more fully to human needs (Wajcman 2004; Rosenberger 2018). As stated earlier, there is both scope and a track record of technologies created for a specific purpose being used for another. Think of the internet, which was originally intended to be used for military communication before it was adapted for and by the research elite and then re-adapted as a tool of communication (Naughton 2016; Feenberg 1991 and 2019). Feminists in particular have demonstrated how existing technologies can be repurposed for novel ends as in the case of women using cell phones to help perform care work more seamlessly (Frizzo-Barker and

Chow-White 2012), or their demand for the re-design of military cockpits which had been created in a manner that did not accommodate women's bodies (Weber 1997). Racialized communities have demanded similar kinds of changes as in the case of medical technologies that discount for race. An important example is the spirometer which, for decades, assumed a lower baseline of lung capacity for Black patients, and the pulse oximeter which does not factor in darker skin when calculating blood oxygen levels (Braun 2014; Sjoding et al. 2020). This approach, finding ways to subvert existing technologies, merges technofeminism with a critical theory of technology to form a new plank in critical STS studies. What unites them is a conception of technology as malleable, mutually shaping, underdetermined, and constituted by degree of interpretive flexibility (Bijker 2001; Wajcman 2007; Hsu and Pinch 2008; Feenberg 2017).

The question then becomes whether it is possible to take the technologies I have examined – dietary trackers (GetFit), genetic-based diet plans (GenoPalate), and decontextualized superfoods (Aduna) – and re-conceptualize them and their objectives towards ends that are truly 'health' orientated. This approach does not see technologies as either oppressive or liberating (as an either/or) but as having the capacity to be shaped towards liberatory ends and experiences – ones that attend to inequality and embrace flexible design, democratization, inclusion, and collective, embodied action. The question to ask is whether this can be done using existing technologies (i.e. those taken up in the preceding chapters). Put another way, we might ask: can we take trackers, superfoods, and genetic-based diets and re-contextualize and construct them as technologies that resist hegemonic good health and, perhaps, articulate a new conception of what it means to be well?

Aduna

With respect to superfoods, deploying an STS and technofeminist reappraisal is difficult since baobab is a foodstuff that, while still a technology broadly defined, has its own 'affordances' –which means that it needs to be thought of differently. An argument, for example, could be made about the need to find ways to consume and enjoy baobab and other foods from the Global South outside of corporate nutritionism, the fetishization of Otherness (i.e. as way to accumulate cultural capital by way of 'exotic' ingredients), and/or capitalist production/ marketing. Consuming foodstuffs that are imported, in which nature and culture are co-constituted, would also need to consider the impact of superfoods storage and transport on the environment (Scrinis 2008; Guthman 2011; Heldke 2015; Dreher 2018). Additionally, for this kind of consumption to be truly ethical, and connected to larger circuits of transformed health norms, it would have to be divorced from simple functionalism and made to be attentive to the history of the food, its cultural significance, and the embodied pleasures it elicits. A perspective I find particularly useful is that of econutritionism, which takes an 'ecological [and anti-colonial] approach to food and nutrition' and 'considers food systems as a whole, prefers variety and biodiversity, and is concerned with the impact of food systems and dietary patterns on other aspects of life and the whole living and physical world' (Cannon and Leitzmann 2005, 792).

This approach could be coupled with a socio-cultural understanding of food as a requisite part of building and preserving community as well as working to instil an ethic of belonging, care, and comfort (Abbots and Lavis 2013). The lived experience of consuming food and performing relational work around it is important, as is sensory engagement with the food itself and the context in which it is consumed.

This is not unlike the approach put forth by new materialists (wherein nature and culture are co-constituted) who see the natural world as retaining its own form of vital material agency and 'enchanted' interrelationality. As noted, Donna Haraway refers to this as the Chthuluscene, a symbiotic reconceptualization of the world which asserts that 'a microbial world of complex and intermingled relationships' exists,

> ... between microscopic and macroscopic life. These discoveries have profoundly challenged the generally accepted view of "individuals". Symbiosis is becoming a core principle of contemporary biology, and it is replacing an essentialist conception of "individuality" with a conception congruent with the larger systems approach now pushing the life sciences in diverse directions. These findings lead us into directions that transcend the self/non-self, subject-object dichotomies that have characterized Western thought.
>
> (Haraway 2013, 326)

Health, in this sense, is an enacted state – one that intermingles with and through the larger constellation of a just society. This just world is an outcome of ethical structures and relations over which people feel a sense of (dispersed) responsibility. Binaries and absolutes, as a result, are shown the front door.

GenoPalate

The case of GenoPalate is especially difficult with respect to how one might envision repurposing it for pro-social and justice-oriented ends. This is because its objectives are so thoroughly imbricated with hegemonic good health norms.

One way might be to centre the citizen-consumer so that they have control over collected health and diet data and decision-making (wherein what is considered private is self-determined) and are able to deploy this knowledge for the benefit of the communities in which they live. This is in line with data governance and sovereignty movements in which the collection of data is permitted, but cannot be shared by default (Hummel et al. 2021). There are substantial limits to this approach – particularly since it does little to attend to the concerns around exploitative technical structures. Moreover, GenoPalate is, at its core, a technology that uses less than rigorous techniques to make outsized predictive claims about customer health status. Layered on top of this is an intentional deployment of hegemonic good health norms, wherein the genetic data collected is re-assembled and categorized in order to make dispositive dietary recommendations despite the fact that, as we well know, health and disease are constructed states and much, much more than a product of one's biology (Korthals 2009; Lerner 2021; Sikka 2021a).

The only way in which I can see this technology being harnessed for more prosocial ends is by acting on and pushing forward some of its more pleasurable aspects. Namely, by building on the desire for self-knowledge and discovery as a way to mitigate uncertainty (Bergoth 2019). Some users do feel a sense of reassurance, clarity, relief, and pleasure in the self-regulation involved in this kind of normative healthwork and this, I argue, needs to be taken seriously (Lupton 2016b). It does not, however, mean that a robust critique of tracking technologies is unwarranted. Rather, it provides a space from which to think about what users find pleasurable and finding ways to preserve this ethos.

Subverting the deployment of hegemonic good health in the context of GenoPalate would require that GB, PN and the sociomaterial discourses surrounding it are transformed such that the science it practices and claims is made clear, veracious, and stripped of its neoliberal and healthist presuppositions. Placing knowledge about one's genetic makeup in the 'broader dimensions of space and time, history and politics [and environment]' is essential since it helps cultivate a non-reductionist and social conception of health in the first instance (Lock 2015, 161). Also required is what Ruckstein describes as a redefinition of personal lifeworlds – ones that use 'genetic testing … [to]promote a more reflective and collective approach to genetic information rather than merely tying people to poorly defined health risks and population histories' (Ruckstein 2017, 1036). What this might look like in practice remains to be seen.

GetFit

GetFit offers some more avenues for repurposing and resistance when taken up as a technology that is mutually shaping from the perspective of design and use (Carstensen and Winker 2007). One of the most thought-provoking approaches I have come across is what Horst et al. (2020) describe as 'quotidian care at a distance' in which technologies like the Apple Watch and its health app are utilized by younger users to monitor the health status of their elderly parents and as a locus through which to build conversation and connection with them. Another way in which fitness apps have been taken up in prosocial ways is as a form of care for the self which involves using functional monitoring to reflect on the 'irreconcilability between lived experience and the datalogical construction of it' – particularly when one's embodied experience conflicts with the app (Thornham 2019, 180). It is also possible that the hegemonic good health oriented self-reflection instigated by GetFit and similar apps might push users to question their politics, to 'turn them inside out', in ways that force the renegotiation of one's understanding of health and wellbeing (Greenfield 2016). Ethnographic and interview-based studies of how users take up these technologies have found that the relations they elicit can be deeply contextual, experiential, and gendered (Markula 2003). Some users, for example, refuse to record certain data, interpret unfavourable data as irrelevant or incorrect, and/ or intentionally give precedence to feeling over data (Esmonde 2020). Making moves to disentangle these technologies from gender norms and beauty regimes opens up possibilities for different modes of self-discovery, world-building, and ways of experiencing the body. As Sanders argues,

> If digitally assisted body projects could be unmoored from goals informed by health and beauty norms, and in a spirit of openness and non-attachment to outcome, then their practitioners may find they are able to be more mindful of how they feel in the moment of movement, and to observe their data synopses without (or with less) judgment or self-criticism.
>
> (Sanders 2017, 21)

Some of this embodied re-construction of the relational self is already occurring. In addition to the self-initiated adoption of these apps and subsequent de/ reconstruction of the data they provide, micro and macro resistances can be found in workplaces in which employees challenge their usefulness, question their infringement on privacy (e.g. the release of sensitive health data), complain about the amount of uncompensated labour they require, and query the potential for the loss of agency and control (Rosenblat and Kneese 2014; Perrault, Hildenbrand, and Rnoh 2020). While not offering a 'way out', these conversations provide sites of resistance and renegotiation in ways that encourage critical reflection. Apps that are gendered, racialized, heteronormative, and/or inhospitable to disabled subjects, continue to be challenged in ways that expose hierarchy and cultivate new ways of thinking about health and bodies. Gonzalez-Polledo calls this a 'cosmopolitical orientation', one that encourages users to transform their relation with digital technologies like apps and trackers in ways that,

> afford new contexts in which new kinds of health politics come to matter, demanding recognition of forms of living which do not neatly fit neatly mainstream biomedical models … these uses of technology evince how technological mediations re-situate health experience in pre-digital inequalities, as well as new data centric logics, to pursue health agendas that are not pre-given, but emerge as a result of sociotechnical interactions, making possible to demand health rights through data, and participation in changing conversations about healthcare futures.
>
> (Gonzalez-Polledo 2018, 634)

I can envision this being applied GetFit with respect to accessibility, control over data, a de/reconstruction of discourse and a reconfigured approach to movement – one that is less about body norms and more about pleasure, engagement, and relational wellbeing. A final example I find particularly interesting and ripe with possibility emerges out of work being done in creative spaces in which the data collected from health trackers and apps are utilized in imaginative ways. Sicchio and Baker, in a paper titled 'Stich, Bitch, Make/Perform', discusses a project in which the data from a fitness tracker was scored and performed through dance. The performance itself speaks to issues of mediated bodily knowledge, boundaries, and biomedical wellbeing. It also,

> raises issues over who is the owner of this data – the choreographer or the performer who is now taking this data and reinterpreting it to their own ends. It may be considered a metaphor for the corporate appropriation of personal data collected through fitness trackers.
>
> (Baker and Sicchio 2015)

While this latter approach might be outside of the kinds of everyday entanglements individuals have with these technologies, it does allow for a discussion of more creative, posthuman, and nomadic forms of engagement. Apps like GetFit have some more room for manoeuvre as compared to

GenoPalate, whose telos is concretized in a diet plan that is explicitly tied to one's genetic makeup and rhetorically bound to hegemonic good health, GB, and PN. This makes it difficult to challenge or reappropriate it over and above interrogating its findings, challenging its conclusions, and, perhaps, pushing for the basic technology to be used for different purposes. I see more potential for creative re-articulations of Aduna and GetFit – particularly when coupled with a transformed conception of 'good health'.

Also important are the larger political economic structures that would likely prevent these rearticulations. There is a significant amount of pressure to retain and encourage profitable levels of consumption tied to market logics which are supported by health ideologies that also encourage unsustainable levels of consumption. This is not without precedent. Hopes that online spaces, smart phones, and a variety of apps might be used for prosocial ends have largely resulted in disappointment. I am thus unable to see how tinkering around the edges of these technologies could offer an authentic alternative.

Before venturing into a discussion of a substantive redefinition of, in the following sections I examine some existing alternatives, namely, health justice/equity and sovereignty and fat justice. Each of these has much to offer as well as some significant limitations.

Health justice and health equity

Current studies of health justice and health equity tend to focus on mapping and addressing inequalities related to access to health care, medicines, culturally appropriate food, space to move, clean air and water, education, and employment. This perspective takes for granted that these inequalities are unnecessary, avoidable, and unfair (Margaret 1991; Braverman 2003). In response, several definitions of health justice and health sovereignty have emerged which critique, deconstruct, and, in some cases, reconstruct a conception of health that is more attuned to human(e) needs. Shared by many of these approaches is the belief that a right to health is an inextricable part of the value extended to all human beings as actors with a right to fair treatment and equal opportunity not solely as individuals, but as naturecultural matterings (Pitts-Taylor 2016). These matterings reflect the fact that we remain discursively constructed as particular kinds of health subjects and thus embody health states in relation to human and nonhuman others.

Contemporary understandings of health justice consider health to be a positive ideal, right, or asset. Lennart Nordenfelt (1995), for example, discusses health justice in terms of human welfare and wellbeing wherein the capacity to realize one's life goals and gain access to basic happiness is seen as essential. Norman Daniels (2001), on the other hand, focuses on *access* to health care as a fundamental right – one that facilitates the maintenance of 'minimal functioning' so that citizens can participate and compete in society. For others, health justice is treated as a capability that every human being has a moral right. Sridhar Venkatapuram's (2013), for example, uses this approach to make the case for the positive entitlement to be healthy. Drawing on Amartya Sen and Marta Nussbaum, Venkatapuram supports the bringing of 'rights, health, and capabilities together in a way that could be practicable as well as philosophically coherent' (Venkatapuram 2016, 50). When health is connected to other capabilities in this way, it distinguises itself from discussions of utility (utilitarianism – cost–benefit analysis) and Rawlsian conceptions of fairness – where health is seen as a natural good to which we all have a right (Daniels 1996; Wolff and De-Shalit 2007). Whether conceptualized as a need, right, or capability, these perspectives draw on philosophical, legal, moral, and political principles – all of which aim to contend with health in terms of resource distribution, access, and public policy.

Health sovereignty, on the other hand, aims to address questions of access, control, and empowerment as it relates to *public* health in particular. Ian Werkehseiser, a noted scholar of critical health studies, describes health sovereignty as the development of 'self-organised community viability' around the definition and enactment of health systems where 'cultural practices, ecological knowledge ... [and] environmental sustainability' (Werkehseiser 2014, 142) are centred. This approach sees health as: 1. prioritizing holistic wellbeing over economic objectives; 2. elevating local systems, healthways, and shared knowledge; and 3. acting in close relation to the natural world (Baumflek 2015; Madsen 2015). It is also co-constituted with and by discourses around food sovereignty and land sovereignty in the Global South as well as indigenous groups and postcolonial countries that continue to try and disentangle themselves from oppressive colonial structures (Schanbacher 2010; Flora 2011; Cooper, Kirton, Lisk, and Besada 2016).

Environmental and food sovereignty movements intersect with health sovereignty on a number of levels. First, health sovereignty owes much of its theoretical inheritance to the food sovereignty movement via its focus on sustainability, ownership, local needs as well as the desire to dismantle corporate structures, and 'delegitimize the economic controls of competing national sovereignties, pitting one sovereignty against another – the nation state versus local communities' (Epting 2018, 596). Health justice is realized in the process of enacting this sovereignty and using it to address health challenges by reconnecting to the land and community and allying with feminist science to enact structural change. This is a decidedly posthuman framework in that it de-centres individuals as the loci of necessary behavioural change in favour of a more bio and eco-social approach. An example of this in action is Uma Hochokma's framework which grew out of a research project conducted with Houma women on alternative models of health sovereignty. What resulted, as Figure 6.1 illustrates, is a robust ethic of care through which to reconceptualize health as co-constituted with and by place, land, history, body, mind, and others:

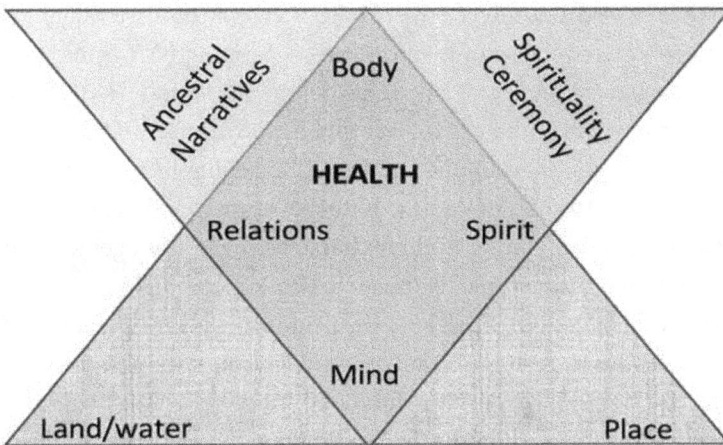

Figure 6.1 Johnson-Jennings, Billiot, and Walters 2020 (http://creativecommons. org/licenses/by/4.0/).

These perspectives, health justice and sovereignty specifically, are essential to understand how we might conceive of health by identifying some of our objectives going forward. They are also, however, open to co-optation as I discuss below. Moreover, it is also the case that these frameworks tend to lack a much-needed sociological analysis of health as it relates to cultures, affects, and technologies. Which is to say that any reformulation of hegemonic health must consider the ecologies that surrounds it inclusive of norms, expectations, and media/consumer representations. Fat health justice offers such an approach, one that is embodied, contextual, and sociomaterial.

Fat health justice

Fat health justice takes on a much more capacious and embodied conception of good health. This has been expressed through movements like Health at Every Size (HAES), fat acceptance, and body positivity. Body positivity, broadly defined, is an ideological framework that seeks to change conversations around bodies by resisting norms that pathologize fatness and, instead, encourage ones that promote the acceptance of all bodies as good bodies (Sastre 2014; Stevens 2020). Empowerment, self-acceptance, fat advocacy, and resistance against stigma has, since the 1970s, formed the crux of the body positivity movement. Fat acceptance is one pillar of body positivity turned inward, requiring the cultivation of 'unconditional self-acceptance' (Gay 2017 139), and then outward, necessitating that we strive to 'show that fat embodiment, instead of being "deviant," involves a type of embodiment that fits within the range of human body diversity' (Slatman 2021, 2). HAES is also a *social* movement based on body positive values that call for less weight-centred forms of medical care, separating BMI from health (or binning it all together), and generally de-pathologizing fatness. HAES advocates argue that focus needs to be on the acceptance of diverse bodies, on satiety and pleasure in eating, trust in one's body, and engaging in enjoyable physical activity (LeBesco 2010; Abbots and Lavis 2013). Respect and life enhancement are seen as its key pillars – what Rodney characterizes as salutogenic (getting at the origins of health), rather than pathogenic (Rodney 2018).

A more recent iteration of HAES worth noting is HIER (Health in Every Respect) which aims to push HAES and movements like it towards a more social justice and equity-oriented positionality (Aphramor and Gingras 2011). One that challenges healthism and calls for more public models of health justice by seeking to 'interrupt the canon of fat-phobia and sizeism and promote different, more politicised, compassionate, and thus more effective ways of thinking and acting in the public health domain' (Mansfield and Rich 2013, 366).

While this all sounds fantastic, in its focus on inclusion, diversity and resistance against regulative hegemonic health norms, there are also possible pitfalls to note. Criticisms of HAES, body positivity, and fat acceptances include their tendency to hold fast to healthism by encouraging behaviours consistent with what Gibson refers to as the 'good fatty', which includes a reliance on a rhetoric of innocence in which fat people are still expected make the 'right' food and fitness choices (so that they are considered 'healthy' in a biomedical sense). The 'bad fatty', as Gibson puts it, are 'people who do not work hard to become thin, they are often presented as a caricature in mainstream media' (Gibson

2021, 6). As a result, they are seen as less than and to blame for not performing the hegemonic health duties required of everyone, even those inhabiting fat bodies. Even HIER, while being very much a work in progress, has been unable to make the move from revealing injustice (through consciousness raising) to addressing it.

Other shortcomings of these three inter-related movements include their white, middle-class ethos as well as their ableism and heteronormativity. Those situated at the intersections of marginalized subject positions, i.e. Black, queer, poor, brown, and disabled, are not only 'left out' but erased in ways that have material consequences on their lives. This is something Virgie Tovar discusses at length in her book *The Self-Love Revolution: Radical Body Positivity for Girls of Color*, as does Aubrey Gordon in *What We Don't Talk About When We Talk About Fat* (Gordon 2020b; Tovar 2020; also see Williams 2017; Doherty et al. 2021). Finding ways to engage in conversations about how fat Black bodies are pathologized (and pathologized in different ways as it relates to gender), and how disabled fat bodies are often pigeon-holed within the unsuitable strictures of a biomedical, hegemonic model of health is necessary.

It is also the case that body positivity, fat acceptance, and HAES have increasingly been co-opted by and through neoliberal corporate doublespeak which divorces these movements from their activist roots and, instead, uses their popularity to sell products (Morris 2019b). Body neutrality is a particular case in point which, as a form of activism that aims to change the value we place on women's bodies, has increasingly been used by corporations to individualize what are structural problems (i.e. as in the case of a popular t-shirt that reads: 'You're are more than a body'). Body neutrality also be depoliticizing by failing to acknowledge that some bodies (racialized bodies, disabled bodies) do not have the luxury of being considered neutral. Body positivity in particular has become an industry in and of itself with companies as diverse as Nike and Versace making their clothing in larger sizes, choosing to feature 'plus-size' models and mannequins, and generally seeking to gain the trust of a consumer base who generally do not fit into their clothing (Cwynar-Horta 2016). In the US, a full 70 million women are believed to fall into the 'plus size' category (Schlossbery 2016).

With respect to health and diets, many diet-oriented and nutritional companies have followed a similar track by toning down the language of weight loss, thinness, and youthful beauty for a discourse of 'fitness,' 'strength,' and 'beauty' (Poshekova 2021). This is in keeping with digital media offering spaces for the self-representation of more diverse bodies which can be seen in the accounts of fat activists on Instagram and Tiktok, for example. However, it also means that companies whose apps still come with calorie counts, a place to log in weight, and whose models have bodies that are slightly outside of the ideal, are still committed to hegemonic good health as an goal wherein, as Zavattaro (2021) puts it, individual bodies are consumed and made sexually attractive for the heterosexual Other. As such, over the years, what was a radical movement has "become its own 'economy, and people with bodies that have been marginalized are no longer the centre of their own creation' (Dionne 2017).

HAES, I argue, has much more promise because of its radicality, intersectionality, and rejection of fat stigma by refusing to make even the discussion of weight part of its modus operandi. However, its language of empowerment has also been co-opted by economic interests, as in the case of WW (formerly Weight Watchers) whose turn to diverse health discourses betrays other interests. As Chastain puts it,

> It's easy to see the profit rationale for their hypocrisy. They get to continue selling their program to people, who they spent years successfully convincing to hate their bodies, and try to open up a new market amongst the people who have crawled and scratched their way up and out of the diet culture that Weight Watchers, excuse me, WW, immersed them in. So, it will likely make money, but that doesn't make it right.

> (Chastain 201)

A final problem touches on issues of embodiment and is a product of how these approaches rely on a conception of the self as the centre of how health knowledge is produced. That is, a significant amount of HAES, body positive, and fat acceptance discourse relies on an understanding of the individual as *the* source of what is good for them (e.g. by re-learning internal hunger cues, what healthfulness feels like etc.). This fails to consider that what and how much we eat, how we feel, and how we define health is social, cultural, and political (Lupton 2012b). Taken together, while potentially radical when taken up by the likes of Tovar and Gordon, HAES, body positivity, and fat acceptance all, in their own way, have become enmeshed in and co-opted by hegemonic good health, GB, PN, and the 'dietary-genomic-functional/superfood industrial complex'. Suffice to say, Aduna, GenoPalate, and GetFit, while drawing on some of the language of empowerment and sustainability that form the crux of the fat justice and body sovereignty movements, do not reflect a commitment to either, or to making the kinds of changes that would be necessary to do so.

This, chapter has delved into and explored several possibilities through which the technologies I engaged with in Chapters 3 to 5 (Aduna, GenoPalate, and GetFit) could be used for more transformative ends by taking advantage of their interpretive flexibility at the level of design and use. Overall, I argue these refashionings are promising but require much more to produce transformative change. I then examined two existing frameworks that challenge hegemonic good health, GB, PN, and the 'dietary-genomic-functional/superfood industrial complex' – namely, health justice and sovereignty and fat health justice. Yet, I argue that even these progressive frameworks and sociomaterial refashionings of existing technology remain insufficient. Alternative apps like Storeywell, which ties non-instrumental movement to storytelling in a family setting, and Diamante, a trial app that uses adaptive mobile message to encourage physical activity amongst vulnerable and low-income communities, are promising but still require that we transform the conception of health that underlies it (Sasksono 2020; Adrian et al. 2020).

7

Conclusion

In this book, I have taken the reader on a rather lengthy journey, beginning with the careful re-construction of our contemporary understanding of 'good health' while also engaging in an examination of some of the ways in which it has been made manifest. I then drew on a multi-modal method of analysis using political economy of culture, critical discourse analysis, new materialism, and auto-ethnography to unpack the ways in which our hegemonic conception of good health (*a co-produced state of idealized expectations, performances, embodiments, and patterns of consumption dominated by gendered and raced technophilic knowledge regimes that reproduce regimented and coercive western standards of health and wellbeing*), PN (personalized nutrition), and GB (genetic biomolecularization) work to uphold an increasingly hegemonic 'dietary-genomic-functional/superfood industrial complex'. After providing some context and background vis-à-vis our current health juggernaut, I examined how this assemblage is made manifest in and through three different technologies – namely, Aduna's baobab superfood, GenoPalate, the genetic-based diet company, and GetFit a popular fitness tracker.

The case studies began with Aduna's baobab superfood which, using political economy and CDA, was revealed to be a company discursively committed to social justice but nevertheless reliant on conventional forms of exploitative market capitalism, nutritionism, and implicit modes of racialization that intersect with gender and postcolonial commodity fetishism. The materialist cuts I made home in on Aduna's particular manifestation of health norms and superfood subcultures, as well as the significance of tradition, the role of social justice, and the production of wellness as a purchasable commodity. Consuming Aduna's baobab powder for two weeks brought to the fore considerations around what constitutes 'good food', eating 'difference', cultural appropriation, food choice and identity, health capital, risk and Covid-19, race and social stratification, and pleasure.

Next was GenoPalate, a nutrigenomic company that deploys a form of biocapitalism which seeks to exploit our vital potential (genetic information) for profit in ways that are lucrative for the company while also being framed as empowering for its users. Further analysis of how this impacts our contemporary understandings of science, race, gender, and disability, as well as the processes of commodification and surveillance, illustrates how this technology (emerging out of a network of intra-acting forces and sociomaterial affects) has had very real effects on how we understand ideal femininity and the roots of biologized and constructed racial and health differences. The commodification of DNA as a biogenetic, saleable commodity was also considered as it relates to this new 'vital economy'. Privacy thus becomes an important site of contestation in that it is undermined consistently, while the cultivation and normalization of self-surveillance produces its own hegemonic good health juggernaut. My 'journey' using GenoPalate, and following its prescriptions for two weeks, validates this analysis while also bringing to the fore novel insights about race, restriction, food and pleasure, the rational mind/embodied body dichotomy, lost sociality, food nostalgia, and guilt/shame. This works together with the preceding sections to paint a robust picture of our dominant understanding of health as a mediated, embodied, normative, discursive, and material construct.

Finally, we have GetFit – a fitness app which reflects some of the same assumptions, discursive formations, and political economic beliefs as Aduna's baobab and GenoPalate but which extends the commodification of data to encompass movement and, in doing so, reproduces hegemonic good health in ways that demand further self-quantification. Surveillance is deeply invovled in this process and is supported by the instrumentalization of the sharing economy which is used to paper over technoscientific values and norms. PN plays an important role in this context by discursively buttressing neoliberal individualism, as does the promise of algorithmically precise health advice. The application of agential cuts draws attention to the inadequacy of the energy-deficit model (which GetFit relies upon), the need to see bodies as corporeal and lived, and the notion that health should be understood as a complex, multi-faceted assemblage. The relation between data and trust was then shown to be co-constructed in ways that promise fidelity and control, but which fail on both counts.

Also discussed in these cuts was the relationship between fatness and health wherein fat stigma and fat phobia, through the total absence of fat bodies from the app and the rhetorical work done by idealized images and text promising hegemonic good health and desirability to come, works to exalt the slim, white body above all others. This body is also able-bodied, and thus the app excludes those who identify as disabled from participation. The exercises are also highly gendered, with the app categorizing some of the plans through the lens of reproduction which is then inscribed by a postfeminist ethic. Moreover, the app makes racializing moves that intersect with gender as it relates to inclusion and representation, as well as to the prejudicial ways in which it shapes public policy and workplace dynamics. Aesthetics, colourism, and post-racial ideologies were also discussed in this section. My two week auto-ethnographic account of using this app elicited revelations around the significance of a 'health journey,' the discourse of wellness, and the relationship between movement and sociality. Also of note was the affective experience of engaging in the scheduled workouts – most of which were pleasurable but which also adhered to hegemonic good health norms. The transformation of that pleasure into capital, coupled with the app's hierarchization of movement, led me to consider how exercise itself was gendered and how it could be used to produce novel forms of capital and status. Moves to resist optimizing logics did not go as well as I had hoped but did push me to think about how hegemonic good health could have pernicious effects on one's sense of embodiment and how it risks engendering a kind of intersectional disempowerment characterized by stigma and blame. Health labour and racialized absences were also discussed.

It is worth pausing here to say a few words about how these three case studies relate to and intra-act with one another. To do this, I return to the framework of the assemblage and ecosystem thinking that I have relied on throughout the book. To begin with, I contend that each of these three hegemonic good health technologies represents an economic, ideological, and cultural node in our larger dominant 'good health' assemblage. For Aduna it is food and nutrients, GenoPalate, biotechnology and genetics, and GetFit, bioinformatics and fitness. Together, these technologies provide an important snapshot of the state of play as it relates to contemporary understandings of good health. However, it is also the case that each node bleeds into one another with each technology serving multiple purposes (i.e. GenoPalate *also* focuses on food, Aduna is *also* interested in the cultivation of wellbeing, and GetFit *also* encourages biological improvement – thus demonstrating that these nodes cannot be siloed). As such, I assert that they represent a heterogenous but tractable set of forces, materialities, affects, desires, interests, and institutions that, as Bennett argues, 'are themselves bonafide agents rather than … instrumentalities, techniques of power, recalcitrant objects, or social constructs' (Bennett 2010a, 47). Their separation into chapters represents agential cutting used to enact 'determinate boundaries, properties and meanings, as well as … the "measured object" ("cause") within the phenomenon' (Barad 2007, 340), necessary for them to be made legible.

On the level of content, similar themes can be found in each of the case study chapters – particularly as it relates to Aduna, GenoPalate, and GetFit's shared neoliberal political economic imperatives, gendering of health, collective racialization of wellness culture, reliance on healthist ideologies, eliding of marginalized subject positions (as in the case of dis/ability), and adoption of individualistic health ideologies. Drawing out and thinking carefully about the resemblances and alignments between them speaks to how they are self-reinforcing and demonstrates how each case study, and the technologies they take up, feed into, and prop up our current hegemonic understanding of good health (within which we too are taken up as part of larger material arrangements). Their differences, however, are also significant with the analysis of Aduna bringing to the fore unique insights about persistent colonial sensibilities as it relates to health; the study of GenoPalate identifying the role the biologizing of race continues to play; and the GetFit chapter focusing in on how movement continues to be commodified and instrumentalized in pursuit of hegemonic health norms. What is important to keep in mind is that this assemblage, made up of us, technologies, health ideologies, norms, institutions, non-human agents, and infrastructures, are emergent, dynamic, and contain openings for new forms of affect and action.

Working with these unique case studies alongside a rather idiosyncratic collection of methodologies was quite an education. First, it allowed me to think through each technology as distinct (when engaging in close analysis), but also related in their overriding objectives as it relates to hegemonic good health. Second, it also allowed me to integrate empirical and experiential knowledge within an intersectional framework that is necessary when studying such a complex subject area. Finally, the autoethnographies pushed me to think through my own experience and hopes about health futures which are reflected in the new approach I articulate below.

Having summarized some of the key findings of this book with a focus on how hegemonic health as a discourse works in and through material institutions (political economy), technologies, practices, and relations, I now explore what a more capacious conception of 'good health' might involve. Not the *co-produced state of idealized expectations, performances, embodiments, and patterns of consumption dominated by gendered and raced technophilic knowledge regimes that reproduce regimented and coercive western standards of health and wellbeing,* but as something more reflective of what could be.

There is a plethora of existing research capable of constructing this ideal as well as an abundance of activists currently working towards this end. In addition to the approaches discussed in the previous chapter, recent scholarship around food justice is especially salient as it relates to the study of injustice, race, and queerness by bringing 'an intersectional perspective to food-related social issues, [and] providing diverse solutions for different communities' (Alkin and Agyeman 2011; Parsons 2018, 111; Smith 2019).

A reconstructed understanding of 'good health' will, at least provisionally, need to assess and repurpose a number of principles and values that already exist in hegemonic good health. For example, it will likely still be co-produced and constituted by embodiments and performances. However, this new framework will eschew harmful idealizations, constraining expectations, unchallenged technophilia, normative coercion, and Western-centric norms. Moreover, 'patterns of consumption' might be replaced with something like 'moments of engagement' and wellness/wellbeing must be understood much more explansively.

My site of departure for such a reconceptualization, at first glance, is likely to seem a little peculiar or even somewhat 'basic'. Prior to writing this book, I had been preparing a lecture in which I provided first year students with a simple explanation of intersectionality and how it can be used as an analytic lens through which to centre forms of oppression involving more than one identity position (Crenshaw 2017; Collins and Bilge 2020). One student, in attempting to reinforce their understanding, asked how it might apply to Covid-19. After discussing statistics about the disproportionate rates of infection and mortality amongst racialized communities, which intersects with class and gender (with poorer Black and minority ethnic men facing worse outcomes), I began to talk about the roots of intersectional thinking stretching back to the Combahee River Collective (Office of National Statistics 2020). We talked about the importance of centring of marginality as *the* necessary first step to affecting social change. Taking a cue from this short conversation, I found myself thinking seriously about how equitable conceptions of 'good health' must take the impetus from these early justifications of intersectionality – particularly as it relates to addressing the needs and experiences of the most marginalized. Barbara Smith's oft-cited quote, 'until Black women are free, none of us will be free', and the Collective's statement asserting that 'If Black women were free, it would mean that everyone else would have to be free since our freedom would necessitate the destruction of all the systems of oppression', makes this clear (Combahee River Collective 1977).

This insight then drew me back into research I had been doing on food justice and trauma and in particular the work by Rachel Slocum and K. Valentine Cadieux (2015) who map out an operationalized theory of food justice. They do this by highlighting the history and structures of injustice that co-produce inequality in the first place. Racism, patriarchy, neoliberalism, settler colonialism, colonization, and environmental destruction, they contend, are sources of trauma that are somatic, felt, and 'settles into bodies'. A commodious and just conception of 'good health', therefore, must also start from this position and situate individuals and groups conjuncturally (culturally, socio-historically, and politically) and account for the differentiated structures from which they emerge.

Also required, as I have argued throughout this book, is a robust understanding of culture and technology, embodied experience, materiality and discourse as well as values and norms. Biltekoff makes this clear in her discussion of diets, but I contend it also applies to health. She states, 'dietary health is inseparable from cultural values' and, as such, 'defining a good diet is also inevitably a social, political and moral act' (Biltekoff 2013, 151–3). Thus, a more just conception of health must not be used to divide, differentiate, or hierarchize based on gender, race, class, sexuality, and/or dis/ability. On the subject of culture, it is the case that 'good health' remains firmly ensconced in a matrix of whiteness, heterosexuality, youth, slimness, able-bodiedness, and conventional attractiveness. Its political economy needs to be shorn of capitalist exploitation and expropriation as well as corporate control. The accoutrements of hegemonic good health, in the form of clothing (pricey athleisure), food (superfoods), gadgets, devices (trackers), and services (personalized diets), also do not feature in my new definition of good health, at least not how they exist presently. Medico-moralizations, moral panics, healthism, nutritionism, and optimization are other elements which are not part of this definition – to which I now turn.

Good health redux

The definition of good health I have settled on would act as an empirical and ethical alternative or ideal type/regulative ideal, in a Kantian sense, as something we strive towards and which acts as a horizon towards which we direct our action (Kant 1906). This approach also requires that we engage in acts of prospective world building in which wilful objects, subjects, sociomaterial matterings, institutions, and norms are refashioned in ethical ways. This definition is not particularly succinct, at least in its initial formation, but will be clarified further on.

I argue that good health needs to be understood as an assemblage of intra-acting, co-constituted, and justice-oriented norms, values, institutions, practices, relations, and enfleshments that cultivate states of wellbeing, where wellbeing is understood as an embodied and relational identity captured by how one feels about their place in the world. Health, defined in this way, is affective and empirical, requiring access to resources and services (what we might call the social determinants of health) including equitable health care, clean drinking water, a liveable income, safe environment, access to education, culturally resonant and pleasurable food, room for meaningful movement etc. This understanding of health requires that we challenge sites of inequality, by drawing on an intersectional framework, and intentionally disconnect from commercial interests, neoliberal pressures, and hyperconsumerism. This conception of health is also care-oriented and socializing through its recognition of human actors as relational selves, as members of multiple communities, and as part of a larger world of ecosystems, nonhuman actants, and environments. On the level of affect, this conception of health captures the flow, desire, pleasure, and fun of life, one that is free from pain and 'disease' of course, but also disconnected from circumscribed bodies and presences vis-à-vis gender, race, class, bodily comportment, dis/ability, and sexuality.

If we parse this out into principles and points (a reductionist exercise but one that can be useful), we get a definition of *health as justice* constituted by:

1. *An assemblage of intra-acting, co-constituted, and justice-oriented norms, values, institutions, practices, relations, technologies and enfleshments*

    This point draws attention to the ways in which health is not a singular thing or tangible outcome, but a process built in and through a variety of forces and flows. Technologies that emerge from this must adhere to an ethos of just outcomes and be assessed in and through all the other entities that will be affected.

2. *Wellbeing understood as embodied and relational*

    This tenet speaks to the ways in which health should not be evaluated solely from the position of measurement and medicalization but reflect a life-world approach in which wellness is understood as the ability to lead a good and flourishing life (capaciously defined). This brings to the fore the importance of diverse forms of knowledge – especially knowledge that is lived, experiential, situated, and co-constituted with others and the environment.

3. *The social determinants of health*

This dimension of health as justice brings into focus all of the structures outside of individual choice that shape one's health. This includes access to a stable income, clean drinking water, culturally appropriate food, education, healthcare, a safe and enjoyable way to move, housing, etc.

4. *Intersectionality and the addressing of inequality*

Any analysis of health, as I have argued throughout this book, must be oriented towards attending to human needs starting from the position that we are complex and irreducible subjects that embody multiple overlapping identity positions. Engaging with these intersections means understanding how intersecting sites of inequality are materially and discursively enacted.

5. *Care-oriented on the level of self, Other, community, and the environment (human and non)*

Care, in this context, takes on an important role and is grounded in Sara Ahmed's (2010) philosophy of care which is embodied, relational, vulnerable, empathetic, and political. It is also expansive enough to include non-humans and the rich ecologies and environments we are part of. Care is also feminist (understood in a non-essentialist way) and confirmed by 'those practices of human life that are reflective of our dependence on each other' (Ben- Porath 2008, 65).

6. *Freedom from pain and disease*

This tenet reflects the principle that everyone has the moral 'right' (broadly defined) to quality, affirmative, and robust healthcare that assists them in living a fruitful and comfortable life. In addition to asserting that medical care should be free at the point of access, it also involves attending to the structural impediments that impede this including racism, sexism, ableism, homophobia, transphobia, and an injured environment.

7. *Pleasure-oriented as it relates to food and movement*

This principle is often overlooked and is informed by my analysis of the case studies as well as the autoethnographies. It is meant to bring to the fore the sense that food and movement should not be understood using a healthist lens. Instead, this definition calls for an orientation to food and movement that is tied to what feels pleasurable, sociable, joyful – what Sobal and Nelson refers to as tied to an ethic of commensality (Sobal and Nelson 2003).

8. *Anti-commercial and anti-consumerist*

As noted, health has increasingly come to be defined through profit, commodification, and consumerism. Health as justice eschews this form of political economy and pushes back against the hegemonic good health norms and values embedded in technological design and social discourse.

9. *Counter-hegemonic with respect to bodies and difference*

This, final, principle speaks to how health as justice aims to centre those bodies (fat bodies, disabled bodies, queer bodies, trans bodies, racialized bodies, nonbinary bodies) and any experiences that have been ignored, stigmatized, erased, and violated by dominant health practices. The health experiences and objectives of these communities are key. Intersectionality is used here as a living methodology to 'disrupt dominant narratives and open possibilities for more just ways of living' in bodies that do not conform. (Rice et al. 2020, 182)

This conception of health, *health as justice*, is by no means dispositive and more like a work in progress – something to collectively strive towards. Fleshing it out to attend to issues of sovereignty, policy, political economic structures, etc., will be necessary going forward. However, I argue that cultivating the conditions for this assemblage to be made manifest is something that should be initiated immediately. I recognize that this is an especially difficult ask since it requires that we deconstruct some of our most firmly held neoliberal positions as well as cross-cutting structures, histories, and norms.

If we think about the discourses and political economic structures that would support such an approach, I maintain that they would be collective, queer, decolonizing, anti-racist, fleshy, relational, and posthuman. The creation of a robust, publicly funded health care system supported by policies that are inclusive and participatory, and which draws upon the *public's* affective power, is as important as the dismantling of hegemonic good health, PN, GB, and the 'dietary-genomic-functional/superfood industrial complex'. New discourses that reflect *health as justice* are necessary as is the creation of new prosocial technologies and services that would support it. Not by fiat of course, but through a vital materialist democratic movement that sees health as a socio-somatic enterprise. Reconstructed and novel technologies that facilitate this move must have characteristics, agencies, and performative expectancies aligned with this new modality of health (Ulucanlar et al. 2013). In my own vision, this would culminate in the superseding of any need for 'superfoods' or of technologies/ services that promise hegemonic good health.

Instead, dietary personalization and proscriptive workouts would be carefully circumscribed and may even be judged to be unnecessary or irrelevant. The creation of technologies that cultivate a *health as justice* ethos must follow an ethic of participatory design, public pedagogy, as well as human and nonhuman relations (Barad 2007; Robertson and Simonsen 2012; Farrington and Farrington 2018). This framing does not aim to consolidate singular universal 'truth' (i.e. one 'correct' conception of health or perfect technology) but, instead, deploys a 'particular kind of empiricism … to find condition under which something new is produced' (Coleman and Ringrose 2013, 10; Ray 2019). A socio-material and technofeminist orientation to the development of new health technologies would be invaluable and could be used to incorporate an ethos of mutual shaping, social articulation, and material ethics. This will likely include genetic science, biotechnological surveillance, and instrumental supplementation to some degree, but in pursuit of *entirely different ends* – ones that refrain 'from hastily adopted deterministic perspectives on socio-technological progress and, instead, stresses the performative, relational, socio-economic and political character of both the social and the material' (Frey, Shaupp and Wenten 2021, 19). A tracker with no-third party sharing that facilitates non-instrumental self-knowledge, collective engagement, and pleasure in movement, or an at-home genetic test whose health advice was properly contextualized and oriented towards *health as justice* would fit nicely into this new world.

Taken together, this book has engaged in an intersectional, STS-based analysis of contemporary health technologies using a variety of methods with the objective of levelling a considered critique grounded in the socio-material and the technological. Incorporating the study of affect, embodiment, assemblages, relational cuts, political economic analysis, auto-ethnography, and discourse analysis, this project has worked to produce a fulsome account of concrete technologies – ones that are used by millions of people to cultivate their own health subjectivities. Having discussed the limitations of hegemonic good health and its conceptual underpinnings through the analysis of Aduna's baobab, Genopalate, and Getfit, I also considered some pre-existing alternatives (health justice/sovereignty and HAES/fat acceptance) before moving to a new conception of health – what I call 'health as justice'. Future work, for me, will include continuing to refine and build on this definition as well as finding ways to envision, build, and operationalize new technologies. This is something that will be a much more collective effort collaborating with others, academics and non, also interested in working in this field.

Bibliography

Abbots, Emma-Jayne, and Anna Lavis. *Why we eat, how we eat: Contemporary encounters between foods and bodies*. New York: Routledge, 2013.

Abel, Sarah, and Hannes Schroeder. 'From country marks to DNA markers: The genomic turn in the reconstruction of African identities'. *Current Anthropology* 61, no. S22 (2020): S198–S209.

Adams, Carol J. *The sexual politics of meat: A feminist-vegetarian critical theory*. New York, USA: Bloomsbury Publishing, 2015.

Aduna. 'Homepage'. 2021a, https://aduna.com.

Aduna. 'Our story'. Aduna, 2021b, https://aduna.com/pages/our-story-aduna.

Aduna. 'Superfood'. Aduna, 2021c, https://aduna.com/collections/powders-grains.

Aduna. 'Baobab: The immune boosting superfruit'. *Aduna*, 2021d, https://aduna.com/blogs/aduna-world/baobab-the-immune-boosting-superfruit?_pos=1&_sid=eaa8fa4f2&_ss=r.

Aduna. 'Long live the baobabs'. *Aduna*, 2021d, https://aduna.com/blogs/aduna-world/long-live-the-baobabs.

AFP. 'Of quinoa, roots and berries: Overproduction threatens Andes superfood haven'. *Agence France-Press*, 25 March 2018, www.hindustantimes.com/more-lifestyle/of-quinoa-roots-and-berries-overproduction-threatens-andes-superfood-haven/story-zOqqhlOmKSkPui65qiJO7M.html.

Agar, Nicholas. 'Liberal eugenics'. *Public Affairs Quarterly* 12, no. 2 (1998): 137–55.

Aguilera, Adrian, et al. 'mHealth app using machine learning to increase physical activity in diabetes and depression: Clinical trial protocol for the DIAMANTE Study'. *BMJ open* 10, no. 8 (2020), https://bmjopen.bmj.com/content/10/8/e034723.abstract.

Ahmed, Sara. '"You end up doing the document rather than doing the doing": Diversity, race equality and the politics of documentation'. *Ethnic and Racial Studies* 30, no. 4 (2007): 590–609.

Ahmed, Sara. *The promise of happiness*. Durham: Duke University Press, 2010.

Ahmed, Sara. *On being included: Racism and diversity in institutional life*. Durham: Duke University Press, 2012.

Ajana, Btihaj, ed. *Metric culture: Ontologies of self-tracking practices*. Bradford: Emerald Group Publishing, 2018.

Ajana, Btihaj. 'Digital health and the biopolitics of the quantified self'. *Digital Health* 3 (2017): 1–18.

Alcoff, Linda Martín. *The problem of speaking for others*. London: Routledge, 2008.

Alkon, Alison Hope, and Julian Agyeman, eds. *Cultivating food justice: Race, class, and sustainability*. Massachusetts: MIT Press, 2011.

Allen-Collinson, Jacquelyn, Lee Crust, and Christian Swann. '"Endurance work": Embodiment and the mind–body nexus in the physical culture of high-altitude mountaineering'. *Sociology* 52, no. 6 (2018): 1324–41.

Allen-Collinson, Jacquelyn. '14 Running embodiment, power and vulnerability'. In *Women and Exercise: The Body, Health and Consumerism*, edited by Eileen Kennedy and Pirkko Markula. London: Routledge, 2010, https://www.taylorfrancis. com/chapters/edit/10.4324/9780203839300-23/running-embodiment-power-vulnerability-notes-toward-feminist-phenomenology-female-running.

Allison, Conor. 'Xiaomi leads wearable sales, with Apple and Fitbit slipping behind'. *Wareable*, 4 December 2018, https://www.wareable.com/xiaomi/xiaomi-wearable-sales-q3-idc-6793.

Almerico, Gina M. 'Food and identity: Food studies, cultural, and personal identity'. *Journal of International Business and Cultural Studies* 8 (2014): 1–8.

Almuhimedi, Hazim, et al. 'Your location has been shared 5,398 times! A field study on mobile app privacy nudging'. In *Proceedings of the 33rd Annual ACM Conference on Human Factors in Computing Systems*, 787–96. 2015.

Andersen, Shaneda Warren, William J. Blot, Xiao-Ou Shu, Jennifer S. Sonderman, Mark Steinwandel, Margaret K. Hargreaves, and Wei Zheng. 'Associations between neighborhood environment, health behaviors, and mortality'. *American Journal of Preventive Medicine* 54, no. 1 (2018): 87–95.

Anderson, L. V. 'Workplace wellness programs are a sham'. *Slate*, 1 September 2016, http://www.slate.com/articles/health_and_science/the_ladder/2016/09/workplace_wellness_programs_are_a_sham.html.

Anderson, R. J., and W. W. Sharrock. 'Radical reflexivity'. University of Manchester and University of Nottingham (2015), https://www.sharrockandanderson.co.uk/wp-content/uploads/2017/04/Reflexivity-Publication-Version.pdf.

Anderson, Warwick. 'From subjugated knowledge to conjugated subjects: Science and globalisation, or postcolonial studies of science?' *Postcolonial Studies* 12, no. 4 (2009): 389–400.

Andersson, Karin, and Jesper Andreasson. 'Being a group fitness instructor during the COVID-19 Crisis: Navigating professional identity, social distancing, and community'. *Social Sciences* 10, no. 4 (2021): 118–34.

Anthias, Floya. 'Rethinking social divisions: Some notes towards a theoretical framework'. *The Sociological Review* 46, no. 3 (1998): 505–35.

Aphramor, Lucy, and Jacqui Gingras. 'Helping people change: Promoting politicised practice in the health care professions'. In *Debating Obesity*, edited by Emma Rich, Lee F. Monaghan, and Lucy Aphramor, 192–218. London: Palgrave Macmillan, 2011.

Arnold, J. E. M., and M. Ruiz Pérez. 'The role of non-timber forest products in conservation and development'. *Incomes From the Forest: Methods for the Development and Conservation of Forest Products for Local Communities* (1998): 17–42.

Arora, Saurabh, Barbara Van Dyck, Divya Sharma, and Andy Stirling. 'Control, care, and conviviality in the politics of technology for sustainability'. *Sustainability: Science, Practice and Policy* 16, no. 1 (2020): 247–62.

Åsberg, Cecilia. 'The timely ethics of posthumanist gender studies'. *Feministische Studien* 31, no. 1 (2013): 7–12.

Askegaard, Søren, Nailya Ordabayeva, Pierre Chandon, Tracy Cheung, Zuzana Chytkova, Yann Cornil, Canan Corus, et al. 'Moralities in food and health research'. *Journal of Marketing Management* 30, no. 17–18 (2014): 1800–32.

Atkinson, Paul. 'Rescuing autoethnography'. *Journal of Contemporary Ethnography* 35, no. 4 (2006): 400–4.

Aydin, Aysun. 'The concept of pleasure: Plato versus Greek's manner of life'. *Ethos: Dialogues in Philosophy and Social Sciences* 6, no. 2 (2013). https://philpapers.org/rec/AYDTCO-2

Ayers, David Franklin. 'Neoliberal ideology in community college mission statements: A critical discourse analysis'. *The Review of Higher Education* 28, no. 4 (2005): 527–49.

Ayo, Nike. 'Understanding health promotion in a neoliberal climate and the making of health conscious citizens'. *Critical Public Health* 22, no. 1 (2012): 99–105.

Azzarito, Laura. 'The rise of the corporate curriculum'. In *Biopolitics and the 'Obesity Epidemic': Governing Bodies*, edited by Jan Wright and Valerie Harwood, 83–95. Hoboken: Routledge, 2008.

Azzarito, Laura. 'The rise of the corporate curriculum: Fatness, fitness, and whiteness'. In *Biopolitics and the 'Obesity Epidemic'*, edited by Jan Wright and Valerie Harwood, 191–204. New York: Routledge, 2012.

Babuya, Neo. *Aduna*, 2021, https://aduna.com/blogs/our-producers-case-studies/neo-babuya.

Bacon, Linda, and Lucy Aphramor. *Body respect: What conventional health books get wrong, leave out, and just plain fail to understand about weight*. Dallas: BenBella Books, Inc., 2014.

Baeck, Peter, Liam Collins, and Bryan Zhang. 'Understanding alternative finance'. *The UK Alternative Finance Industry Report* (2014), https://media.nesta.org.uk/documents/understanding-alternative-finance-2014.pdf.

Bahra, Ramanpreet Annie. 'You can only be happy if you're thin! Normalcy, happiness, and the lacking body'. *Fat Studies* 7, no. 2 (2018): 193–202.

Baker, Camille N., and Kate Sicchio. 'Stitch, bitch, make/perform: Wearables and performance'. Working Paper (2015), https://ucl.scienceopen.com/document_file/2b48c91f-6a41-4b36-b2b4-1e7418457182/ScienceOpen/247_Baker.pdf.

Banner, Olivia. *Communicative biocapitalism: The voice of the patient in digital health and the health humanities*. Ann Arbor: University of Michigan Press, 2017.

Baptiste, et al. 'Racial discrimination in health care: An "us" problem'. *Journal of Clinical Nursing* (2020): 4415–17.

Barad, Karen. 'Meeting the universe halfway: Realism and social constructivism without contradiction'. *Feminism, Science and the Philosophy of Science*, edited by Lynn Hankinson Nelson and Jack Nelson, 161–94. Dordrecht: Kluwer, 1996.

Barad, Karen. 'Posthumanist performativity: Toward an understanding of how matter comes to matter'. *Signs: Journal of Women in Culture and Society* 28, no. 3 (2003): 801–31.

Barad, Karen. *Meeting the universe halfway: Quantum physics and the entanglement of matter and meaning*. Durham: Duke University Press, 2007.

Barad, Karen. 'Diffracting diffraction: Cutting together-apart'. *Parallax* 20, no. 3 (2014): 168–87.

Barkho, Gabriela. 'The wearable tech industry is expected to hit $54 billion by 2023'. *Observer*, 12 December 2019, https://observer.com/2019/08/wearable-tech-industry-hit-54-billion-by-2023/.

Barta, Kristen, and Gina Neff (2014, May). 'Technologies for sharing: Lessons from the quantified self movement about the political economy of platforms'. In *International Communication Association Conference, Seattle, WA, USA* (Vol. 22): 1–28.

Bartky, Sandra Lee. 'Suffering to be beautiful'. *Gender Struggles: Practical approaches to contemporary feminism* (2002): 241–56.

Bartky, Sandra Lee. *Femininity and domination: Studies in the phenomenology of oppression*. New York: Routledge, 2015.

Bartky, Sandra Lee. 'Foucault, femininity, and the modernization of patriarchal power'. In *Feminist Theory Reader* edited by Carole McCann, Seung-kyung Kim, and Emek Ergun, 342–52, London: Routledge, 2020.

Barua Maan. 'Encounter: Living lexicon for the environmental humanities'. *Environmental Humanities* 7 (2015): 265–70.

Barua, Maan. 'Nonhuman labour, encounter value, spectacular accumulation: The geographies of a lively commodity'. *Transactions of the Institute of British Geographers* 42, no. 2 (2017): 274–88.

Baumflek, Michelle. 'Stewardship, health sovereignty and biocultural diversity: Contemporary medicinal plant use in indigenous communities of Maine, USA and New Brunswick, Canada'. 2015. Dissertation, Cornell University, https://ecommons.cornell.edu/bitstream/handle/1813/39383/mjb235.pdf?sequence=1.

Bayer Global. 'Bayer acquires majority stake in care/of'. *Bayer Global*, 17 November 2020, https://media.bayer.com/baynews/baynews.nsf/id/Bayer-Acquires-Majority-Stake-in-Care-of.

Beckmann, Andrea. 'Representing "healthy" and "sexual" bodies: the media, "disability" and consensual "SM"'. In *Representing Health: Discourses of Health and Illness in the Media*, edited by Martin King and Katherine Watson, 206–33. Basingstoke: Palgrave Macmillan, 2005.

Bellemare, Marc F., Johanna Fajardo-Gonzalez, and Seth R. Gitter. 'Foods and fads: The welfare impacts of rising quinoa prices in Peru'. *World Development* 112 (2018): 163–79.

Beltrán, Mary. '"Fast and Bilingual: Fast & Furious" and the Latinization of racelessness'. *Cinema Journal* (2013): 75–96.

Ben-Porath, Sigal. 'Care ethics and dependence—rethinking jus post bellum'. *Hypatia* 23, no. 2 (2008): 61–71.

Bender, Melinda S., et al. 'Digital technology ownership, usage, and factors predicting downloading health apps among Caucasian, Filipino, Korean, and Latino

Americans: The digital link to health survey'. *JMIR mHealth and uHealth* 2, no. 4 (2014): e3710.

Benjamin, Ruha. *Race after technology: Abolitionist tools for the new Jim Code*. New Jersey: John Wiley & Sons, 2019.

Bennett, Jane. 'The force of things: Steps toward an ecology of matter'. *Political Theory* 32, no. 3 (2004): 347–72.

Bennett, Jane. 'A vitalist stopover on the way to a new materialism'. In *New Materialisms: Ontology, Agency, and Politics*, edited by Jane Bennett, Pheng Cheah, Melissa A. Orlie, and Elizabeth Grosz, 47–69. Durham: Duke University Press, 2010a.

Bennett, Jane. *Vibrant matter: A political ecology of things*. Durham: Duke University Press, 2010b.

Bennett, Jane. *The enchantment of modern life*. New Jersey: Princeton University Press, 2016.

Bennett, Jane, Pheng Cheah, Melissa A. Orlie, and Elizabeth Grosz. *New Materialisms: Ontology, Agency, and Politics*. Duke University Press, 2010.

Berbary, Lisbeth A. 'Theory practicing differently: Re-imagining the public, health, and social research'. *Leisure Sciences* (2020): 1–9.

Bergroth, Harley. '"You can't really control life": Dis/assembling self-knowledge with self-tracking technologies'. *Distinktion: Journal of Social Theory* 20, no. 2 (2019): 190–206.

Bijker, Wiebe E. 'Understanding technological culture through a constructivist view of science, technology, and society'. In *Visions of STS: Counterpoints in Science, Technology and Society Studies*, edited by S. H. Cutcliffe and Carl Mitcham, 19–34. New York: State University of New York, 2001.

Biltekoff, Charlotte. *Eating right in America: The cultural politics of food and health*. Durham: Duke University Press, 2013.

Biltekoff, Charlotte, Jessica Mudry, Aya H. Kimura, Hannah Landecker, and Julie Guthman. 'Interrogating moral and quantification discourses in nutritional knowledge'. *Gastronomica: The Journal of Food and Culture* 14, no. 3 (2014): 17–26.

Birch, Kean, and David Tyfield. 'Theorizing the bioeconomy: Biovalue, biocapital, bioeconomics or ... what?' *Science, Technology, & Human Values* 38, no. 3 (2013): 299–327.

Blakey, Michael L. 'Scientific racism and the biological concept of race'. *Literature and Psychology* 45, no. 1/2 (1999): 29–43.

Bliss, Catherine. 'Biomedicalization in the postgenomic age'. In *Routledge Handbook of Genomics, Health and Society*, edited by Sahra Gibbon, Barbara Prainsack, Stephen Hilgartner, and Janelle Lamoreaux, 15–23. London: Routledge, 2018.

Bobrow-Strain, Aaron. 'White bread bio-politics: Purity, health, and the triumph of industrial baking'. *Cultural Geographies* 15, no. 1 (2008): 19–40.

Bochner, Arthur P., and Carolyn Ellis. 'An introduction to the arts and narrative research: Art as inquiry'. *Qualitative Inquiry* 9, no. 4 (2003): 506–14.

Bødker, Mads, and Alan Chamberlain. 'Affect theory and autoethnography in ordinary information systems'. *Nottingham University*, 2016, https://nottingham-repository. worktribe.com/preview/795350/ECIS%202016.pdf.

Bodunrin, Temitope Sarah, and Tim Stone. 'Consuming well-being and happiness through epicurean ingestion'. *Qualitative Market Research: An International Journal* (2019), https://www.emerald.com/insight/content/doi/10.1108/QMR-06-2018-0061/ full/html?casa_token=mwUTPr10l6EAAAAA:_2WLinqvxDCZVVZEtLWetSB QAIQpMzRAdQDS5iox6qxCir3iWX4OFrAdX3Tz38dnclgJnXLMm2Tr yWChFplk1C8z57_IyIvRkPf4hRPe9isakTrrOMI7.

Bonham, Vence L., Shawneequa L. Callier, and Charmaine D. Royal. 'Will precision medicine move us beyond race?' *The New England Journal of Medicine* 374, no. 21 (2016): 2003–5.

Boni, Federico. 'Framing media masculinities: Men's lifestyle magazines and the biopolitics of the male body'. *European Journal of Communication* 17, no. 4 (2002): 465–78.

Bordo, Susan. *Unbearable weight: Feminism, Western culture, and the body*. Berkeley: University of California Press, 2004.

Bordo, Susan. *Reading the slender body*. New York: Routledge, 2018.

Bourdieu, Pierre. *Distinction: A social critique of the judgement of taste*. New York: Routledge, 2018.

Bourreau, Marc, et al. 'Google/Fitbit will monetise health data and harm consumers'. *Vox EU: CEPR*, 30 September 2020, https://voxeu.org/article/googlefitbit-will-monetise-health-data-and-harm-consumers.

Boyd, Danah, and Kate Crawford. 'Critical questions for big data: Provocations for a cultural, technological, and scholarly phenomenon'. *Information, Communication & Society* 15, no. 5 (2012): 662–79.

Braidotti, Rosi. 'Teratologies'. In *Deleuze and Feminist Theory*, edited by Ian Buchanan and Claire Colebrook, 156–72. Edinburgh: Edinburgh University Press, 2000.

Braidotti, Rosi. *Transpositions: On nomadic ethics*. New York: Polity, 2006.

Braidotti, Rosi. 'Feminist epistemology after postmodernism: Critiquing science, technology and globalisation'. *Interdisciplinary Science Reviews* 32 no. 1 (2007): 65–74.

Braidotti, Rosi. 'Affirmation, pain and empowerment'. *Asian Journal of Women's Studies* 14, no. 3 (2008): 7–36.

Braidotti, Rosi. *Nomadic theory: The portable Rosi Braidotti*. New York: Columbia University Press, 2011.

Braidotti, Rosi. 'Posthuman humanities'. *European Educational Research Journal* 12, no. 1 (2013a): 1–19.

Braidotti, Rosi. *The posthuman*. New Jersey: John Wiley & Sons, 2013b.

Braidotti, Rosi. 'Posthuman critical theory'. In *Critical Posthumanism and Planetary Futures*, edited by Debashish Banerji and Makarand R. Paranjape. New Delhi: Springer, New Delhi, 2016, https://doi.org/10.1007/978-81-322-3637-5_2.

Braidotti, Rosi. *Posthuman knowledge*. Cambridge: Polity Press, 2019a.

Braidotti, Rosi. 'A theoretical framework for the critical posthumanities'. *Theory, Culture & Society* 36 no. 6 (2019b): 31–61.

Brandt-Rauf, Paul W., and Sherry I. Brandt-Rauf. 'Genetic testing in the workplace: Ethical, legal, and social implications'. *Annual Review of Public Health* 25 (2004): 139–53.

Braun, Lundy. *Breathing race into the machine: The surprising career of the spirometer from plantation to genetics*. Minneapolis: University of Minnesota Press, 2014.

Braveman, Paula, and Laura Gottlieb. 'The social determinants of health: It's time to consider the causes of the causes'. *Public Health Reports* 129, no. 1 (2014): 19–31.

Braveman, Paula, and Sofia Gruskin. 'Defining equity in health'. *Journal of Epidemiology & Community Health* 57, no. 4 (2003): 254–8.

Braveman, Paula, Susan Egerter, and David R. Williams. 'The social determinants of health: coming of Age'. *Annual Review of Public Health* 32 (2011): 281–398.

Brett, Lorna. 'From superfood to super profits'. *Dynamic Business*, 19 November 2012, https://dynamicbusiness.com.au/leadership-2/entrepreneur-profile/from-superfood-to-super-profits-16112012.html.

Brody, Jane E. 'The pandemic as a wake-up call for personal health'. *The New York Times*, 15 March 2021, https://www.nytimes.com/2021/03/15/well/live/pandemic-health-obesity.html.

Brondízio, Eduardo S. 'From staple to fashion food: Shifting cycles and shifting opportunities in the development of açai palm fruit economy in the Brazilian estuary'. *Working Forests in the Neotropics: Conservation through Sustainable Management* (2004): 339–65.

Brown, Wendy. 'Neo-liberalism and the end of liberal democracy'. *Theory & Event* 7, no. 1 (2003), 10.1353/tae.2003.0020.

Buchmann, Christine, Sarah Prehsler, Anna Hartl, and Christian R. Vogl. 'The importance of baobab (Adansonia digitata L.) in rural West African subsistence—suggestion of a cautionary approach to international market export of baobab fruits'. *Ecology of Food and Nutrition* 49, no. 3 (2010): 145–72.

Burchell, Graham, Arnold Davidson, and Michel Foucault. *The birth of biopolitics: Lectures at the Collège de France, 1978–1979*. New York: Springer, 2008.

Butler, Ruth, and Hester Parr, eds. *Mind and body spaces: Geographies of illness, impairment and disability*. London: Routledge, 2005.

Butz, David, and Kathryn Besio. 'Autoethnography'. *Geography Compass* 3, no. 5 (2009): 1660–74.

Byrne, Christine. 'Weight isn't the Problem with COVID-19. How we talk about it is'. *Huffpost*, 3 October 2020, https://www.huffingtonpost.co.uk/entry/fat-covid-19-pandemic-obesity_l_5f736f60c5b6e99dc3336e3e.

Cagle, Van M. 'The language of cultural studies: An analysis of British subculture theory'. *Studies in Symbolic Interaction* 10 (1989): 301–13.

Cairns, Kate, and Josée Johnston. 'Choosing health: Embodied neoliberalism, postfeminism, and the "do-diet"'. *Theory and Society* 44, no. 2 (2015): 153–75.

Cairns, Kate, Josée Johnston, and Shyon Baumann. 'Caring about food: Doing gender in the foodie kitchen'. *Gender & Society* 24, no. 5 (2010): 591–615.

Calabrese, Andrew, and Colin Sparks. 'Toward a political economy of culture'. *Toward a Political Economy of Culture: Capitalism and Communication in the Twenty-first Century* (2004): 1–12.

Calogero, Rachel M., and J. Kevin Thompson. 'Gender and body image'. In *Handbook of gender research in psychology*, 153–84. New York: Springer, 2010.

Calogero, Rachel M., and J. Kevin Thompson. 'Gender and body image'. In *Handbook of Gender Research in Psychology*, edited by Joan C. Chrisler and Donald R. McCreary, 153–84. New York: Springer, 2010.

Calvard, Thomas. 'Integrating social scientific perspectives on the quantified employee self'. *Social Sciences* 8, no. 9 (2019): 262–81.

Calvert, Amy. 'You are what you (m) eat: Explorations of meat-eating, masculinity and masquerade'. *Journal of International Women's Studies* 16, no. 1 (2014): 18–33.

Camp, Kathryn M., and Elaine Trujillo. 'Position of the academy of nutrition and dietetics: Nutritional genomics'. *Journal of the Academy of Nutrition and Dietetics* 114, no. 2 (2014): 299–312, https://jandonline.org/article/s22122672(13)01783-8/fulltext.

Campbell, Fiona Kumari. 'Refusing able (ness): A preliminary conversation about ableism'. *M/C Journal* 11, no. 3 (2008), https://journal.media-culture.org.au/index.php/mcjournal/article/view/46.

Campos, Paul F. *The obesity myth: Why America's obsession with weight is hazardous to your health*. New York: Penguin Press, 2004.

Cannon, Geoffrey, and Claus Leitzmann. 'The new nutrition science project'. *Public Health Nutrition* 8, no. 6a (2005): 673–94.

Caplan, Pat. *Food, health and identity*. London: Routledge, 2013.

Cardona, Beatriz. 'The pitfalls of personalization rhetoric in time of health crisis: COVID-19 pandemic and cracks on neoliberal ideologies'. *Health Promotion International* (2020): 1–10.

Carroll, Anthony J. 'Disenchantment, rationality and the modernity of Max Weber'. *Forum Philosophicum* 16, no. 1 (2011): 117–37.

Carstensen, Tanja, and Gabriele Winker. 'E-empowerment of heterogenous feminist networks'. In *Gender designs IT: Construction and Deconstruction of Information Society Technology*, edited by Isabel Zorn, Susanne Maass, Els Rommes, Carola Schirmer, and Heidi Schelhowe, 109–20. Wiesbaden: Verlag für Sozialwissenschaften, 2007.

Casilli, Antonio A., and Julian Posada. 'The platformization of labor and society'. In *Society and the Internet: How Networks of Information and Communication Are Changing Our Lives*, edited by Mark Graham, and William H. Dutton, 293–306. Oxford: Oxford University Press, 2019.

Catlaw, Thomas J., and Billie Sandberg. 'The quantified self and the evolution of neoliberal self-government: An exploratory qualitative study'. *Administrative Theory & Praxis* 40, no. 1 (2018): 3–22.

Cavanah, Cassandra, and Beth McGroarty. 'Nutrition gets very personalized'. *Global Wellness Summit*, 2019, https://www.globalwellnesssummit.com/2019-global-wellness-trends/nutrition-gets-very-personalized/.

Cetina, Karin Knorr. 'Sociality with objects: Social relations in postsocial knowledge societies'. *Theory, Culture & Society* 14, no. 4 (1997): 1–30.

Chan, Yuk Wah, and James Farrer. 'Introduction: Asian food and culinary politics: Food governance, constructed heritage and contested boundaries'. *Asian Anthropology* 20, no. 1 (2021): 1–11.

Chapman, Carolyn Riley, Kripa Sanjay Mehta, Brendan Parent, and Arthur L. Caplan. 'Genetic discrimination: Emerging ethical challenges in the context of advancing technology'. *Journal of Law and the Biosciences* 7, no. 1 (2020): lsz016.

Charmaz, Kathy, and Richard G. Mitchell. 'The myth of silent authorship: Self, substance, and style in ethnographic writing'. *Symbolic Interaction* 19, no. 4 (1996): 285–302.

Chastain, Regan. 'We all know what WW stands for: Why the weight watchers rebrand is BS'. *Ravishly*, 28 September 2018, https://www.ravishly.com/weight-watchers-rebrand.

Chazan, May, and Stephanie Kittmer. 'Defying, producing, and overlooking stereotypes? The complexities of mobilizing "grandmotherhood" as political strategy'. *Journal of Women & Aging* 28, no. 4 (2016): 297–308.

Chen, Julie Yujie, and Ping Sun. 'Temporal arbitrage, fragmented rush, and opportunistic behaviors: The labor politics of time in the platform economy'. *New Media & Society* 22, no. 9 (2020): 1561–79.

Chiappetta, Margaret, and Kean Birch. 'Limits to biocapital'. In *Handbook of Genomics, Health and Society*. New York: Routledge, 2018.

Chouliaraki, Lilie, and Norman Fairclough. *Discourse in late modernity: Rethinking critical discourse analysis*. Edinburgh: Edinburgh University Press, 1999.

Chrisler, Joan C. 'Teaching health psychology from a size-acceptance perspective'. *Fat Studies* 7, no. 1 (2018): 33–43.

Christopher, Allison, John P. Bartkowski, and Timothy Haverda. 'Portraits of veganism: A comparative discourse analysis of a second-order subculture'. *Societies* 8, no. 3 (2018): 55.

Cifor, Marika, and Patricia Garcia. 'Gendered by design: A duoethnographic study of personal fitness tracking systems'. *ACM Transactions on Social Computing* 2, no. 4 (2020): 1–22.

Clark, Adrian, and Daphne Bugler. 'Best bakuchiol skincare products for a better alternative to retinol'. *British GQ*, 10 Febrary 2021, https://www.gq-magazine.co.uk/grooming/gallery/best-bakuchiol-skincare-products.

Clark, Andy. *Natural-born cyborgs: Minds, technologies, and the future of human intelligence*. Oxford: Oxford University Press, 2003.

Clark, Laren. 'Diabetes diet: THIS "superfood" fruit could manage blood sugar levels'. 17 October 2017. *Express*.

Clarke, Adele E., Laura Mamo, Jennifer Ruth Fosket, Jennifer R. Fishman, and Janet K. Shim, eds. *Biomedicalization: Technoscience, health, and illness in the US*. Durham: Duke University Press, 2010.

Clarke, Laura Hurd. *Facing age: Women growing older in anti-aging culture*. Vol. 1. Lanham: Rowman & Littlefield Publishers, 2010.

Clough, Patricia T. 'The affective turn: Political economy, biomedia and bodies'. *Theory, Culture & Society* 25, no. 1 (2008): 1–22.

Clough, Patricia Ticineto. 'Comments on setting criteria for experimental writing'. *Qualitative Inquiry* 6, no. 2 (2000): 278–91.

CNET. 'Fitness by GetFit: Daily workout. Exercise at home for Android'. *CNET*, 2021, https://download.cnet.com/Fitness-by-GetFit-Daily-workout-Exercise-at-home/3000-2129_4-78266295.html.

Coates, Rodney D., Abby L. Ferber, and David L. Brunsma. *The matrix of race: Social construction, intersectionality, and inequality*. New York: Sage Publications, 2017.

Coffey, Julia. 'Creating distance from body issues: Exploring new materialist feminist possibilities for renegotiating gendered embodiment'. *Leisure Sciences* 41, no. 1–2 (2019): 72–90.

Coleman, Rebecca, and Jessica Ringrose. 'Introduction: Deleuze and research methodologies'. *Deleuze and Research Methodologies* (2013): 1–22.

Collier, Roger. 'The DNA-based diet'. *The Canadian Medical Association* (2017): E40–E41.

Collins, Patricia Hill. *Intersectionality as critical social theory*. Durham: Duke University Press, 2019.

Collins, Patricia Hill, and Sirma Bilge. *Intersectionality*. New Jersey: John Wiley & Sons, 2020.

Collins, Paul D., Jerald Hage, and Frank Hull. 'A framework for analyzing technical systems in complex organizations'. *Research in the Sociology of Organizations* 6 (1986): 81–100.

Colls, Rachel. 'Materialising bodily matter: Intra-action and the embodiment of "fat"'. *Geoforum* 38, no. 2 (2007): 353–65.

Colvonen, Peter J., Pamela N. DeYoung, Naa-Oye A. Bosompra, and Robert L. Owens. 'Limiting racial disparities and bias for wearable devices in health science research'. *Sleep* 43, no. 10 (2020): https://doi.org/10.1093/sleep/zsaa159.

Comaroff, John L., and Jean Comaroff. *Of revelation and revolution, Vol. 2: The dialectics of modernity on a South African frontier*. Chicago: University of Chicago Press, 1997.

The Combahee River Collective. 'The Combahee River Collective statement'. The Combahee River Collective, 1977, https://www.blackpast.org/african-american-history/combahee-river-collective-statement-1977/.

Conrad, Peter. 'Medicalization and social control'. *Annual Review of Sociology* 18, no. 1 (1992): 209–32.

Coole, Diana, and Samantha Frost. 'Introducing the new materialisms'. In *New Materialisms: Ontology, Agency, and Politics*, edited by Jane Bennett, Pheng Cheah, Melissa A. Orlie, and Elizabeth Grosz, 1–43. Durham: Duke University Press, 2010.

Cooper, Andrew F., John J. Kirton, Franklyn Lisk, and Hany Besada, eds. *Africa's health challenges: sovereignty, mobility of people and healthcare governance*. New York: Routledge, 2016.

Cooper, Daniel. 'You can't buy an ethical smartphone today'. *Engadget*, 6 February 2018, https://www.engadget.com/2018-02-06-ethical-smartphone-conscious-consumption.htm.

Cornil, Yann, and Pierre Chandon. 'Pleasure as an ally of healthy eating? Contrasting visceral and Epicurean eating pleasure and their association with portion size preferences and wellbeing'. *Appetite* 104 (2016): 52–9.

Costanza-Chock, Sasha. 'Design justice, AI, and escape from the matrix of domination'. *Journal of Design and Science* (2018): https://doi.org/10.21428/96c8d426.

Counihan, Carole M. 'Food rules in the United States: Individualism, control, and hierarchy'. *Anthropological Quarterly* no. 2 (1992): 55–66.

Coveney, John, and Robin Bunton. 'In pursuit of the study of pleasure: Implications for health research and practice'. *Health* 7, no. 2 (2003): 161–79.

Coveney, John. *Food, morals and meaning: The pleasure and anxiety of eating*. New York: Routledge, 2019.

Crawford, Robert. 'Healthism and the medicalization of everyday life'. *International Journal of Health Services* 10, no. 3 (1980): 365–88.

Crawshaw, Paul. 'Governing at a distance: Social marketing and the (bio) politics of responsibility'. *Social Science & Medicine* 75, no. 1 (2012): 200–7.

Crawshaw, Trisha L. 'Rock and rolls: Exploring body positivity at Girls Rock Camp'. *Fat Studies* 9, no. 1 (2020): 17–36.

Crenshaw, Kimberle. 'Mapping the margins: Intersectionality, identity politics, and violence against women of color'. *Stanford Law Review* 43 (1990): 1241.

Crenshaw, Kimberlé W. *On intersectionality: Essential writings*. New York: The New Press, 2017.

Crosset, Todd, and Becky Beal. 'The use of "subculture" and "subworld" in ethnographic works on sport: A discussion of definitional distinctions'. *Sociology of Sport Journal* 14, no. 1 (1997): 73–85.

Crumley, Carole L. 'Heterarchy and the analysis of complex societies'. *Archeological Papers of the American Anthropological Association* 6, no. 1 (1995): 1–5.

Cukier, Wendy, Ojelanki Ngwenyama, Robert Bauer, and Catherine Middleton. 'A critical analysis of media discourse on information technology: Preliminary results of a proposed method for critical discourse analysis'. *Information Systems Journal* 19, no. 2 (2009): 175–96.

Cunningham, Hilary. 'Prodigal bodies: Pop culture and post-pregnancy'. *Michigan Quarterly Review* 41, no. 3 (2002): https://quod.lib.umich.edu/cgi/t/text/text-idx?cc=mqr;c=mqr;c=mqrarchive;idno=act2080.0041.314;rgn=main;view=text;xc=1;g=mqrg.

Cuthbert, Denise. 'Beg, borrow or steal: The politics of cultural appropriation'. *Postcolonial Studies: Culture, Politics, Economy* 1, no. 2 (1998): 257–62.

Cwynar-Horta, Jessica. 'The commodification of the body positive movement on Instagram'. *Stream: Culture/Politics/Technology* 8, no. 2 (2016): 36–56.

Daniels, Jessie. 'Race and racism in Internet studies: A review and critique'. *New Media & Society* 15, no. 5 (2013): 695–719.

Daniels, Norman. *Justice and justification: Reflective equilibrium in theory and practice*. Cambridge: Cambridge University Press, 1996.

Daniels, Norman. 'Justice, health, and healthcare'. *American Journal of Bioethics* 1, no. 2 (2001): 2–16.

Datta, Anisha, and Indranil Chakraborty. 'Are you neoliberal fit? The politics of consumption under neoliberalism'. In *The SAGE Handbook of Consumer Culture*, edited by Olga Kravets et al., 453–77. Thousand Oaks: Sage, 2018.

Davies, Will. 'The political economy of pulse: Techno-somatic rhythm and real-time data'. *Ephemera* 19, no. 3 (2019): 513–36.

De Laet, Marianne, and Annemarie Mol. 'The Zimbabwe bush pump: Mechanics of a fluid technology'. *Social Studies of Science* 30, no. 2 (2000): 225–63.

Dean, Megan. 'Eating identities,"Unhealthy" eaters, and damaged agency'. *Feminist Philosophy Quarterly* 4, no. 3 (2018).

Dean, Mitchell. 'Foucault, government and the enfolding of authority'. In *Foucault and Political Reason: Liberalism, Neo-liberalism and Rationalities of Government*, edited by Andrew Barry, Thosmas Osborne and Nikolas Rose, 209–29. New York: Routledge, 1996.

Deleuze, Gilles. *Spinoza: Practical philosophy*. San Francisco: City Lights Books, 1988.

Deleuze, Gilles. *Difference and repetition*. New York: Columbia University Press, 1994.

Deleuze, Gilles. *Anti-oedipus*. London: A&C Black, 2004.

Deleuze, Gilles, Felix Guattari, and Brian Massumi. *Nomadology: The war machine*. New York: Semiotext(e), 1986.

Deleuze, Gilles, and Félix Guattari. *A thousand plateaus: Capitalism and schizophrenia*. London: Bloomsbury Publishing, 1988.

Delgado, Richard, and Jean Stefancic. *Critical race theory: An introduction*. Vol. 2. New York: NYU Press, 2017.

Denshire, Sally. 'On auto-ethnography'. *Current Sociology* 62, no. 6 (2014): 831–50.

Denzin, Norman K. *Interpretive interactionism*. Vol. 16. London: Sage, 2001.

DeVault, Marjorie L. *Feeding the family: The social organization of caring as gendered work*. Chicago: University of Chicago Press, 1994.

Devlin, Edward. 'Aduna targets £1bn baobab market via tree-planting partnership'. *The Grocer*, 25 February 2020, https://www.thegrocer.co.uk/supply-chain/aduna-targets-1bn-baobab-market-via-tree-planting-partnership/602285.article.

Dhillion, Shivcharn S., and Gunnar Gustad. 'Local management practices influence the viability of the baobab (Adansonia digitata Linn.) in different land use types, Cinzana, Mali'. *Agriculture, Ecosystems & Environment* 101, no. 1 (2004): 85–103.

Didžiokaitė, Gabija, Paula Saukko, and Christian Greiffenhagen. 'The mundane experience of everyday calorie trackers: Beyond the metaphor of Quantified Self'. *New Media & Society* 20, no. 4 (2018): 1470–87.

Diener, Samuel. 'New materialisms'. *The Year's Work in Critical and Cultural Theory* 28, no. 1 (2020): 44–65. https://doi.org/10.1093/ywcct/mbaa003.

Diop, Aïda Gabar, Mama Sakho, Manuel Dornier, Mady Cisse, and Max Reynes. 'Le baobab africain (Adansonia digitata L.): principales caractéristiques et utilisations'. *Fruits* 61, no. 1 (2006): 55–69.

Diop, Aïda Gabar, et al. 'Fruit du baobab: étude de la transformation de la pulpe en nectar'. *Maîtrise des Procédés en vue d'améliorer la qualité et la sécurité des aliments, Utilisation des OGM, Analyse des risques en agroalimentaire. Ouagadougou* (2005): 8–11.

Dionne, Evette. 'The fragility of body positivity'. *bitchmedia*, 2017, https://www.bitchmedia.org/article/fragility-body-positivity.

Dixon, Jane. 'Authority, power and value in contemporary industrial food systems'. *The International Journal of Sociology of Agriculture and Food* 11 (2003): 31–9.

Dixon, Jane. 'From the imperial to the empty calorie: How nutrition relations underpin food regime transitions'. *Agriculture and Human Values* 26, no. 4 (2009): 321–33.

DNAfit. 'Homepage'. *DNAfit*. 2021, https://www.dnafit.com.

Dodd-Butera, Teresa, Margaret Beaman, and Marissa Brash. 'Environmental health equity: A concept analysis'. *Annual Review of Nursing Research* 38, no. 1 (2020): 183–202.

Doherty, Sarah, Shana McDavis-Conway, Adrienne Hill, Elaine Lee, Sydney Lewis, Aaminah Shakur, and Cicely Smith. 'A conversation about fat activism among activists in community with Nolose'. *Fat Studies* (2021): 1–20.

Douglas, Mary. *Purity and danger: An analysis of concepts of pollution and taboo.* New York: Routledge, 2003.

Dr. Y. 'The baobab: Symbol of power, presence, strength, and grace'. *African Heritage*, 15 November 2011, https://afrolegends.com/2011/11/15/the-baobab-symbol-of-presence-strength-and-grace/.

Dreher, Nick. 'Food from nowhere: Complicating cultural food colonialism to understand matcha as superfood'. *Graduate Journal of Food Studies* 5, no. 1 (2018): 1–20.

Duncan, Margot. 'Autoethnography: Critical appreciation of an emerging art'. *International Journal of Qualitative Methods* 3, no. 4 (2004): 28–39.

Durham, Meenakshi Gigi, and Douglas M. Kellner, eds. *Media and cultural studies: Keyworks.* New Jersey: John Wiley & Sons, 2012.

Durkheim, Emile. *Suicide: A study in sociology.* New York: Routledge, 2005.

Durocher, Myriam. 'From the digitalization of society to the production of a biomedicalized food culture'. *Digitalization of Society and Socio-political Issues 1: Digital, Communication and Culture* (2019): 201–8.

Duster, Troy. *Backdoor to eugenics.* Sussex: Psychology Press, 2003.

Duster, Troy. 'A post-genomic surprise. The molecular reinscription of race in science, law and medicine'. *The British Journal of Sociology* 66, no. 1 (2015): 1–27.

Earp, Brian D. 'Addressing polarisation in science'. *Journal of Medical Ethics* 41, no. 9 (2015): 782–4.

The Editors. The strategist haul: What the editors bought in February. *The Strategist*, 26 February 2021, https://nymag.com/strategist/2021/02/what-the-editors-bought-in-february-2021.html.

Edkins, M. T., L. M. Kruger, K. Harris, and J. J. Midgley. 'Baobabs and elephants in Kruger National Park: Nowhere to hide'. *African Journal of Ecology* 46, no. 2 (2008): 119–25.

Ehley, Brianna. 'Workplace wellness programs may cost more than they're worth'. *Fiscal Times*, 16 December 2014, http://www.thefiscaltimes.com/ 2014/12/16/Workplace-Wellness-Programs-May-Cost-More-They-re-Worth.

EJWS. Editorial: Celebrating intersectionality? Debates on a multi-faceted concept in gender studies: Themes from a conference? *European Journal of Women's Studies* 16, no. 3 (2009): 203–10.

El-ojeili, Chamsy, and Dylan Taylor. "'The Future in the Past": Anarcho-primitivism and the critique of civilization today'. *Rethinking Marxism* 32, no. 2 (2020): 168–86.

Ellingson, Laura, and Carolyn Ellis. 'Autoethnography as constructionist project'. In *Handbook of Constructionist Research*, edited by James A. Holstein and Jaber F. Gubrium, 446–66. London: The Guildford Press, 2008.

Ellis, Carolyn. 'What counts as scholarship in communication? An autoethnographic Response'. *American Communication Journal* 1, no. 2 (1998): 1–5. http://nacjournal. org/holdings/vol1/Iss2/special/ellis.htm.

Ellis, Carolyn, Tony E. Adams, and Arthur P. Bochner. 'Autoethnography: An overview'. *Historical Social Research/Historische Sozialforschung* (2011): 273–90.

Elmer, Greg. 'A diagram of panoptic surveillance'. *New Media & Society* 5, no. 2 (2003): 231–47.

Epting, Shane. 'Advancing food sovereignty through interrogating the question: What is food sovereignty?' *Journal of Agricultural and Environmental Ethics* 31, no. 5 (2018): 593–604.

Emontspool, Julie, and Carina Georgi. 'A cosmopolitan return to nature: How combining aesthetization and moralization processes expresses distinction in food consumption'. *Consumption Markets & Culture* 20, no. 4 (2017): 306–28.

Engmann, Rachel Ama Asaa. 'Under imperial eyes, black bodies, buttocks, and breasts: British colonial photography and Asante "fetish girls"'. *African rts* 45, no. 2 (2012): 46–57.

Ereshefsky, Marc. 'Defining "health" and "disease"'. *Studies in History and Philosophy of Science Part C: Studies in History and Philosophy of Biological and Biomedical Sciences* 40, no. 3 (2009): 221–7.

Ernsberger, Paul. 'BMI, body build, body fatness, and health risks'. *Fat Studies* 1, no. 1 (2012): 6–12.

Esmonde, Katelyn. "'There's only so much data you can handle in your life": Accommodating and resisting self-surveillance in women's running and fitness tracking practices'. *Qualitative Research in Sport, Exercise and Health* 12, no. 1 (2020): 76–90.

Evans, Daniel. 'My FitnessPal'. *British Journal of Sports Medicine* 51, no. 14. July 2016, https://bjsm.bmj.com/content/51/14/1101.

Evans, John, and Brian Davies. 'New directions, new questions? Social theory, education and embodiment'. *Sport, Education and Society* 16, no. 3 (2011): 263–78.

Evans, Nicholas G., and Jonathan D. Moreno. 'Children of capital: Eugenics in the world of private biotechnology'. *Ethics in Biology, Engineering and Medicine: An International Journal* 6, no. 3–4 (2015): 285–97.

Fairclough, Norman. 'Discourse and text: Linguistic and intertextual analysis within discourse analysis'. *Discourse & Society* 3, no. 2 (1992): 193–217.

Fairclough, Norman. 'Critical discourse analysis and the marketization of public discourse: The universities'. *Discourse & Society* 4, no. 2 (1993): 133–68.

Fairclough, Norman. 'Critical discourse analysis as a method in social scientific research'. *Methods of Critical Discourse Analysis* 5, no. 11 (2001): 121–38.

Fairclough, Norman. *Critical discourse analysis: The critical study of language.* London: Routledge, 2013.

Fairclough, Norman, and Ruth Wodak. 'Critical discourse analysis'. In *Discourse Studies: A Multidisciplinary Introduction*. Vol. 2., edited by Teun van Dijk, 258–84. London: Sage, 1997.

Fanon, Frantz. *The wretched of the earth.* New York: Grove/Atlantic, Inc., 2007.

Farrell, Amy Erdman. *Fat shame.* New York: New York University Press, 2011.

Farrington, Rebecca, and Conor Farrington. 'Quantified lives and vital data. Exploring health and technology through personal medical devices'. *Health, Technology and Society: Critical Inquiries* (2020): 56.

Fee, Margery. 'Racializing narratives: Obesity, diabetes and the "Aboriginal" thrifty genotype'. *Social Science & Medicine* 62, no. 12 (2006): 2988–97.

Feenberg, Andrew. *Critical theory of technology.* Vol. 5. New York: Oxford University Press, 1991.

Feenberg, Andrew. 'Critical theory of technology and STS'. *Thesis Eleven* 138, no. 1 (2017): 3–12.

Ferdinand, Keith C., and Daphne P. Ferdinand. 'Race-based therapy for hypertension: Possible benefits and potential pitfalls'. *Expert Review of Cardiovascular Therapy* 6, no. 10 (2008): 1357–66.

Ferrando, Francesca. 'Why space migration must be posthuman'. In *The Ethics of Space Exploration*, edited by James S. J. Scwartz and Tony Milligan, 137–52. Basel: Springer, Cham, 2016.

Ferreira, Eduarda. 'The co-production of gender and ICT: Gender stereotypes in schools'. *First Monday* (2017): https://journals.uic.edu/ojs/index.php/fm/article/download/7062/6546.

Ferrier, Morwenna. 'Baobab fruit takes off as a "superfood" with sharp rise in UK sales'. *The Guardian*, 20 March 2018, https://www.theguardian.com/lifeandstyle/2018/mar/30/baobab-fruit-takes-off-superfood-sharp-rise-uk-sales.

Fields, Karen E., and Barbara Jeanne Fields. *Racecraft: The soul of inequality in American life.* London: Verso Trade, 2014.

Finn, S. Margot. *Discriminating taste: How class anxiety created the American food revolution.* New Jersey: Rutgers University Press, 2017.

Fiore-Gartland, Brittany, and Gina Neff. 'Communication, mediation, and the expectations of data: Data valences across health and wellness communities'. *International Journal of Communication* 9 (2015): 1466–84.

Fischler, Claude. 'Food, self and identity'. *Social Science Information* 27, no. 2 (1988): 275–92.

Fisher, Mark. *Capitalist realism: Is there no alternative?* Winchester, UK: John Hunt Publishing, 2009.

Fitbit. 'Homepage'. *Fitbit*, 2021, https://www.fitbit.com/global/uk/home.

Fitzgerald, Maggie. Personalized nutrition could be the next plant-based meat, worth $64 billion by 2040, says UBS. *CNBC*, 19 January 2020, https://www.cnbc.com/2020/01/19/personalized-nutrition-could-be-the-next-plant-based-meat-worth-64-billion-by-2040-says-ubs.html.

Flora, C. 'Book Review: Schanbacher, William D.: The politics of food: The global conflict between food security and food sovereignty'. *Journal of Agricultural and Environmental Ethics* 24, no. 5 (2011): 545–7.

Ford, Chandra L., and Collins O. Airhihenbuwa. 'The public health critical race methodology: Praxis for antiracism research'. *Social Science & Medicine* 71, no. 8 (2010): 1390–8.

Fortune Business Insights. 'Fitness tracker market size, share & COVID-19 impact analysis …'. *Fortune Business Insights*, 2021, https://www.fortunebusinessinsights.com/fitness-tracker-market-103358.

Foster, John Bellamy, and Robert W. McChesney. 'Surveillance capitalism: Monopoly-finance capital, the military-industrial complex, and the digital age'. *Monthly Review* 66, no. 3 (2014): 1.

Fotopoulou, Aristea, and Kate O'Riordan. 'Training to self-care: Fitness tracking, biopedagogy and the healthy consumer'. *Health Sociology Review* 26, no. 1 (2017): 54–68.

Foucault, Michel. *L'ordre du discours*. Paris: Gallimard, 1972.

Foucault, Michel. 'Truth and power'. In *Power/Knowledge: Selected Interviews and Other Writings 1972–1977*, trans. and edited by Colin Gordon, 107–33. Brighton. Sussex: The Harvester Press, 1980a.

Foucault, Michel. *Power/knowledge: Selected interviews and other writings, 1972–1977*. New York: Vintage, 1980b.

Foucault, Michel. *The Foucault reader*. New York: Pantheon, 1984.

Foucault, Michel. *Technologies of the self: A seminar with Michel Foucault*. Amherst: University of Massachusetts Press, 1988.

Foucault, Michel. *The use of pleasure: The history of sexuality*. Vol. 2. Harmondsworth: Penguin, 1992.

Foucault, Michel. *Discipline and punish: The birth of the prison*. Durham: Duke University Press, 2007.

Foucault, Michel, Arnold I. Davidson, and Graham Burchell. *The birth of biopolitics: Lectures at the Collège de France, 1978–1979*. Berline: Springer, 2008.

Fox, Nick J. 'Personal health technologies, micropolitics and resistance: A new materialist analysis'. *Health* 21, no. 2 (2017): 136–53.

Fox, Nick J. 'Refracting "health": Deleuze, Guattari and body-self'. *Health* 6, no. 3 (2002): 347–63.

Fox, Nick J., and Pam Alldred. 'New materialist social inquiry: Designs, methods and the research-assemblage'. *International Journal of Social Research Methodology* 18, no. 4 (2015): 399–414.

Fox, Nick J., and Pam Alldred. 'New materialism'. In *SAGE research methods foundations*. New York: Sage Publications, 2019.

France24. 'South African villagers tap into trend for "superfood" baobab'. *France24*, 24 September 2018, https://www.france24.com/en/20180924-south-african-villagers-tap-trend-superfood-baobab.

Fredengren, Christina. 'Unexpected encounters with deep time enchantment. Bog bodies, crannogs and "otherworldly" sites. The materializing powers of disjunctures in time'. *World Archaeology* 48, no. 4 (2016): 482–99.

Frey, Philipp, Simon Schaupp, and Klara-Aylin Wenten. 'Towards emancipatory technology studies'. *Nanoethics* (2021): 1–9.

Friese, Colin. Response to 'A post-genomic surprise. The molecular reinscription of race in science, law and medicine'. *British Journal of Sociology* 66, no. 1 (2015): 53–7, doi: 10.1111/1468-4446.12117_4. PMID: 25789803.

Frith, Jordan, and Didem Özkul. 'Mobile media beyond mobile phones'. *Mobile Media and Communications* 7, no. 3 (2019): 293–302.

Frizzo-Barker, Julie, and Peter A. Chow-White. '"There's an App for That" Mediating mobile moms and connected careerists through smartphones and networked individualism'. *Feminist Media Studies* 12, no. 4 (2012): 580–9.

Fu, Chen-Ping, Catherine E. Welsh, Fernando Pardo-Manuel de Villena, and Leonard McMillan. 'Inferring ancestry in admixed populations using microarray probe intensities'. In *Proceedings of the ACM Conference on Bioinformatics, Computational Biology and Biomedicine*, 105–12. 2012.

Fuchs, Christian. 'Some theoretical foundations of critical media studies: Reflections on Karl Marx and the media'. *International Journal of Communication* 3 (2009): 34.

Fuchs, Christian. 'Web 2.0, prosumption, and surveillance'. *Surveillance & Society* 8, no. 3 (2011): 288–309.

Fuchs, Christian. *Digital labour and Karl Marx*. New York: Routledge, 2014.

Fuchs, Christian. 'Towards a critical theory of communication as renewal and update of Marxist humanism in the age of digital capitalism'. *Journal for the Theory of Social Behaviour* 50, no. 3 (2020): 335–56.

Fujimura, Joan H., and Ramya Rajagopalan. 'Different differences: The use of "genetic ancestry" versus race in biomedical human genetic research'. *Social Studies of Science* 41, no. 1 (2011): 5–30.

Fullagar, Simone. 'Negotiating the neurochemical self: Anti-depressant consumption in women's recovery from depression'. *Health* 13, no. 4 (2009): 389–406.

Fullagar, Simone. 'Diffracting mind-body relations: Feminist materialism and the entanglement of physical culture in women's recovery from depression'. In *Sport, Physical Culture, and the Moving Body: Materialism, Technologies, Ecologies*, edited by Joshua Newman, Holly Thorpe, and David Andrews. 1–37. New Jersey: Rutgers University Press, 2017.

Fullagar, Simone. 'Post-qualitative inquiry and the new materialist turn: Implications for sport, health and physical culture research'. *Qualitative Research in Sport, Exercise and Health* 9, no. 2 (2017): 247–57.

Fullagar, Simone. 'A physical cultural studies perspective on physical (in) activity and health inequalities: The biopolitics of body practices and embodied movement'. *Revista Tempos e Espaços em Educação* 12, no. 28 (2019): 63–76.

Fullagar, Simone, and Adele Pavlidis. 'Feminist theories of emotion and affect in sport'. In *The Palgrave Handbook of Feminism and Sport, Leisure and Physical Education*, edited by Louise Mansfield et al., 447–62. London: Palgrave Macmillan, 2018.

Fullagar, Simone, Diana C. Parry, and Corey W. Johnson. 'Digital dilemmas through networked assemblages: Reshaping the gendered contours of our future'. In *Digital Dilemmas*, edited by Diana Parry et al., 225–43. London: Palgrave Macmillan, Cham, 2019.

Fullwiley, Duana. 'The biologistical construction of race: Admixture technology and the new genetic medicine'. *Social Studies of Science* 38, no. 5 (2008): 695–735.

Fullwiley, Duana. 'Race, genes, power'. *The British Journal of Sociology* 66, no. 1 (2015): 36–45.

Galton, Francis. *Inquiries into human faculty and its development*. London: Macmillan, 1883.

Gamboa, Cindybell, Monica Schuster, Eddie Schrevens, and Miet Maertens. *The Quinoa Boom and the Welfare of Smallholder Producers in the Andes*. No. 1067-2017-1142. 2017.

Garcia, Antero, and Roberto Santiago de Roock. 'Civic dimensions of critical digital literacies: Towards an abolitionist lens'. *Pedagogies: An International Journal* 16, no. 2 (2021): 187–201.

Garcia, Megan. 'Racist in the machine: The disturbing implications of algorithmic bias'. *World Policy Journal* 33, no. 4 (2016): 111–17.

Garfield, Craig F., Anthony Isacco, and Timothy E. Rogers. 'A review of men's health and masculinity'. *American Journal of Lifestyle Medicine* 2, no. 6 (2008): 474–87.

Garner, Samual A., and Jiyeon Kim. 'The privacy risks of direct-to-consumer genetic testing: A case study of 23andme and ancestry'. *Washington University Law Review* 96 (2018): 1219.

Garnham, Nicholas. *Capitalism and communication: Global culture and the economics of information*. California: Sage Publications, 1990.

Garver, Kenneth L., and Bettylee Garver. 'Eugenics: Past, present, and the future'. *American Journal of Human Genetics* 49, no. 5 (1991): 1109.

Gay, Roxane. *Hunger: A memoir of (my) body*. London, UK: HarperCollins, 2017.

Geertz, Clifford. 'Thick description: Toward an interpretive theory of culture'. *Turning Points in Qualitative Research: Tying Knots in a Handkerchief* 3 (1973): 143–68.

GenoPalate. 'What is insulin?' *GenoPalate*, 2019, https://www.genopalate.com/blogs/genopalate-glossary/insulin?_pos=1&_sid=2cd2b0238&_ss=r.

GenoPalate. 'Do you need a multi-vitamin?' *GenoPalate*, 8 May 2020, https://www.genopalate.com/blogs/news/do-you-need-a-multi-vitamin?_pos=5&_sid=ee93ac489&_ss=r.

GenoPalate. '5 Things you should know to maintain a healthy blood pressure'. GenoPalate. 10 November 2020, https://www.genopalate.com/blogs/ genopalate-digest/5-things-you-should-know-to-maintain-a-healthy-blood-pressure?_pos=3&_sid=2cd2b0238&_ss=r.

GenoPalate. 'A personalized approach to losing weight while living with type 2 diabetes'. *GenoPalate*, 10 November 2020, https://www.genopalate.com/blogs/genopalate-digest/weight-loss-type-2-diabetes?_pos=7&_sid=ee93ac489&_ss=r.

GenoPalate. 'Can a DNA test really tell you how to eat?' GenoPalate, 2020, https://www.genopalate.com/pages/our-science.

GenoPalate. 'Homepage'. *GenoPalate*, 2021, https://www.genopalate.com.

Gerber, Nina, Paul Gerber, and Melanie Volkamer. 'Explaining the privacy paradox: A systematic review of literature investigating privacy attitude and behavior'. *Computers & Security* 77 (2018): 226–61.

Gernalzick, Nadja. 2018. 'Sugar and the global south: Substance of new'.

GetFit App Google Play. GetFit apps. *Google Play*, 2021, https://play.google.com/store/apps/details?id=com.appyfurious.getfit&hl=en_GB&gl=US.

GetFit Apps. 'Homepage'. *GetFit Apps*, 2021, https://getfitapps.com.

GetFit: App Store. Home fitness workout by GetFit. *App Store*, 2021, https://apps.apple.com/gb/app/home-fitness-workout-by-getfit/id1273749004#?platform=appleWatch.

Ghita, Cristina. 'In defence of subjectivity: Autoethnography and studying technology non-use'. In *The 27th European Conference on Information Systems (ECIS), Stockholm & Uppsala, June 8–14, 2019.* Association for Information Systems (AIS), 2019.

Gibson, Gemma. 'Health (ism) at every size: The duties of the "good fatty"'. *Fat Studies* (2021): 1–14.

Giddens, Laurie, Ester Gonzalez, and Dorothy Leidner. 'I track, therefore I Am: Exploring the impact of wearable fitness devices on employee identity and well-being'. (2016): https://core.ac.uk/download/pdf/301368690.pdf.

Giesler, Markus, and Ela Veresiu. 'Creating the responsible consumer: Moralistic governance regimes and consumer subjectivity'. *Journal of Consumer Research* 41, no. 3 (2014): 840–57.

Gilford, Dawn. 'Are superfoods bad for the environment'. *Small Footprint Family*, 2020, https://www.smallfootprintfamily.com/are-superfoods-bad-for-environment.

Gill, Rosalind. 'Postfeminist media culture: Elements of a sensibility'. *European Journal of Cultural Studies* 10, no. 2 (2007): 147–66.

Gill, Rosalind, and Christina Scharff, eds. *New femininities: Postfeminism, neoliberalism and subjectivity.* New York: Springer, 2013.

Gill, Rosalind. 'Postfeminism and the new cultural life of feminism'. *Diffractions* 6 (2016): 1–8.

Gill, Rosalind. 'The affective, cultural and psychic life of postfeminism: A postfeminist sensibility 10 years on'. *European Journal of Cultural Studies* 20, no. 6 (2017): 606–26.

Gillborn, David, and Gloria Ladson-Billings. *Critical race theory.* Thousand Oaks: Sage Publications Limited, 2020.

Gillespie, Stuart, and Mara van den Bold. 'Agriculture, food systems, and nutrition: Meeting the challenge'. *Global Challenges* 1, no. 3 (2017): 1600002 (1–12).

Gilmore, Ruth Wilson. *Golden gulag: Prisons, surplus, crisis, and opposition in globalizing California*. Vol. 2. Berkeley: University of California Press, 2007.

Gilroy, Paul. 'Nationalism, history and ethnic absolutism'. *History Workshop*, no. 30. Oxford: Oxford University Press, 1990.

Gimpel, Henner, Marcia Nißen, and Roland Görlitz. 'Quantifying the quantified self: A study on the motivations of patients to track their own health'. *VAIS eLibrary* (2013), https://aisel.aisnet.org/icis2013/proceedings/HealthcareIS/3/.

Gkiouleka, Anna, Tim Huijts, Jason Beckfield, and Clare Bambra. 'Understanding the micro and macro politics of health: Inequalities, intersectionality & institutions-A research agenda'. *Social Science & Medicine* 200 (2018): 92–8.

Godsland, Ian F. 'Metabolism, biopower, and race'. *The Lancet Diabetes & Endocrinology* 5, no. 3 (2017): 164.

Gonzalez-Polledo, Elena. 'Can digital health save democracy? Meeting the cosmopolitical challenge of digital worlds'. *Journal of Social and Political Psychology* 6, no. 2 (2018): 631–43.

Goody, Jack, and John Rankine Goody. *Cooking, cuisine and class: A study in comparative sociology*. Cambridge: Cambridge University Press, 1982.

Gordon, Aubrey. 'As coronavirus rages, we need to talk about medical anti-fat bias'. *Shape*, 21 December 2020a, https://www.self.com/story/coronavirus-medical-anti-fat-bias.

Gordon, Aubrey. *What we don't talk about when we talk about fat*. Boston: Beacon Press, 2020b.

Gough, Annette, and Hilary Whitehouse. 'Challenging amnesias: Re-collecting feminist new materialism/ecofeminism/climate/education'. *Environmental Education Research* 26, no. 9–10 (2020): 1420–34.

Govinnage, Sunili. 'Coconut oil, teff and quinoa: Increased "superfoods" demand hits the south in the guts'. *The Guardian*, September 2014, https://www.theguardian.com/commentisfree/2014/sep/24/coconut-oil-teff-and-quinoa-increased-superfoods-demand-hits-the-south-in-the-guts.

Graham, Phil. 'Issues in political economy'. *Handbook of Media Management and Economics* (2006): 493–519.

Grand View Research. 'Superfoods Market Size, Share & Trends Analysis Report by Type (Fruits, Vegetables, Grains & Seeds), by Application (Bakery & Confectionery, Snacks, Beverages), by Region, and Segment Forecasts, 2019–2025'. *Grand View Research*, October 2019, https://www.grandviewresearch.com/industry-analysis/superfood-market.

Greco, Monica. 'Psychosomatic subjects and the "duty to be well". Personal agency within'. *Economy and Society* 22, no. 3 (1993): 357–72.

Greely, Henry T. 'Genetic genealogy'. In *Revisiting Race in a Genomic Age*, edited by Jonathan Marks, et al., 215–34. New Jersey: Rutgers University Press, 2008.

Green, Kenneth. 'Shaping technologies and shaping markets: Creating demand for biotechnology'. *Technology Analysis & Strategic Management* 3, no. 1 (1991): 57–76.

Greenfield, Dana 'Deep data: Notes on the n of 1'. In *Quantified: Biosensing Technologies in Everyday Life*, edited by Dawn Nafus, 123–47. Cambridge: MIT Press, 2016.

Greenhalgh, Susan. *Fat-talk nation*. Ithaca: Cornell University Press, 2015.

Griffin, Meghan. 'Somatechnologies of body size modification: Posthuman embodiment and discourses of health'. 2012. PhD. Dissertation, University of Central Florida, https://stars.library.ucf.edu/etd/2387/.

Grosz, Elizabeth A. *Volatile bodies: Toward a corporeal feminism*. Bloomington: Indiana University Press, 1994.

Grosz, Elizabeth A. eds. *Becomings: Explorations in time, memory, and futures*. New York: Cornell University Press, 1999.

Guraseh, Baby. 'Baby Guraseh'. *Aduna*, 2021, https://aduna.com/blogs/our-producers-case-studies/baby-guraseh.

Gurrieri, Lauren, Jan Brace-Govan, and Josephine Previte. 'Neoliberalism and managed health: Fallacies, façades and inadvertent effects'. *Journal of Macromarketing* 34, no. 4 (2014): 532–8.

Guthman, Julie, and Melanie DuPuis. 'Embodying neoliberalism: Economy, culture, and the politics of fat'. *Environment and Planning D: Society and Space* 24, no. 3 (2006): 427–48.

Guthman, Julie. *Weighing in: Obesity, food justice, and the limits of capitalism*. Berkeley: University of California Press, 2011.

Guthman, Julie. 'Fatuous measures: The artifactual construction of the obesity epidemic'. *Critical Public Health* 23, no. 3 (2013): 263–73.

Gutin, Iliya. 'Essential (ist) medicine: Promoting social explanations for racial variation in biomedical research'. *Medical Humanities* 45, no. 3 (2019): 224–34.

Haggerty, Kevin D., and Richard V. Ericson. 'The surveillant assemblage'. *The British Journal of Sociology* 51, no. 4 (2000): 605–22.

Hale, Timothy M., Wen-Ying Sylvia Chou, Shelia R. Cotton, and Aneka Khilnani, eds. *eHealth: Current evidence, promises, perils and future directions*. Bradford: Emerald Publishing Limited, 2018.

Hall, Stuart. 'Cultural studies and the centre: Some problematics and problems'. *Culture, Media, Language* (1980): 15–47.

Hall, Stuart. 'Cultural identity and diaspora'. In *Colonial Discourse and Postcolonial Theory*, edited by R. J. Patrick Williams and Laura Chrisman, 392–403. New York: Columbia University Press, 1994.

Hall, Stuart, and Bram Gieben. 'The west and the rest: Discourse and power'. *Race and Racialization, 2E: Essential Readings* (1992): 85–95.

Hall, Stuart, and Paul Du Gay, eds. *Questions of cultural identity*. London: Sage, 2006.

Hall, Stuart. 'The problem of ideology: Marxism without guarantees'. In *Stuart Hall: Critical Dialogues in Cultural Studies*, edited by Kuan-Hsing Chen and David Morley, 25–46. London: Routledge, 1997.

Hannah-Moffat, Kelly. 'Actuarial sentencing: An "unsettled" proposition'. *Justice Quarterly* 30, no. 2 (2013): 270–96.

Hansen, Mark Boris Nicola. *New philosophy for new media*. Massachusetts: MIT Press, 2004.

Haraway, Donna. 'Situated knowledges: The science question in feminism and the privilege of partial perspective'. *Feminist Studies* 14, no. 3 (1988): 575–99.

Haraway, Donna J., and Thyrza Goodeve. *Modest_Witness@ Second_Millennium. FemaleMan_Meets_OncoMouse: Feminism and technoscience*. New York: Routledge, 1997.

Haraway, Donna Jeanne. *The Haraway reader*. Sussex: Psychology Press, 2004.

Haraway, Donna. 'When species meet: Staying with the trouble'. *Environment and Planning D: Society and Space* 28, no. 1 (2010): 53–5.

Haraway, Donna. *Simians, cyborgs, and women: The reinvention of nature*. New York: Routledge, 2013.

Haraway, Donna. 'Anthropocene, capitalocene, plantationocene, chthulucene: Making kin'. *Environmental Humanities* 6, no. 1 (2015): 159–65.

Haraway, Donna J. *Manifestly Haraway*. Vol. 37. Minneapolis: University of Minnesota Press, 2016a.

Haraway, Donna J. *Staying with the trouble: Making kin in the Chthulucene*. Durham: Duke University Press, 2016b.

Haraway, Donna. 'Staying with the trouble for multispecies environmental justice'. *Dialogues in Human Geography* 8, no. 1 (2018): 102–5.

Harbers, Hans. *Inside the politics of technology: Agency and normativity in the co-production of technology and society*. Amsterdam: Amsterdam University Press, 2005.

Hardey, Mariann. 'On the body of the consumer: Performance-seeking with wearables and health and fitness apps'. *Sociology of Health & Illness* (2019): 991–1004.

Harding, Sandra G., ed. *The feminist standpoint theory reader: Intellectual and political controversies*. Sussex: Psychology Press, 2004.

Harding, Sandra. *Sciences from below: Feminisms, postcolonialities, and modernities*. Durham: Duke University Press, 2008.

Harper, A. Breeze, ed. *Sistah vegan: Black female vegans speak on food, identity, health, and society*. New York: Lantern Books, 2009.

Harris, Nathan. 'How to create a corporate wellness plan using nutrigenomics'. *Ease Academy*, 15 March 2019, https://itsease.com/academy/how-to-create-a-corporate-wellness-plan/.

Harris, Oliver J. T., and John Robb. 'Multiple ontologies and the problem of the body in history'. *American Anthropologist* 114, no. 4 (2012): 668–79.

Harrison, Christy. *Anti-Diet: Reclaim your time, money, well-being, and happiness through intuitive eating*. Hachette: Little Brown, 2019.

Hatch, Anthony Ryan. *Blood sugar: Racial pharmacology and food justice in Black America*. Minnesota: University of Minnesota Press, 2016.

Hayes-Conroy, Allison, and Jessica Hayes-Conroy. 'Feminist nutrition: Difference, decolonization, and dietary change'. In *Doing Nutrition Differently: Critical Approaches to Diet and Dietary Intervention*, edited by Alison Hayes-Conroy, 173–88. New York: Routledge, 2013.

Hayes-Conroy, Allison, and Jessica Hayes-Conroy. 'Political ecology of the body: A visceral approach'. In *The International Handbook of Political Ecology*, edited by Raymond Bryant, 659–672. Cheltanham: Edward Elgar Publishing, 2015.

Hayles, Katherine N. 'Revealing and transforming: How literature revalues computational practice'. *Performance Research* 11, no. 4 (2006): 5–16.

Hayles, Katherine N. *How we became posthuman: Virtual bodies in cybernetics, literature, and informatics*. Chicago: University of Chicago Press, 2008.

Health Warrior. 'Homepage'. *Health Warrior*. 2021a, https://www.healthwarrior.com.

Health Warrior. 'Our beginnings: A story rooted in seeds'. *Health Warrior*. 2021b, https://www.healthwarrior.com/pages/a-story-rooted-in-seeds.

Heath, Deborah, Rayna Rapp, and Karen-Sue Taussig. 'Genetic citizenship'. In *A Companion to the Anthropology of Politics*, edited by Joan Vincent, 152–67. New York: John Wiley & Sons, 2004.

Hebdige, Dick. *Subculture and the meaning of style*. London: Metheun Press, 2012.

Hedegaard, Liselotte, and Valerie Hémar-Nicolas. 'Rethinking food well-being as reconciliation between pleasure and sustainability'. *International Journal of Food Design* 5, no. 1–2 (2020): 157–66.

Heidegger, Martin. *The question concerning technology*. New York: Harper and Row, 1977.

Heldke, Lisa. *Exotic appetites: Ruminations of a food adventurer*. New York: Routledge, 2015.

Henderson, Julie Anne, Paul Russell Ward, John David Coveney, and Anne Taylor. Health is the number one thing we go for: Healthism, citizenship and food choice. *The Future of Sociology Conference*, 2009, http://www.tasa.org.au/tasa-conference/past-tasa-conferences/2009-tasa-conference/.

Henderson, Tonya L., and D. M. Gly Solutions. 'Sociomaterial fractals in a quantum storytelling frame'. Big Story Conference 2015 Los Angeles, CA. https://davidboje.com/quantum/pdfs_Proceedings_BigStory_2015/Henderson%20Fractals%20&%20QST%202015%20FINAL.pdf.

Heyes, Cressida J. 'Foucault goes to weight watchers'. *Hypatia* 21, no. 2 (2006): 126–49.

Hill Collins, Patricia. *Black feminist thought: Knowledge, consciousness, and the politics of empowerment*. New York: Routledge, 1991.

Hinton, Peta, Tara Mehrabi, and Josef Barla. 'New materialisms/New colonialisms'. Unpublished manuscript, Åbo Akademi University, Finland, 2015.

Hinze, Susan W., Jielu Lin, and Tanetta E. Andersson. 'Can we capture the intersections? Older Black women, education, and health'. *Women's Health Issues* 22, no. 1 (2012): e91–e98.

Hird, Myra J. 'The corporeal generosity of maternity'. *Body & Society* 13, no. 1 (2007): 1–20.

Hite, Adele H. 'A material-discursive exploration of "healthy food" and the dietary guidelines for Americans'. PhD diss., North Carolina State University, 2019.

Ho, Calvin WL, Joseph Ali, and Karel Caals. 'Ensuring trustworthy use of artificial intelligence and big data analytics in health insurance'. *Bulletin of the World Health Organization* 98, no. 4 (2020): 263–9.

Holford, W. David. 'An agential realist perspective on the construction and flow of knowledge: The case of dynamic entanglement and "cuts" within an aircraft engine manufacturing workplace'. *Journal of Knowledge Management* (2018): https://doi.org/10.1108/JKM-08-2017-0342.

Holt, Nicholas L. 'Representation, legitimation, and autoethnography: An autoethnographic writing story'. *International Journal of Qualitative Methods* 2, no. 1 (2003): 18–28.

Hood, Jacob. 'Making the body electric: The politics of body-worn cameras and facial recognition in the United States'. *Surveillance & Society* 18, no. 2 (2020): 157–69.

hooks, bell. *Feminist theory: From margin to center*. Boston: South End Press, 1988.

hooks, bell. 'Eating the other: Desire and resistance'. In *Media and Cultural Studies: Key Works*, edited by M. G. Durham and Douglas Kellner, 424–48. Malden, MA: Blackwell Publishers, 1992.

hooks, bell. *Black looks: Race and representation*. London: Routledge, 2019.

Horst, Heather, et al. 'Quotidian care at a distance'. In *Digital Media Practices in Households: Kinship through Data*, edited by Hjorth et al., 163–86. Amsterdam: Amsterdam University Press, 2020.

Hosman, Elliot. 'Genetic surveillance: Consumer genomics and DNA forensics'. *Biopolitical Times*, 29 October 2015, https://www.geneticsandsociety.org/biopolitical-times/genetic-surveillance-consumer-genomics-and-dna-forensics.

Howe, Jeff. *Crowdsourcing: How the power of the crowd is driving the future of business*. New York: Random House, 2008.

Hoyer, Wayne D., and Nicola E. Stokburger-Sauer. 'The role of aesthetic taste in consumer behavior'. *Journal of the Academy of Marketing Science* 40, no. 1 (2012): 167–80.

Hsu, Hansen, and Trevor Pinch. 'Affordances and theories of materiality in STS'. (2008), https://www.academia.edu/download/54003408/Materiality_Paper.pdf.

Huggan, Graham. *The postcolonial exotic: Marketing the margins*. New: York: Routledge, 2002.

Hultman, Karin, and Hillevi Lenz Taguchi. 'Challenging anthropocentric analysis of visual data: A relational materialist methodological approach to educational research'. *International Journal of Qualitative Studies in Education* 23, no. 5 (2010): 525–42.

Hummel, Patrik, Matthias Braun, Max Tretter, and Peter Dabrock. 'Data sovereignty: A review'. *Big Data & Society* 8, no. 1 (2021): 2053951720982012.

Hussey, Ian, and Joe Curnow. 'Fair Trade, neocolonial developmentalism, and racialized power relations'. *Interface* 5, no. 1 (2013): 40–68.

Hynnä, Kaisu, and Katariina Kyrölä. '"Feel in your body": Fat activist affects in blogs'. *Social Media+Society* 5, no. 4 (2019): 2056305119879983.

Ingold, Tim. *The perception of the environment: Essays on livelihood, dwelling and skill.* New York: Routledge, 2002.

Intrado. 'Global superfoods market (2020 to 2026) – by type, application, region, industry analysis and forecast'. *Intrado: Global News Wire*, 19 May 2020, https://www.globenewswire.com/news-release/2020/05/19/2035483/0/en/Global-Superfoods-Market-2020-to-2026-By-Type-Application-Region-Industry-Analysis-and-Forecast.html.

Ivancic, Sonia R. 'Body sovereignty and body liability in the wake of an "obesity epidemic": A poststructural analysis of the soda ban'. *Health Communication* 33, no. 10 (2018): 1243–56.

Jackson, Peter. 'Food stories: Consumption in an age of anxiety'. *Cultural Geographies* 17, no. 2 (2010): 147–65.

Jäger, Siegfried. 'Discourse and knowledge: Theoretical and methodological aspects of a critical discourse and dispositive analysis'. *Methods of Critical Discourse Analysis* 1 (2001): 32–63.

Jensen, Casper Bruun. 'Developing/development cyborgs'. *Phenomenology and the Cognitive Sciences* 7, no. 3 (2008): 375–85.

Johnson-Jennings, Michelle, Shanondora Billiot, and Karina Walters. 'Returning to our roots: Tribal health and wellness through land-based healing'. *Genealogy* 4, no. 3 (2020): 91.

Johnson, Lauren. 'Adapting and combining constructivist grounded theory and discourse analysis: A practical guide for research'. *International Journal of Multiple Research Approaches* 8, no. 1 (2014): 100–16.

Johnston, Josée, and Shyon Baumann. 'Democracy versus distinction: A study of omnivorousness in gourmet food writing'. *American Journal of Sociology* 113, no. 1 (2007): 165–204.

Johnston, Josée, and Shyon Baumann. *Foodies: Democracy and distinction in the gourmet foodscape.* London: Routledge, 2014.

Johnston, Josée, Andrew Biro, and Norah MacKendrick. 'Lost in the supermarket: The corporate-organic foodscape and the struggle for food democracy'. *Antipode* 41, no. 3 (2009): 509–32.

Kaboré, Donatien, Hagrétou Sawadogo-Lingani, Bréhima Diawara, Clarisse S. Compaoré, Mamoudou H. Dicko, and Mogens Jakobsen. 'A review of baobab (Adansonia digitata) products: Effect of processing techniques, medicinal properties and uses'. *African Journal of Food Science* 5, no. 16 (2011): 833–44.

Kahn, Jonathan. *Race in a bottle: The story of BiDil and racialized medicine in a post-genomic age.* New York: Columbia University Press, 2012.

Kamphuis, Carlijn BM, Tessa Jansen, Johan P. Mackenbach, and Frank J. Van Lenthe. 'Bourdieu's cultural capital in relation to food choices: A systematic review of cultural capital indicators and an empirical proof of concept'. *PloS One* 10, no. 8 (2015): e0130695.

Kant, Immanuel. *Immanuel Kant* (Vol. 1). Norderstedt: Agentur des Rauhen Hauses, 1906.

Kant, Immanuel. 'Critique of pure reason. 1781'. In *Modern Classical Philosophers*. Cambridge: Houghton Mifflin, 1908.

Kapoor, Ilan. 'Hyper-self-reflexive development? Spivak on representing the Third World "Other"'. *Third World Quarterly* 25, no. 4 (2004): 627–47.

Katwala, Amit. 'The spurious, questionable science behind DNA testing kits'. *Wired*, 30 May 2019, https://www.wired.co.uk/article/dna-testing-kits-science.

Kbv Research. 'Superfood market size. Kbv Research'. May 2020, https://www.kbvresearch.com/superfoods-market/.

Kennedy, Brett Patrick. *Masculinity, eating, and exercise: The relationship of men to their bodies*. Berkeley: California School of Professional Psychology-Berkeley/Alameda, 2000.

Kent, Rachael. 'Self-tracking health over time: From the use of Instagram to perform optimal health to the protective shield of the digital detox'. *Social Media+Society* 6, no. 3 (2020): 2056305120940694.

Kimura, Aya Hirata. '2. Charismatic nutrients'. In *Hidden Hunger*, 19–38. Ithaca: Cornell University Press, 2013a.

Kimura, Aya Hirata. *Hidden hunger: Gender and the politics of smarter foods*. Ithaca: Cornell University Press, 2013b.

Kirkpatrick, Keith. 'Battling algorithmic bias: How do we ensure algorithms treat us fairly?' *Communications of the ACM* 59, no. 10 (2016): 16–17.

Kittles, Rick A., and Kenneth M. Weiss. 'Race, ancestry, and genes: Implications for defining disease risk'. *Annual Review of Genomics and Human Genetics* 4, no. 1 (2003): 33–67.

Klosowski, Thorin. 'We checked 250 iPhone apps—this is how they're tracking you'. *The New York Times*, 6 May 2021, https://www.nytimes.com/wirecutter/blog/how-iphone-apps-track-you/.

KnowTheChain. 'Xiaomi Corp'. *KnowTheChain*, 2020, https://knowthechain.org/wp-content/uploads/2020_KTC_ICT_Scorecard_Xiaomi.pdf.

Koerber, A. 'Toward a feminist rhetoric of technology'. *Journal of Business and Technical Communication* 14, no. 1 (2000): 58–73.

Korthals, Michiel. 'Food styles and the future of nutrigenomics'. In *Nutrition and Genomics: Issues of Ethics, Law, Regulation and Communication*, edited by David Castle and Nola Ries, 263–79. Cambridge: Academic Press, 2009.

Kozel, Susan. 'Re-Embodiment: New strategies for teaching embodied interaction'. In *CUMULUS Kolding 2017, Kolding, Denmark (2017)*, 107–16. Cumulus International Association of Universities and Colleges of Art, Design and Media, 2017.

Kronfli, Basil. 'Xiaomi is undercutting the whole tech industry. And it's working'. *Wired*, 20 February 2021, https://www.wired.co.uk/article/xiaomi-product-guide.

Krupar, Shiloh, and Nadine Ehlers. 'Target: Biomedicine and racialized geo-body-politics' (2013). Faculty of Law, Humanities and the Arts – Papers. 2056. https://ro.uow.edu.au/lhapapers/2056.

Kukla, Rebecca. 'Medicalization,"normal function," and the definition of health'. In *The Routledge Companion to Bioethics*, edited by John D. Arras, Elizabeth Fenton, and Rebecca Kukla, 539–54. London: Routledge, 2014.

Laczo, Lilla. Why Jason Loewy built MyMacros+ the best diet tracking app. 20 Minute Fitness Episode 60, 2018, https://www.shapescale.com/blog/20-minute-fitness-podcast/why-jason-loewy-built-mymacros-a-diet-tracking-app/.

Lakkis, Jacqueline, Lina A. Ricciardelli, and Robert J. Williams. 'Role of sexual orientation and gender-related traits in disordered eating'. *Sex Roles* 41, no. 1 (1999): 1–16.

Lamb, Sarah. 'On being (not) Old: Agency, self-care, and life-course aspirations in the United States'. *Medical Anthropology Quarterly* 33, no. 2 (2019): 263–81.

Lange, Jochen. 'Platform stabilization: an autoethnographic exploration of the multiple relations and role of data behind the interface of online tutoring software'. *Critical Studies in Education* 62, no. 1 (2020): 1–15.

Langley, Paul. 'Crowdfunding in the United Kingdom: A cultural economy'. *Economic geography* 92, no. 3 (2016): 301–21.

Larsen, Kristian, Anette Lykke Hindhede, Mikkel Haderup Larsen, Mathias Holst Nicolaisen, and Frederik Møller Henriksen. 'Bodies need yoga? No plastic surgery! Naturalistic versus instrumental bodies among professions in the Danish healthcare field'. *Social Theory & Health* (2020): 1–20.

Laslett, Barbara. 'Personal narratives as sociology'. *Contemporary Sociology* 28, no. 4 (1999): 391–401.

Latour, Bruno. *Science in action: How to follow scientists and engineers through society.* Cambridge: Harvard University Press, 1987.

Latour, Bruno. 'Technology is society made durable'. *The Sociological Review* 38, no. 1 suppl (1990): 103–31.

Latour, Bruno. *Politics of nature: How to bring the sciences into democracy.* Cambridge: Harvard University Press, 2004.

Latour, Bruno. *Reassembling the social: An introduction to actor-network-theory.* Oxford: Oxford University Press, 2005.

Latour, Bruno. 'Nonhumans'. In *Patterned Ground: Entanglements of Nature and Culture*, edited by Stephen Harrison, Steve Pile, and Nigel Thrift, 224–7. London: Reaktion, 2004.

Lawrence, Jane. 'The Indian health service and the sterilization of Native American women'. *American Indian Quarterly* 24, no. 3 (2000): 400–19.

Lazuka, Rebecca F., Madeline R. Wick, Pamela K. Keel, and Jennifer A. Harriger. 'Are we there yet? Progress in depicting diverse images of beauty in Instagram's body positivity movement'. *Body Image* 34 (2020): 85–93.

Le Billon, Philippe, and Lauren Shykora. 'Conflicts, commodities and the environmental geopolitics of supply chains'. In *A Research Agenda for Environmental Geopolitics.* Cheltenham: Edward Elgar Publishing, 2020.

LeBesco, Kathleen. 'Fat panic and the new morality'. In *Against Health*, edited by Jonathan Metzl, Anna Kirkland, and Anna Rutherford Kirkland, 72–82. New York University Press, 2010.

Leichter, Howard M. 'Lifestyle correctness and the new secular morality'. In *Morality and Health*, edited by Allan M. Brandt and Paul Rozin, 359–78. New York: London: Routledge, 1997.

Leighten, Patricia. 'The white peril and L'art nègre: Picasso, primitivism, and anticolonialism'. *The Art Bulletin* 72, no. 4 (1990): 609–30.

Lemke, Thomas. 'New materialisms: Foucault and the "government of things"'. *Theory, Culture & Society* 32, no. 4 (2015): 3–25.

Leone, Massimo. 'Critique of the culinary reason'. *Semiotica* 2016, no. 211 (2016): 165–86.

Leone, Massimo. 'Time and meaning: A cultural semiotics of temporal and aspectual ideologies'. *LEXIA*, (2017): 17–63.

Lerner, Richard M. 'Promoting positive development, health, and social justice through dismantling genetic determinism'. In *Individuals as Producers of Their Own Development*, edited by Richard M. Lerner, 367–84. New York: Routledge, 2021.

Levinson-Waldman, Rachel. 'Cellphones, law enforcement, and the right to privacy'. *Brennan Center for Justice*, 20 December 2018, https://www.brennancenter.org/sites/default/files/publications/2018_12_CellSurveillanceV3.pdf.

LinkedIn. 'GetFit Apps'. LinkedIn, 2021, https://www.linkedin.com/company/getfit-apps/about/.

Lisao, Klushetile, Coert Johannes Geldenhuys, and Paxie W. Chirwa. 'Assessment of the African baobab (Adansonia digitata L.) populations in Namibia: Implications for conservation'. *Global Ecology and Conservation* 14 (2018): https://doi.org/10.1016/j.gecco.2018.e00386.

Lisao, Klushetile, Coert Johannes Geldenhuys, and Paxie W. Chirwa. 'Traditional uses and local perspectives on baobab (Adansonia digitata) population structure by selected ethnic groups in northern Namibia'. *South African Journal of Botany* 113 (2017): 449–56.

Lloyd, Genevieve. 'Spinoza on the distinction between intellect and will'. In *Spinoza: Issues and Directions*, edited by Edwin M. Curley and Pierre-François Moreau, 113–23. Leiden: Brill, 1990.

Lock, Margaret. 'Comprehending the body in the era of the epigenome'. *Current Anthropology* 56, no. 2 (2015): 151–77.

Long, Lisa A. 'Contemporary women's roles through Hmong, Vietnamese, and American eyes'. *Frontiers: A Journal of Women Studies* 29, no. 1 (2008): 1–36.

Longhurst, Robyn. 'Becoming smaller: Autobiographical spaces of weight loss'. *Antipode* 44, no. 3 (2012): 871–88.

Loomba, Ania. *Colonialism/postcolonialism*. London: Routledge, 2007.

López, Nancy. 'Contextualizing lived race-gender and the racialized-gendered social determinants of health'. *Mapping 'race': Critical Approaches to Health Disparities Research* (2013): 179–211.

Loyer, Jessica. 'The social lives of superfoods'. PhD diss. University of Adelaide, 2016, https://digital.library.adelaide.edu.au/dspace/handle/2440/101777.

Loyer, Jessica. 'The cranberry as food, health food, and superfood: Challenging or maintaining hegemonic nutrition?' *Graduate Journal of Food Studies* 4, no. 2 (2017): https://gradfoodstudies.org/2017/11/11/cranberry-as-superfood/.

Loyer, Jessica, and Christine Knight. 'Selling the "Inca superfood": Nutritional primitivism in superfoods books and maca marketing'. *Food, Culture & Society* 21, no. 4 (2018): 449–67.

Lukes, Erin. 'Rihanna just revealed Fenty skin's first products – and we have the details'. *InStyle*, 27 July 2020, https://www.instyle.com/beauty/skin/rihanna-fenty-skin-products.

Lupton, Deborah. 'M-health and health promotion: The digital cyborg and surveillance society'. *Social Theory & Health* 10, no. 3 (2012a): 229–44.

Lupton, Deborah. 'A sociological critique of the Health at Every Size movement'. *This Sociological Life*, 24 September 2012b, https://simplysociology.wordpress.com/2012/09/24/a-sociological-critique-of-the-health-at-every-size-movement/.

Lupton, Deborah. 'Quantifying the body: Monitoring and measuring health in the age of health technologies'. *Critical Public Health* 23, no. 4 (2013): 393–403.

Lupton, Deborah. 'Apps as artefacts: Towards a critical perspective on mobile health and medical apps'. *Societies* 4, no. 4 (2014a): 606–22.

Lupton, Deborah. 'Self-tracking cultures: Towards a sociology of personal informatics'. In *Proceedings of the 26th Australian Computer-human Interaction Conference on Designing Futures: The Future of Design*, 77–86, 2014b.

Lupton, Deborah. 'Self-Tracking modes: Reflexive self-monitoring and data practices paper for the "Imminent Citizenships: Personhood and Identity Politics in the Informatic Age" workshop, 27 August 2014'. *ANU, Canberra* (2014c).

Lupton, Deborah. 'Fabricated data bodies: Reflections on 3D printed digital body objects in medical and health domains'. *Social Theory & Health* 13, no. 2 (2015): 99–115.

Lupton, Deborah. 'Towards critical digital health studies: Reflections on two decades of research in health and the way forward'. *Health* 20, no. 1 (2016a): 49–61.

Lupton, Deborah. *The quantified self*. New Jersey: John Wiley & Sons, 2016b.

Lupton, Deborah. 'The diverse domains of quantified selves: Self-tracking modes and dataveillance'. *Economy and Society* 45, no. 1 (2016c): 101–22.

Lupton, Deborah. 'Lively data, social fitness and biovalue: The intersections of health self-tracking and social media'. *SSRN* (2017a). https://papers.ssrn.com/sol3/papers.cfm?abstract_id=3088205.

Lupton, Deborah. *Digital health: Critical and cross-disciplinary perspectives*. London: Routledge, 2017b.

Lupton, Deborah. '"I just want it to be done, done, done!" Food tracking apps, affects and agential capacities'. *Multimodal Technologies and Interaction* 2, no. 2 (2018a): 1–15.

Lupton, Deborah. 'Vitalities and visceralities: Alternative body/food politics in new digital media'. In *Alternative Food Politics: From the Margins to the Mainstream*, edited by Michelle Phillipov and Katherine Kirkwood. London: Routledge, 2018b.

Lupton, Deborah. *Fat*. London: Routledge, 2018c.

Lupton, Deborah. '"It's made me a lot more aware": A new materialist analysis of health self-tracking'. *Media International Australia* 171, no. 1 (2019): 66–79.

Lupton, Deborah. 'Caring dataveillance: Women's use of apps to monitor pregnancy and children'. In *The Routledge Companion to Digital Media and Children*, edited by Leila Green, 393–402. London: Routledge, 2020a.

Lupton, Deborah. 'Data mattering and self-tracking: What can personal data do?' *Continuum* 34, no. 1 (2020b): 1–13.

Lupton, Deborah. 'Sharing Is Caring'. *Australian Self-Trackers' Concepts and Practices of Personal Data Sharing and Privacy. Frontiers in Digital Health* (2021), doi: 10.3389/fdgth.

Lupton, Deborah, and Sarah Maslen. 'The more-than-human sensorium: Sensory engagements with digital self-tracking technologies'. *The Senses and Society* 13, no. 2 (2018): 190–202.

Lutz, Helma. 'Intersectionality as method'. *DiGeSt. Journal of Diversity and Gender Studies* 2, no. 1–2 (2015): 39–44.

Lyles, Courtney R., Robert M. Wachter, and Urmimala Sarkar. 'Focusing on digital health equity'. *JAMA* 326, no. 18 (2021): 1795–1796.

MacGregor, Casimir, Alan Petersen, and Christine Parker. 'Hyping the market for "anti-ageing" in the news: From medical failure to success in self-transformation'. *BioSocieties* 13, no. 1 (2018): 64–80.

Macia, Enguerran, Priscilla Duboz, and Dominique Chevé. 'The paradox of impossible beauty: Body changes and beauty practices in aging women'. *Journal of Women & Aging* 27, no. 2 (2015): 174–87.

MacNevin, Audrey. 'Exercising options: Holistic health and technical beauty in gendered accounts of bodywork'. *The Sociological Quarterly* 44, no. 2 (2003): 271–89.

Madden, Mary, Michele Gilman, Karen Levy, and Alice Marwick. 'Privacy, poverty, and big data: A matrix of vulnerabilities for poor Americans'. *Washington University Law Review* 95, no. 1 (2017): 53–125.

Madsen, Deborah L., ed. *The Routledge companion to native American literature*. New York: Routledge, 2015.

Mannur, Anita. 'Culinary nostalgia: Authenticity, nationalism, and diaspora'. *Melus* 32, no. 4 (2007): 11–31.

Mansell, Robin. 'Bits of power: Struggling for control of information and communication networks'. *The Political Economy of Communication* 5, no. 1 (2017), http://www.polecom.org/index.php/polecom/article/view/75.

Mansfield, Louise, and Emma Rich. 'Public health pedagogy, border crossings and physical activity at every size'. *Critical Public Health* 23, no. 3 (2013): 356–70.

Markula, Pirkko. 'The technologies of the self: Sport, feminism, and Foucault'. *Sociology of Sport Journal* 20, no. 2 (2003): 87–107.

Masson, Estelle, Sandrine Bubendorff, and Christèle Fraïssé. 'Toward new forms of meal sharing? Collective habits and personal diets'. *Appetite* 123 (2018): 108–13.

Massumi, Brian. *Politics of affect*. New Jersey: John Wiley & Sons, 2015.

Masuoka, Natalie. 'Reconsidering race: Social science perspectives on racial categories in the age of genomics'. *Perspectives on Politics* 17, no. 2 (2019): 587–9.

Matsuda, Mari. 'Grounding intersectionality: Critical foundations and trajectories'. Paper presented at the 4th Annual Critical Race Studies Annual Symposium on Intersectionalities, Los Angeles, CA, 11 March 2011.

Mauss, Marcel. *The gift: The form and reason for exchange in archaic societies*. New York: Routledge, 2002.

Mayes, Christopher. *The biopolitics of lifestyle: Foucault, ethics and healthy choices*. New York: Routledge, 2015.

McAfee, Kathleen. 'Neoliberalism on the molecular scale. Economic and genetic reductionism in biotechnology battles'. *Geoforum* 34, no. 2 (2003): 203–19.

McBlane, Angus. 'Expressing corporeal silence: Phenomenology, Merleau-Ponty, and posthumanism'. *Word and Text: A Journal of Literary Studies and Linguistics* 6, no. 1 (2016): 149–61.

McCarthy, Michael. 'Experts warn on data security in health and fitness apps'. *BMJ: British Medical Journal (Online)* 347 (2013).

McChesney, Robert W. *The political economy of media: Enduring issues, emerging dilemmas*. New York: New York University Press, 2008.

McDonald, Whitney S., et al. 'Genetic testing and employer-sponsored wellness programs: An overview of current vendors, products, and practices'. *Molecular Genetics & Genomic Medicine* 8, no. 10 (2020): 1–19.

McDonell, Emma. 'Miracle foods: Quinoa, curative metaphors, and the depoliticization of global hunger politics'. *Gastronomica* 15, no. 4 (2015): 70–85.

McGillivray, David. 'Fitter, happier, more productive: Governing working bodies through wellness'. *Culture and Organization* 11, no. 2 (2005): 125–38.

McMahon, Don D., et al. 'Digital health, fitness, and wellness tools for students with disabilities'. *Journal of Special Education Technology* (2022): https://journals.sagepub.com/doi/abs/10.1177/01626434221094795?casa_token=YegUDfvXDJMAA AAA:MVmv3FHPPaCWYpH7Z7TfTFx9t0hU6UeuLV05YdFRfKnU56jB_ uTLDyjP9sl-6DLvgQmm7N15Ir4HTw.

McMillan Cottom, Tressie. 'Where platform capitalism and racial capitalism meet: The sociology of race and racism in the digital society'. *Sociology of Race and Ethnicity* 6, no. 4 (2020): 441–9.

McNaughton, Darlene. 'From the womb to the tomb: Obesity and maternal responsibility'. *Critical Public Health* 21, no. 2 (2011): 179–90.

McRobbie, Angela. *The aftermath of feminism: Gender, culture and social change*. Los Angeles: Sage, 2009.

McRuer, Robert. 'Compulsory able-bodiedness and queer/disabled existence'. In *The Disability Studies Reader* 3, edited by Lennard J. Davis, 383–92. New York: Routledge, 2010.

McRuer, Robert. 'Queer/disabled existence'. In *The Disability Studies Reader*, edited by Lennard J. Davis, 88–90. London: Routledge, 2016.

McWhorter, Ladelle. 'From scientific racism to neoliberal biopolitics'. (2017), https://scholarship.richmond.edu/wgss-faculty-publications/11/.

Mellor, Philip A., and Chris Shilling. 'Body pedagogics and the religious habitus: A new direction for the sociological study of religion'. *Religion* 40, no. 1 (2010): 27–38.

Meneley, Anne. 'The olive and imaginaries of the Mediterranean'. *History and Anthropology* 31, no. 1 (2020): 66–83.

Menezes, Ellen, Rosires Deliza, Ho Lim Chan, and Jean-Xavier Guinard. 'Preferences and attitudes towards açaí-based products among North American consumers'. *Food Research International* 44, no. 7 (2011): 1997–2008.

Merleau-Ponty, Merleau. *Phenomenology of perception*. New Jersey: The Humanities Press, 1962.

Merleau-Ponty, Maurice. *Maurice Merleau-Ponty: Basic writings*. Sussex: Psychology Press, 2004.

Mersha, Tesfaye B., and Andrew F. Beck. 'The social, economic, political, and genetic value of race and ethnicity in 2020'. *Human Genomics* 14, no. 1 (2020): 1–5.

Merz, Sibille. '"Health and ancestry start here": Race and prosumption in direct-to-consumer genetic testing services'. *Ephemera: Theory & Politics in Organization* 16, no. 3 (2016): 1–20.

Metzl, Jonathan, Anna Kirkland, and Anna Rutherford Kirkland, eds. *Against health: How health became the new morality*. New York: NYU Press, 2010.

Meyer, Jochen, Steven Simske, Katie A. Siek, Cathal G. Gurrin, and Hermie Hermens. 'Beyond quantified self: Data for wellbeing'. In *CHI'14 Extended Abstracts on Human Factors in Computing Systems*, 95–8, 2014.

Meyerding, Stephan G. H., Annemone Kürzdörfer, and Birgit Gassler. 'Consumer preferences for superfood ingredients—The case of bread in Germany'. *Sustainability* 10, no. 12 (2018): 4667.

Miller, Amara Lindsay. 'Eating the other yogi: Kathryn Budig, the yoga industrial complex, and the appropriation of body positivity'. *Race and Yoga* 1, no. 1 (2016): 1–23.

Miller, Peter, and Nikolas Rose. 'Governing economic life'. *Economy and Society* 19, no. 1 (1990): 1–31.

Mintz, Sidney W., and Christine M. Du Bois. 'The anthropology of food and eating'. *Annual Review of Anthropology* 31, no. 1 (2002): 99–119.

Mintz, Sidney Wilfred. *Tasting food, tasting freedom: Excursions into eating, culture, and the past*. Boston: Beacon Press, 1996.

Mitchell, David, and Sharon Snyder. 'The eugenic Atlantic: Race, disability, and the making of an international eugenic science, 1800–1945'. *Disability & Society* 18, no. 7 (2003): 843–64.

Mitchell, Ronald B. 'Technology is not enough: Climate change, population, affluence, and consumption'. *The Journal of Environment & Development* 21, no. 1 (2012): 24–7.

Mogashoa, Tebogo. 'Understanding critical discourse analysis in qualitative research'. *International Journal of Humanities Social Sciences and Education* 1, no. 7 (2014): 104–13.

Mohanty, Chandra Talpade, Ann Russo, and Lourdes Torres, eds. *Third world women and the politics of feminism*. Vol. 632. Bloomington: Indiana University Press, 1991.

Mol, Annemarie. *The body multiple*. Durham: Duke University Press, 2003.

Mollow, Anna. 'Disability studies gets fat'. *Hypatia* 30, no. 1 (2015): 199–216.

Morder Intelligence. 'Superfoods market – growth, trends, Covid-19 impact, and forecasts (2021–2026)' *Mordor Intelligence*, 2021, https://www.mordorintelligence.com/industry-reports/superfoods-market.

Morello-Frosch, et al. 'Embodied health movements: Responses to a' scientized" world'. In *The New Political Sociology of Science: Institutions, Networks, and Power*, edited by Scott Frickel and Kelly Moore, 244–171. Madison: University of Wisconsin Press, 2006.

Morris, Amelia. 'Fat activism and body positivity: Freedom from dieting?' In *The Politics of Weight*, edited by Amelia Morris, 143–79. Stuttgart: Palgrave Macmillan, 2019a.

Morris, Amelia. *The politics of weight: Feminist dichotomies of power in dieting*. Berlin: Springer, 2019b.

Mosco, Vincent. 'Political economic theory and research: Conceptual foundations and current trends'. In *The Handbook of Media and Mass Communication Theory*, edited by Robert S. Fortner, P. Mark Fackler, 37–55. New York: John Wiley & Sons, 2014.

Motta, Sara, and A. Gunvald Nilsen, eds. *Social movements in the Global South: Dispossession, development and resistance*. New York: Springer, 2011.

Mudry, Jessica. *Measured meals: Nutrition in America*. Albany: Suny Press, 2009a.

Mudry, Jessica. 'The mindful measurement of food: Quantification, the food pyramid and discourses of taste'. *Material Culture Review/Revue de la culture matérielle* 70 (2009b): 12–22.

Mullings, Leith, and Amy J. Schulz. 'Intersectionality and health: An introduction'. In, *Gender, Race, Class, & Health: Intersectional Approaches*, edited by A. J. Schulz and L. Mullings, 3–17. San Francisco: Jossey-Bass/Wiley, 2006.

Muoio, Dave. 'Under Armour sells off MyFitnessPal for $345M, will shut down Endomondo by 2021'. *Mobile Health News*, 2 November 2020, https://www.mobihealthnews.com/news/under-armour-sells-myfitnesspal-345m-will-shut-down-endomondo-2021.

Murdock, Graham, and Peter Golding. 'For a political economy of mass communications'. *Socialist Register* 10 (1973): https://socialistregister.com/index.php/srv/article/view/5355.

Murdock, Graham, and Peter Golding. 'Political economy and media production: A reply to Dwyer'. *Media, Culture & Society* 38, no. 5 (2016): 763–9.

Murphy, Margi. 'Google factory workers are "underpaid and overworked."' *The Sunday Telegraph*, 11 November 2018, https://www.telegraph.co.uk/technology/2018/11/10/google-factory-workers-underpaid-overworked/.

Murphy, Michelle. 'Unsettling care: Troubling transnational itineraries of care in feminist health practices'. *Social Studies of Science* 45, no. 5 (2015): 717–37.

Murray, Samantha. *The 'Fat' female body*. New York: Springer, 2008.

Murray, Seb. 'SME Profile: Aduna'. *BusinessBecause*, 2014, https://www.businessbecause.com/news/mba-jobs/2312/sme-profile-aduna.

Mutch, David M., Michael A. Zulyniak, Iwona Rudkowska, and M. Elizabeth Tejero. 'Lifestyle genomics: Addressing the multifactorial nature of personalized health'. *Lifestyle Genomics* 11, no. 1 (2018): 1–8.

My Macros+. 'Homepage'. *My Macros+*, 2021, https://snip.ly/40ih8a#https://getmymacros.com/.

MyFitnessPal. 'Homepage'. *MyFitnessPal*, 2021, https://www.myfitnesspal.com.

Nash, Catherine. *Of Irish descent: Origin stories, genealogy, and the politics of belonging.* Syracuse: Syracuse University Press, 2008a.

Nash, Jennifer C. 'Re-thinking intersectionality'. *Feminist Review* 89, no. 1 (2008b): 1–15.

Nash, Catherine. 'The politics of genealogical incorporation: Ethnic difference, genetic relatedness and national belonging'. *Ethnic and Racial Studies* 40, no. 14 (2017): 2539–57.

Nash, Meredith. 'Let's work on your weaknesses': Australian CrossFit coaching, masculinity and neoliberal framings of "health"and "fitness"'. *Sport in Society* 21, no. 9 (2018): 1432–53.

Nature's Hearth Superfoods. 'Homepage'. *Natures Heart Superfoods*, 2021, https://www.naturesheartsuperfoods.co.uk.

Naughton, John. 'The evolution of the Internet: From military experiment to General Purpose Technology'. *Journal of Cyber Policy* 1, no. 1 (2016): 5–28.

Nelson, Alondra. 'Bio science: Genetic genealogy testing and the pursuit of African ancestry'. *Social Studies of Science* 38, no. 5 (2008): 759–83.

Nelson, Alondra. *The social life of DNA: Race, reparations, and reconciliation after the genome.* Boston: Beacon Press, 2016.

Nelson, Scott. 'Why the wellness business is booming (and how to succeed in the industry)'. *Forbes*, 14 October 2019, https://www.forbes.com/sites/forbesbusinessdevelopmentcouncil/2019/10/14/why-the-wellness-business-is-booming-and-how-to-succeed-in-the-industry/.

Nestlé. 'Nestlé acquires majority interest in Latin American company Terrafertil'. *Nestlé*, 9 February 2018, https://www.nestle.com/media/news/nestle-acquires-majority-interest-in-terrafertil.

Nixon, Brice. 'Dialectical method and the critical political economy of culture'. *tripleC: Communication, Capitalism & Critique. Open Access Journal for a Global Sustainable Information Society* 10, no. 2 (2012): 439–56.

Noble, Safiya Umoja. *Algorithms of oppression: How search engines reinforce racism.* New York: NYU Press, 2018.

Noor, Khairul Baharein Mohd. 'Case study: A strategic research methodology'. *American Journal of Applied Sciences* 5, no. 11 (2008): 1602–4.

Nordenfelt, Lennart Y. *On the nature of health: An action-theoretic approach.* Berlin: Springer Science & Business Media, 1995.

Norman, Moss E. 'Embodying the double-bind of masculinity: Young men and discourses of normalcy, health, heterosexuality, and individualism'. *Men and Masculinities* 14, no. 4 (2011): 430–49.

Novas, Carlos. 'The political economy of hope: Patients' organizations, science and biovalue'. *BioSocieties* 1, no. 3 (2006): 289–305.

Nunes, João Arriscado, and Marília Louvison. 'Epistemologies of the South and decolonization of health: For an ecology of care in collective health'. *Saúde e Sociedade* 29 (2020): https://www.scielosp.org/article/sausoc/2020.v29n3/e200563/en/.

NYRR. 'Homepage'. *New York Road Runners*, 2021: https://www.nyrr.org.

Okidegbe, Ngozi. 'When they hear us: Race, algorithms and the practice of criminal law'. *Kansas Journal of Law and Public Policy* 29 (2019): 329–38.

O.W.N. News Network. 'Mergers and acquisitions'. *Organic and Wellness News*, 2020, https://www.organicwellnessnews.com/?SectionID=19.

O'Connor, Martin. 'On the misadventures of capitalist nature'. *Capitalism Nature Socialism* 4, no. 3 (1993): 7–40.

O'Neill, Rachel. '"Glow from the inside out": Deliciously Ella and the politics of "healthy eating'. *European Journal of Cultural Studies* (2020): 1–22.

Office of National Statistics. 'Why have Black and South Asian people been hit hardest by COVID-19?' *Office of National Statistics*, 14 December 2021, https://www.ons.gov. uk/peoplepopulationandcommunity/healthandsocialcare/conditionsanddiseases/ articles/whyhaveblackandsouthasianpeoplebeenhithardestbycovid19/2020-12-14.

Orlikowski, Wanda J., and Susan V. Scott. '10 sociomateriality: Challenging the separation of technology, work and organization'. *Academy of Management Annals* 2, no. 1 (2008): 433–74.

Otero, Gerardo, Gabriela Pechlaner, and Efe Can Gürcan. 'The neoliberal diet: Fattening profits and people'. In *The Routledge Handbook of Poverty in the United States*, edited by Stephen Haymes, Maria Vidal De Haymes, and Reuben Miller, 504–11. New York: Routledge, 2014.

Oudshoorn, Nelly, Els Rommes, and Marcelle Stienstra. 'Configuring the user as everybody: Gender and design cultures in information and communication technologies'. *Science, Technology, & Human Values* 29, no. 1 (2004): 30–63.

Overend, Alissa, Meredith Bessey, Adele Hite, and Andrea Noriega. 'Introduction to against healthisms: Challenging the paradigm of 'eating right'. *Journal of Critical Dietetics* 5, no. 1 (2020): 1–3.

Owen, William F., Richard Carmona, and Claire Pomeroy. 'Failing another national stress test on health disparities'. *JAMA* 323, no. 19 (2020): 1905–6.

Owens, John, and Alan Cribb. '"My Fitbit Thinks I Can Do Better!" Do health promoting wearable technologies support personal autonomy?' *Philosophy & Technology* 32, no. 1 (2019): 23–38.

Owler. GenoPalate. *Owler*, 2020, https://www.owler.com/company/ genopalate#fundinghistory.

Pantzar, Mika, and Minna Ruckenstein. 'The heart of everyday analytics: Emotional, material and practical extensions in self-tracking market'. *Consumption Markets & Culture* 18, no. 1 (2015): 92–109.

Papacharalampous, Madgalini. 'A business opportunity in food industry: Natural food products that boost health and have healing attributes'. (2017). PhD. Dissertation. National Hellenic University, https://repository.ihu.edu.gr/xmlui/handle/11544/15918.

Papageorgiou, Achilleas, Michael Strigkos, Eugenia Politou, Efthimios Alepis, Agusti Solanas, and Constantinos Patsakis. 'Security and privacy analysis of mobile health applications: The alarming state of practice'. *IEEE Access* 6 (2018): 9390–403.

Parker-Gibson, Necia. 'Quinoa: Catalyst or catastrophe?' *Journal of Agricultural & Food Information* 16, no. 2 (2015): 113–22.

Parsons, Julie M. 'When convenience is inconvenient: "Healthy" family foodways and the persistent intersectionalities of gender and class'. *Journal of Gender Studies* 25, no. 4 (2016): 382–97.

Parsons, Zoe. 'Queering it up: The queering of food justice'. *The Editorial Board* (2018): 110–17, https://scholars.unh.edu/cgi/viewcontent.cgi?article=1014&context=commentary#page=110.

Parviainen, Jaana, and Johanna Aromaa. 'Bodily knowledge beyond motor skills and physical fitness: A phenomenological description of knowledge formation in physical training'. *Sport, Education and Society* 22, no. 4 (2017): 477–92.

Patience, Sara. 'Can healthy eating go too far? Identifying orthorexia'. *Independent Nurse*, no. 2 (2021): 18–21.

Patrut, Adrian, Stephan Woodborne, Roxana T. Patrut, Laszlo Rakosy, Daniel A. Lowy, Grant Hall, and F. Karl. 'The demise of the largest and oldest African baobabs'. *Nature Plants* 4, no. 7 (2018): 423–6.

Pausé, Cat, Jackie Wykes, and Samantha Murray, eds. *Queering fat embodiment*. Oxfordshire: Routledge, 2016.

Peña-Lévano, Luis, Colton Adams, and Shaheer Burney. 'Latin America's superfood economy: Producing and marketing Açaí, Chia Seeds, and Maca Root'. *Choices* 35, no. 3 (2021): 16–20.

Pendenza, Massimo, and Vanessa Lamattina. 'Rethinking self-responsibility: An alternative vision to the neoliberal concept of freedom'. *American Behavioral Scientist* 63, no. 1 (2019): 100–15.

Perrault, Evan K., Grace M. Hildenbrand, and Rachel HeeJoon Rnoh. 'Employees' refusals to participate in an employer-sponsored wellness program: Barriers and benefits to engagement'. *Compensation & Benefits Review* 52, no. 1 (2020): 8–18.

Perry, David. 'When disability and race intersect'. *CNN Opinion*, 4 December 2014, http://www.cnn.com/2014/12/04/opinion/perry-garner-disability-race-intersection/index.html.

Perry, Sara Elizabeth. 'The enchantment of the archaeological record'. *European Journal of Archaeology* 22 (2019): 354–71.

Peters, Michael A., and Priya Venkatesan. 'Biocapitalism and the politics of life'. *Geopolitics, History, and International Relations* 2, no. 2 (2010): 100–22.

Peterson, Alan, and Deborah Lupton. *The new public health: Health and self in the age of risk*. Thousand Oaks: Sage, 1996.

Petrakaki, Dimitra, Eva Hilberg, and Justin Waring. 'Between empowerment and self-discipline: Governing patients' conduct through technological self-care'. *Social Science & Medicine* 213 (2018): 146–53.

Phelan, Sean M., et al. 'Impact of weight bias and stigma on quality of care and outcomes for patients with obesity'. *Obesity Reviews* 16, no. 4 (2015): 319–26.

Pink, Sarah, and Vaike Fors. 'Being in a mediated world: Self-tracking and the mind–body–environment'. *Cultural Geographies* 24, no. 3 (2017): 375–88.

PitchBook. 'Genopalate'. *Pitchbook*, 2021, https://pitchbook.com/profiles/company/179165-44#overview.

Pitts-Taylor, Victoria, ed. *Mattering: Feminism, science, and materialism*. Vol. 1. New York: New York University Press, 2016.

Pizzorno, Alessandro. 'Foucault and the liberal view of the individual'. In *Michel Foucault, Philosopher*, edited by J. Timothy. Armstrong. 204–11. New York: Routledge, 1992.

Popper, Karl, and I. I. I. Bartley. *The open universe: An argument for indeterminism from the postscript to the logic of scientific discovery*. New York: Routledge, 2012.

Poulain, Jean-Pierre. *The sociology of food: Eating and the place of food in society*. London: Bloomsbury Publishing, 2017.

Prentice, Rachel. *Bodies in formation*. Durham: Duke University Press, 2012.

Poshekhova, Olga Stanislavovna. 'Representation of the phenomenon of body positivity in English sports advertising discourse'. *Laplage em Revista* 7, no. 2 (2021): 473–81.

Pulsifer, Rebecah. 'Trolling humanism: New materialist performativity in border'. In *New Feminist Materialism and Queer Studies in the Anthropocene*, edited by Christian David, 7–63. Monterey: Larkspur Press, 2019.

Pun, Ngai, Tommy Tse, and Kenneth Ng. 'Challenging digital capitalism: SACOM's campaigns against Apple and Foxconn as monopoly capital'. *Information, Communication & Society* 22, no. 9 (2019): 1253–68.

Purser, Ronald. *McMindfulness: How mindfulness became the new capitalist spirituality*. London: Repeater, 2019.

Puwar, Nirmal. *Space invaders: Race, gender and bodies out of place*. Berg: Oxford, 2004.

Quinn, Diane M., and Jennifer Crocker. 'When ideology hurts: Effects of belief in the protestant ethic and feeling overweight on the psychological well-being of women'. *Journal of Personality and Social Psychology* 77, no. 2 (1999): 402.

Rabinow, Paul, and Nikolas Rose. 'Biopower today'. *BioSocieties* 1, no. 2 (2006): 195–217.

Rajan, Kaushik Sunder. *Biocapital: The constitution of postgenomic life*. Durham: Duke University Press, 2006.

Ramadan, A., F. M. Harraz, and S. A. El-Mougy. 'Anti-inflammatory, analgesic and antipyretic effects of the fruit pulp of Adansonia digitata'. *Fitoterapia (Milano)* 65, no. 5 (1994): 418–22.

Rao, Sheila. 'Sweet success? Interrogating nutritionism in biofortified sweet potato promotion in Mwasonga, Tanzania'. PhD diss., Carleton University, 2019, https://curve.carleton.ca/system/files/etd/a7ded06b-6df1-428f-94a5-85ca7e4bdec8/etd_pdf/fde32c889036a0e6aaf98e358fe47470/rao-sweetsuccessinterrogatingnutritionisminbiofortified.pdf.

Raphael, Rina. 'These 10 market trends turned wellness into a \$4.2 trillion global industry'. *Fast Company*, 10 August 2018.

Rashford, John. 'The uses of the baobab flower (Adansonia digitata L)'. *Ethnobotany Research and Applications* 14 (2015): 211–29.

Ravindran, T K Sundari. 'Commentary: Beyond the socioeconomic in the health gap: Gender and intersectionality'. *International Journal of Epidemiology* 46, no. 4 (2017): 1321–2.

Ray, John. 'The postqualitative turn in physical cultural studies'. *Leisure Sciences* 41, no. 1–2 (2019): 91–107.

Reed-Danahay, Deborah, ed. *Auto/ethnography: Rewriting the self and the social.* London: Routledge, 2021.

Rekker, Roderik. 'The nature and origins of political polarization over science'. *Public Understanding of Science* 30, no. 4 (2021): 352–68.

Rice, Carla. 'Rethinking fat: From bio-to body-becoming pedagogies'. *Cultural Studies? Critical Methodologies* 15, no. 5 (2015): 387–97.

Rice, Carla, Elisabeth Harrison, and May Friedman. 'Doing justice to intersectionality in research'. *Cultural Studies ↔ Critical Methodologies* 19, no. 6 (2019): 409–20.

Rice, Carla, Karleen Pendleton Jiménez, Elisabeth Harrison, Margaret Robinson, Jen Rinaldi, Andrea LaMarre, and Jill Andrew. 'Bodies at the intersections: Refiguring intersectionality through queer women's complex embodiments'. *Signs: Journal of Women in Culture and Society* 46, no. 1 (2020): 177–200.

Rice, Edbauer Jenny. 'The new "new": Making a case for critical affect studies'. *Quarterly Journal of Speech* 94, no. 2 (2008): 200–12, doi: 10.1080/00335630801975434.

Rich, Emma. 'Digitising fat'–Digital technologies, embodiment and the governance of fat'. In *2nd Annual International Weight Stigma Conference.* 2014, https://researchportal.bath.ac.uk/en/publications/digitising-fat-digital-technologies-embodiment-and-the-governance.

Rich, Emma, and Louise Mansfield. 'Fat and physical activity: Understanding and challenging weight stigma-special issue of fat studies: An interdisciplinary journal of body weight and society'. *Fat Studies* 8, no. 2 (2019): 99–109.

Richardson, L. D., and M. Norris. 'Access to health and health care: How race and ethnicity matter'. *Mount Sinai Journal of Medicine* 77, no. 2 (2010): 166–77.

Riley, Sarah, Adrienne Evans, and Martine Robson. *Postfeminism and health: Critical psychology and media perspectives.* New York: Routledge, 2018.

Riordan, Jesse D., and Joseph H. Nadeau. 'From peas to disease: Modifier genes, network resilience, and the genetics of health'. *The American Journal of Human Genetics* 101, no. 2 (2017): 177–91.

Roberts, Celia, and Adrian Mackenzie. *Living data: Making sense of health biosensing.* Cambridge: Policy Press, 2019.

Roberts, Celia, and Brigit McWade. 'Messengers of stress: Towards a cortisol sociology'. *Sociology of Health & Illness* (2021): https://doi.org/10.1111/1467-9566.1326.

Roberts, Dorothy E. 'What's wrong with race-based medicine: Genes, drugs, and health disparities'. *Minnesota Journal of Science & Technology* 12, no.1 (2011a): 1–21.

Roberts, Dorothy. *Fatal invention: How science, politics, and big business re-create race in the twenty-first century.* New York: New Press/ORIM, 2011b.

Robertson, Steve. *Understanding men and health: Masculinities, identity and well-being.* London: McGraw-Hill Education, 2007.

Robertson, Toni, and Jesper Simonsen. 'Participatory design: An introduction'. In *Routledge International Handbook of Participatory Design*, edited by Jesper Simonsen and Toni Robertson, 21–38. New York: Routledge, 2012.

Rodney, Alexandra. 'Pathogenic or health-promoting? How food is framed in healthy living media for women'. *Social Science & Medicine* 213 (2018): 37–44.

Rose, Nikolas. 'The politics of life itself'. *Theory, Culture & Society* 18, no. 6 (2001): 1–30.

Rose, Nikolas. 'Molecular biopolitics, somatic ethics and the spirit of biocapital'. *Social Theory & Health* 5, no. 1 (2007a): 3–29.

Rose, Nikolas. *The politics of life itself: Biomedicine, power, and subjectivity in the twenty-first century.* New Jersey: Princeton University Press, 2007b.

Rose, Nikolas, and Paul Rabinow. 'Thoughts on the concept of biopower today'. 1 June 2007/2003, http://www.molsci.org/research/publications_pdf/Rose_Rabinow_Biopower_Today.pdf.

Rosenberger, Robert. 'Why it takes both postphenomenology and STS to account for technological mediation'. In *Postphenomenological Methodologies: New Ways in Mediating Techno-human Relationships*, edited by Catherine Adams et al. 171–98 Lanham: Rowman & Littlefield, 2018.

Rosenblat, Alex, and Tamara Kneese. 'Workplace surveillance'. (2014). Data & Society Working Paper, 8 October 2014, https://www.datasociety.net/pubs/fow/WorkplaceSurveillance.pdf.

Ross, Amy A. 'Tracking health and fitness: A cultural examination of self-quantification, biomedicalization, and gender'. In *eHealth: Current Evidence, Promises, Perils and Future Directions.* 123–42. Bingley: Emerald Publishing Limited, 2018.

Roth, Anna, and Tomasz Zawadzki. 'Instagram as a tool for promoting superfood products'. *Annals of Marketing Management & Economics* 4, no. 1 (2018): 101–13.

Roth, Wolff-Michael. *Auto/biography and auto/ethnography: Praxis of research method.* Leiden: Brill, 2005.

Rothgerber, Hank. 'Real men don't eat (vegetable) quiche: Masculinity and the justification of meat consumption'. *Psychology of Men & Masculinity* 14, no. 4 (2013): 363.

Roy, Deboleena, and Banu Subramaniam. 'Matter in the shadows'. *Mattering: Feminism, Science, and Materialism* 1 (2016): 23.

Ruckenstein, Minna. 'Visualized and interacted life: Personal analytics and engagements with data doubles'. *Societies* 4, no. 1 (2014): 68–84.

Ruckenstein, Minna. 'Keeping data alive: Talking DTC genetic testing'. *Information, Communication & Society* 20, no. 7 (2017): 1024–39.

Ruckenstein, Minna, and Mika Pantzar. 'Beyond the quantified self: Thematic exploration of a dataistic paradigm'. *New Media & Society* 19, no. 3 (2017): 401–18.

Ruckenstein, Minna, and Natasha Dow Schüll. 'The datafication of health'. *Annual Review of Anthropology* 46 (2017): 261–78.

Ruger, Jennifer Prah. 'Health and social justice'. *The Lancet* 364, no. 9439 (2004): 1075–80.

Ryan Shuda, M., and Yuri Feito. 'Challenge, commitment, community, and empowerment: Factors that promote the adoption of CrossFit as a training program'. *Transformation* 1 (2017): 1–14.

Sabina, Ifeyinwa, Ajibola Nihmot, and Johnpaul Ifechukwu. 'African baobab: Its role in enhancing nutrition, health, and the environment'. *Trees, Forests and People* (2020): 100043.

Sabina, S. 'Biopolitics to molecular biopolitics: From Michael Foucault to Nikolas Rose'. *The Researchers' International Research Journal* 4, no. 2 (2018): 1–7.

Sadalla, Edward, and Jeffrey Burroughs. 'Profiles in eating-sexy vegetarians and other diet-based social stereotypes'. *Psychology Today* 15, no. 10 (1981): 51.

Saksono, Herman, Carmen Castaneda-Sceppa, Jessica Hoffman, Vivien Morris, Magy Seif El-Nasr, and Andrea G. Parker. 'Storywell: Designing for family fitness app motivation by using social rewards and reflection'. In *Proceedings of the 2020 CHI Conference on Human Factors in Computing Systems*, 1–13, 2020.

Salvatore, Jessica, and Jeanne Marecek. 'Gender in the gym: Evaluation concerns as barriers to women's weight lifting'. *Sex Roles* 63, no. 7 (2010): 556–67.

San-Cristobal, Rodrigo, Fermín I. Milagro, and J. Alfredo Martínez. 'Future challenges and present ethical considerations in the use of personalized nutrition based on genetic advice'. *Journal of the Academy of Nutrition and Dietetics* 113, no. 11 (2013): 1447–54.

Sanders, Rachel. 'Self-tracking in the digital era: Biopower, patriarchy, and the new biometric body projects'. *Body & Society* 23, no. 1 (2017): 36–63.

Sanders, Rachel. 'The color of fat: Racializing obesity, recuperating whiteness, and reproducing injustice'. *Politics, Groups, and Identities* 7, no. 2 (2019): 287–304.

Sandiford, Keith A. *The cultural politics of sugar: Caribbean slavery and narratives of colonialism*. Cambridge: Cambridge University Press, 2000.

Sassatelli, Roberta, and Federica Davolio. 'Consumption, pleasure and politics: Slow food and the politico-aesthetic problematization of food'. *Journal of Consumer Culture* 10, no. 2 (2010): 202–32.

Sastre, Alexandra. 'Towards a radical body positive: Reading the online "body positive movement"'. *Feminist Media Studies* 14, no. 6 (2014): 929–43.

Schalk, Sami. 'Reevaluating the supercrip'. *Journal of Literary & Cultural Disability Studies* 10, no. 1 (2016): 71–87.

Schanbacher, William D. *The politics of food: The global conflict between food security and food sovereignty*. Santa Barbara: ABC-CLIO, 2010.

Schechner, Sam, and Mark Secada. 'You give apps sensitive personal information. Then they tell Facebook'. *Wall Street Journal*, 22 February 2019, https://www.wsj.com/articles/you-give-apps-sensitive-personal-information-then-they-tell-facebook-11550851636?mod=article_inline.

Schiemer, Carolin, Afton Halloran, Kristjan Jespersen, and Petra Kaukua. 'Marketing insects: Superfood or solution-food?' In *Edible Insects in Sustainable Food Systems*, edited by Afton Halloran, Afton, Roberto Flore, Paul Vantomme, and Nanna Roos, 213–36. Berlin: Springer, 2018.

Schlauderaff, Sav. 'The Future is hypernormative: An analysis of bodymind representations in 23andMe's commercials'. *UCLA* (2018): 1–19, https://escholarship.org/content/qt3fs858hf/qt3fs858hf.pdf.

Schlossberg, Mallory. 'I'm part of a huge demographic that retailers largely ignore – here's why it's so frustrating'. *Business Insider*, 7 January 2016, https://www.businessinsider.com.au/petite-problem-story-2015-12.

Schott, Nicole. 'Food marketing as a pedagogical act: Teaching women to consume "skinny"'. *Journal of Social Justice* 5, no. 1 (2015): 1–23.

Schuldt, Jonathon P., Dominique Muller, and Norbert Schwarz. 'The "fair trade" effect: Health halos from social ethics claims'. *Social Psychological and Personality Science* 3, no. 5 (2012): 581–9.

Schüll, Natasha Dow. 'Data for life: Wearable technology and the design of self-care'. *BioSocieties* 11, no. 3 (2016): 317–33.

Schulz, Amy J., and Leith Ed Mullings. *Gender, race, class, & health: Intersectional approaches*. San Francisco: Jossey-Bass, 2006.

Scott, Susie. *Total institutions and reinvented identities*. New York: Springer, 2011.

Scrinis, Gryorgy. 'Nutritionism and functional foods'. In *The Philosophy of Food*, edited by D. Kaplan. Berkeley: University of California Press.

Scrinis, Gyorgy. 'On the ideology of nutritionism'. *Gastronomica* 8, no. 1 (2008): 39–48.

Scrinis, Gyorgy. *Nutritionism: The science and politics of dietary advice*. New York: Columbia University Press, 2013.

Scully, Jackie Leach. 'Disability and the challenge of genomics'. In *Routledge Handbook of Genomics, Health and Society*, edited by Gibbon, et al., 186–94. New York: Routledge, 2018.

Searcey, Dionne. 'Across Senegal, the beloved baobab tree is the "pride of the neighborhood."' *The New York Times*, 20 September 2018, https://www.nytimes.com/2018/09/30/world/africa/senegal-baobabs-climate-change.html.

Seedrs. 'Aduna'. *Seedrs*. 5 July 2018, https://www.seedrs.com/aduna2/sections/idea.

SensorTower. 'GetFit Apps'. *Sensor Tower*, 2021, https://sensortower.com/ios/publisher/getfit-apps/1404979200.

Shakespeare, Tom. 'Debating disability'. *Journal of Medical Ethics* 34, no. 1 (2008): 11–14.

Shapiro, Joseph P. *No pity: People with disabilities forging a new civil rights movement*. London: Broadway Books, 1994.

Shankar, Shalini. 'Racial naturalization, advertising, and model consumers for a new millennium'. *Journal of Asian American Studies* 16, no. 2 (2013): 159–88.

Sharon, Tamar. 'Healthy citizenship beyond autonomy and discipline: Tactical engagements with genetic testing'. *Biosocieties* 10, no. 3 (2015): 295–316.

Sharon, Tamar. 'Self-tracking for health and the quantified self: Re-articulating autonomy, solidarity, and authenticity in an age of personalized healthcare'. *Philosophy & Technology* 30, no. 1 (2017): 93–121.

Shattuck, Annie. 'Alternative food networks: Knowledge, place and politics'. *The Journal of Peasant Studies* 1, no. 3 (2013): 589–92.

Shaw, Andrea Elizabeth. *The embodiment of disobedience: Fat black women's unruly political bodies*. Lanham: Lexington Books, 2006.

Shcherbina, Anna, C. Mikael Mattsson, Daryl Waggott, Heidi Salisbury, Jeffrey W. Christle, Trevor Hastie, Matthew T. Wheeler, and Euan A. Ashley. 'Accuracy in wrist-worn, sensor-based measurements of heart rate and energy expenditure in a diverse cohort'. *Journal of Personalized Medicine* 7, no. 2 (2017): 1–12.

Shilling, Chris, and Philip A. Mellor. 'Cultures of embodied experience: Technology, religion and body pedagogics'. *The Sociological Review* 55, no. 3 (2007): 531–49.

Shilling, Chris. *The body and social theory*. New Jersey: Sage, 2012.

Sibibe, M., and J. T. Williams. 'Baobab–Adansonia digitata Fruits for the future'. In *International Centre of Underutilized Crops*. Southampton, UK: University of Southampton, 2002.

Sidibe, M. Baobab, and Adansonia Digitata L. 'Vol. 4. crops for the future'. *International Centre for Underutilised Crops*, 2002, http://www.boutique-baobab.fr/baobab/Pdf/Adansia_digitata_monography.pdf.

Sikka, Tina. 'The contradictions of a superfood consumerism in a postfeminist, neoliberal world'. *Food, Culture & Society* 22, no. 3 (2019): 354–75.

Sikka, Tina. 'Personalised nutrition: Studies in the biogenetics of race and food'. *Social Identities* 27, no. 3 (2021a): 359–76.

Sikka, Tina. 'Covid-19, fatness, and risk: Medico-media discourses and stigma'. *Platypus: The CASTAC Blog*. 26 January 2021b, http://blog.castac.org/2021/01/covid-19-fatness-and-risk-medico-media-discourses-and-stigma/.

Sikka, Tina. 'The social construction of "good health"'. In *Communication and Health*, edited by Charlene Elliot and Joshua Greenberg, 231–49. Singapore: Palgrave Macmillan, 2022.

Silchenko, Ksenia, and Søren Askegaard. 'Powered by healthism? Marketing discourses of food and health'. *European Journal of Marketing* 55, no. 1 (2020): 133–61.

Silk, Michael L., and David L. Andrews. 'Toward a physical cultural studies'. *Sociology of Sport Journal* 28, no. 1 (2011): 4–35.

Simmel Georgy. 'The sociology of the meal'. In *Simmel on Culture: Selected Writings*, edited by David Frisby and Michael Featherstone. New York: Sage, 1998.

Simone Fullagar. 'Post-qualitative inquiry and the new materialist turn: Implications for sport, health and physical culture research'. *Qualitative Research in Sport, Exercise and Health* 9, no. 2 (2017): 247–57, doi: 10.1080/2159676X.2016.1273896.

Sjoding, Michael W., Robert P. Dickson, Theodore J. Iwashyna, Steven E. Gay, and Thomas S. Valley. 'Racial bias in pulse oximetry measurement'. *New England Journal of Medicine* 383, no. 25 (2020): 2477–8.

Skeggs, Beverley. *Formations of class & gender: Becoming respectable*. Thousand Oaks: Sage, 1997.

Skrabanek, Petr. *The death of humane medicine and the rise of coercive healthism*. Bury St. Edmunds: St. Edmundsbury Press, 1994.

Slatman, Jenny. 'Mobilizing the sense of "Fat": A phenomenological materialist approach'. *Human Studies* 44, no. 4 (2021): 1–18.

Slendier Slim. 'About us'. *Slendier Slim*. 2021, http://www.slendierslim.com.au/about. html.

Slocum, Rachel, and Arun Saldanha, eds. *Geographies of race and food: Fields, bodies, markets*. London: Routledge, 2016.

Slocum, Rachel, and K. Valentine Cadieux. 'Notes on the practice of food justice in the US: Understanding and confronting trauma and inequity'. *Journal of Political Ecology* 22 (2015): 27–52.

Smelik, Anneke M., and Nina Lykke, eds. *Bits of life: Feminism at the intersections of media, bioscience, and technology*. Washington: University of Washington Press, 2010.

Smith, Bobby J. 'Food justice, intersectional agriculture, and the triple food movement'. *Agriculture and Human Values* 36, no. 4 (2019): 825–35.

Smith, Marsha, and John Harvey. 'Social eating initiatives and the practices of commensality'. *Appetite* 161 (2021): 105–7.

Smith, Thomas SJ, and Louise Reid. 'Which "being" in wellbeing? Ontology, wellness and the geographies of happiness'. *Progress in Human Geography* 42, no. 6 (2018): 807–29.

Sobal, Jeffery, and Mary K. Nelson. 'Commensal eating patterns: A community study'. *Appetite* 41, no. 2 (2003): 181–90.

Southam, L., et al. 'Is the thrifty genotype hypothesis supported by evidence based on confirmed type 2 diabetes-and obesity-susceptibility variants?' *Diabetologia* 52, no. 9 (2009): 1846–51.

Sparkes, Andrew C. 'Autoethnography and narratives of self: Reflections on criteria in action'. *Sociology of Sport Journal* 17, no. 1 (2000): 21–43.

Spinks, Rosie. 'We're all losers to a gadget industry built on planned obsolescence'. *The Guardian*, 23 March 2015, https://www.theguardian.com/sustainable-business/2015/mar/23/were-are-all-losers-to-gadget-industry-built-on-planned-obsolescence.

Spinoza, Baruch. *Spinoza: Complete works*. Indianapolis: Hackett Publishing, 2002.

Springgay, Stephanie, and Zofia Zaliwska. 'Diagrams and cuts: A materialist approach to research-creation'. *Cultural Studies? Critical Methodologies* 15, no. 2 (2015): 136–44.

Srnicek, Nick. *Platform capitalism*. New Jersey: John Wiley & Sons, 2017.

Statista. 'Health and wellness food market'. *Statista*, 2021, https://www.statista.com/statistics/502267/global-health-and-wellness-food-market-value/.

Steim, Richard I., and Carol J. Nemeroff. 'Moral overtones of food: Judgments of others based on what they eat'. *Personality and Social Psychology Bulletin* 21, no. 5 (1995): 480–90.

Stern, Alexandra Minna. 'Eugenics, sterilization, and historical memory in the United States'. *História, Ciências, Saúde-Manguinhos* 23 (2016): 195–212.

Stevens, Alicia, and Scott Griffiths. 'Body Positivity (# BoPo) in everyday life: An ecological momentary assessment study showing potential benefits to individuals' body image and emotional wellbeing'. *Body Image* 35 (2020): 181–91.

Stibbe, Arran. 'Health and the social construction of masculinity in Men's Health magazine'. *Men and Masculinities* 7, no. 1 (2004): 31–51.

Strings, Sabrina. 'Obese black women as "social dead weight": Reinventing the "diseased black woman"'. *Signs: Journal of Women in Culture and Society* 41, no. 1 (2015): 107–30.

Strings, Sabrina. *Fearing the black body: The racial origins of fat phobia*. New York: NYU Press, 2019.

Sum, Ngai-Ling, and Bob Jessop. *Towards a cultural political economy: Putting culture in its place in political economy*. Cheltenham: Edward Elgar Publishing, 2013.

Sundar, Aparna, and Frank R. Kardes. 'The role of perceived variability and the health halo effect in nutritional inference and consumption'. *Psychology & Marketing* 32, no. 5 (2015): 512–21.

Swan, Melanie. 'Health 2050: The realization of personalized medicine through crowdsourcing, the quantified self, and the participatory biocitizen'. *Journal of Personalized Medicine* 2, no. 3 (2012): 93–118.

Syed-Abdul, Shabbir, Luis Fernandez-Luque, Wen-Shan Jian, Yu-Chuan Li, Steven Crain, Min-Huei Hsu, Yao-Chin Wang, et al. 'Misleading health-related information promoted through video-based social media: Anorexia on YouTube'. *Journal of Medical Internet Research* 15, no. 2 (2013): e30.

Takahashi, Lico. 'The gender-based digital divide and how design can change it'. *Rhine-Waal University of Applied Sciences Thesis*, 2019, https://www.researchgate.net/profile/Lico-Takahashi/publication/331374388_Designing_Gender_Inclusion_The_gender-based_digital_divide_and_how_design_can_change_it/links/5c88ee8ba6fdcc38174fd645/Designing-Gender-Inclusion-The-gender-based-digital-divide-and-how-design-can-change-it.pdf.

TallBear, Kim. 'Narratives of race and indigeneity in the Genographic Project'. *Journal of Law, Medicine & Ethics* 35, no. 3 (2007): 412–24.

TallBear, Kim. 'Genomic articulations of indigeneity'. *Social Studies of Science* 43, no. 4 (2013a): 509–33.

TallBear, Kim. *Native American DNA: Tribal belonging and the false promise of genetic science*. Minneapolis: University of Minnesota Press, 2013b.

Tangari, Gioacchino, et al. 'Mobile health and privacy: Cross sectional study'. *BMJ* 373 (2021), https://www.bmj.com/content/373/bmj.n1248.

Thomas, D. M., C. K. Martin, S. Lettieri, C. Bredlau, K. Kaiser, T. Church, C. Bouchard, and S. B. Heymsfield. 'Response to "Why is the 3500 kcal per pound weight loss rule wrong?"'. *International Journal of Obesity* 37, no. 12 (2013): 1614–15.

Thornham, Helen. 'Algorithmic vulnerabilities and the datalogical: Early motherhood and tracking-as-care regimes'. *Convergence* 25, no. 2 (2019): 171–85.

Thorpe, Holly, and Marianne Clark. 'Gut Feminism, new materialisms and sportwomen's embodied health: The case of RED-S in endurance athletes'. *Qualitative Research in Sport, Exercise and Health* 12, no. 1 (2020): 1–17.

Throsby, Karen. 'Obesity surgery and the management of excess: Exploring the body multiple'. *Sociology of Health & Illness* 34, no. 1 (2012): 1–15.

Ticineto Clough, Patricia. 'The new empiricism: Affect and sociological method'. *European Journal of Social Theory* 12, no. 1 (2009): 43–61.

Tidgwell, Tracy, May Friedman, Jen Rinaldi, Crystal Kotow, and Emily RM Lind. 'Introduction to the special issue: Fatness and temporality'. *Fat Studies* 7, no. 2 (2018): 115–23.

Tierney, William G. 'Life history's history: Subjects foretold'. *Qualitative Inquiry* 4, no. 1 (1998): 49–70.

Tiggemann, Marika, and Isabella Anderberg. 'Muscles and bare chests on Instagram: The effect of Influencers' fashion and fitspiration images on men's body image'. *Body Image* 35 (2020): 237–44.

Till, Chris. 'Exercise as labour: Quantified self and the transformation of exercise into labour'. *Societies* 4, no. 3 (2014): 446–62.

Tischleder, Babette B. 'Theorising things, building worlds: Why the new materialisms deserve literary imagination'. *Open Cultural Studies* 3, no. 1 (2019): 125–34.

Toffoletti, Kim, Holly Thorpe, and Jessica Francombe-Webb, eds. *New sporting femininities: Embodied politics in postfeminist times*. Berlin: Springer, 2018.

Tovar, Virgie. *The self-love revolution: Radical body positivity for girls of color*. Oakland: New Harbinger Publications, 2020.

Troiano, Alexandra. 'Wearables and personal health data: Putting a premium on your privacy'. *Brooklyn Law Review* 82, no. 4 (2017): 6.

Tuck, Eve, and K. Wayne Yang. 'Decolonization is not a metaphor'. *Decolonization: Indigeneity, Education & Society* 1, no. 1 (2012): 1–40.

Turner Lee, Nicol. 'Detecting racial bias in algorithms and machine learning'. *Journal of Information, Communication and Ethics in Society* 16, no. 3 (2018): 252–60.

Tushnet, Rebecca. 'The difference engine: Perpetuating poverty through algorithms'. *Jotwell: Journal of Things We Like* (2018): https://heinonline.org/HOL/LandingPage?handle=hein.journals/jotwell2018&div=141&id=&page=.

Udler, Miriam S. 'Type 2 diabetes: multiple genes, multiple diseases'. *Current Diabetes Reports* 19, no. 8 (2019): 1–9.

Ulucanlar, Selda, Alex Faulkner, Susan Peirce, and Glyn Elwyn. 'Technology identity: The role of sociotechnical representations in the adoption of medical devices'. *Social Science & Medicine* 98 (2013): 95–105.

UNEP. 'Secrets of the baobabs: Lifeline for a forest on the edge'. *United Nationals Environmental Program*, 10 December 2018, https://www.unep.org/news-and-stories/story/secrets-baobabs-lifeline-forest-edge.

Ureta, Sebastián. 'Selling the sociotechnical sublime: Critical reflections on introducing STS to managers of a Chilean mining corporation'. *Tapuya: Latin American Science, Technology and Society* 1, no. 1 (2018): 138–52.

Van der Tuin, Iris, and Rick Dolphijn. 'The transversality of new materialism'. *Women: A Cultural Review* 21, no. 2 (2010): 153–71.

Van Dijk, Teun A. 'Principles of critical discourse analysis'. *Discourse & Society* 4, no. 2 (1993): 249–83.

van Kraalingen, Imre. 'Cultivating embodied connections in biodynamic agriculture'. Master's thesis, 2019, https://www.duo.uio.no/bitstream/handle/10852/69273/Cultivating-Embodied-Connections-in-Biodynamic-Agriculture—Imre-van-Kraalingen.pdf?sequence=1.

Vartanian, Lenny R., C. Peter Herman, and Janet Polivy. 'Consumption stereotypes and impression management: How you are what you eat'. *Appetite* 48, no. 3 (2007): 265–77.

Venkatapuram, Sridhar. 'On health justice. Some thoughts and responses to critics'. *Bioethics* 30, no. 1 (2016): 49–55.

Viome. 'You, decoded'. *Viome*, 2021, https://www.viome.com.

Vogel, Else, and Annemarie Mol. 'Enjoy your food: On losing weight and taking pleasure'. *Sociology of Health & Illness* 36, no. 2 (2014): 305–17.

Voléry, Ingrid, and Marie-Pierre Julien, eds. *From measuring Rods to DNA sequencing: Assessing the human*. Berlin: Springer Nature, 2020.

Wajcman, Judy. *TechnoFeminism*. Cambridge: Polity, 2004.

Wajcman, Judy. 'From women and technology to gendered technoscience'. *Information, Community and Society* 10, no. 3 (2007): 287–98.

Walajahi, Hina, David R. Wilson, and Sara Chandros Hull. 'Constructing identities: The implications of DTC ancestry testing for tribal communities'. *Genetics in Medicine* 21, no. 8 (2019): 1744–50.

Waldby, Catherine, and Melinda Cooper. 'The biopolitics of reproduction: Post-Fordist biotechnology and women's clinical labour'. *Australian Feminist Studies* 23, no. 55 (2008): 57–73.

Walia, Harsha. *Undoing border imperialism*. Vol. 6. California: Ak Press, 2013.

Wall, Sarah. 'An autoethnography on learning about autoethnography'. *International Journal of Qualitative Methods* 5, no. 2 (2006): 146–60.

Warfield, Katie. 'Becoming method (ologist): A feminist posthuman autoethnography of the becoming of a posthuman methodology'. *Reconceptualizing Educational Research Methodology* 10, no. 2–3 (2019): 147–72.

Warin, Megan. 'Material feminism, obesity science and the limits of discursive critique'. *Body & Society* 21, no. 4 (2015): 48–76.

Warin, Megan, and Anne Hammarström. 'Material feminism and epigenetics: A "Critical Window" for engagement?' *Australian Feminist Studies* 33, no. 97 (2018): 299–315.

Watkins, Patti Lou. 'Fat studies 101: Learning to have your cake and eat it too'. *M/C Journal* 18, no. 3 (2015): https://journal.media-culture.org.au/index.php/mcjournal/index.

Wayne, Michael. 'Post-Fordism, monopoly capitalism, and Hollywood's media industrial complex'. *International Journal of Cultural Studies* 6, no. 1 (2003): 82–103.

Weber, Max, and Stephen Kalberg. *The Protestant ethic and the spirit of capitalism.* New York: Routledge, 2013.

Weber, Rachel. N. 'Manufacturing gender in commercial and military cockpit design'. *Science, Technology and Human Values* 22, no. 2 (1997): 235–53.

Weiler, Anelyse M., Chris Hergesheimer, Ben Brisbois, Hannah Wittman, Annalee Yassi, and Jerry M. Spiegel. 'Food sovereignty, food security and health equity: A meta-narrative mapping exercise'. *Health Policy and Planning* 30, no. 8 (2015): 1078–92.

Weiss, Gilbert, and Ruth Wodak, eds. *Critical discourse analysis.* New York: Palgrave Macmillan, 2007.

Welhausen, Candice A. 'Quantifiable me: Fitness and health trackers and the trope of holisticism'. *Communication Design Quarterly Review* 5, no. 4 (2018): 61–71.

Welltodo. 'Global wellness industry trend report 2018'. *Welltodo Global,* 2018, https://www.welltodoglobal.com/wp-content/uploads/2018/01/WelltodoTrend-Report.pdf.

Werkhseiser, Ian. 'Food sovereignty, health sovereignty, and self-organised community viability'. *Interdisciplinary Environmental Review* 15, no. 2–3 (2014): 134–46.

West, Carolyn M. 'Mammy, Sapphire, and Jezebel: Historical images of Black women and their implications for psychotherapy'. *Psychotherapy: Theory, Research, Practice, Training* 32, no. 3 (1995): 458.

Whitehead, Margaret. 'The concepts and principles of equity and health'. *Health Promotion International* 6, no. 3 (1991): 217–28.

WHO. 'WHO remains firmly committed to the principles set out in the preamble to the Constitution'. *World Health Organization,* 2021, https://www.who.int/about/who-we-are/constitution.

Whyte, Kyle. 'What do indigenous knowledges do for indigenous peoples?' In *Keepers of the Green World: Traditional Ecological Knowledge and Sustainability,* edited by Melissa K. Nelson and Dan Shilling (2017), https://papers.ssrn.com/sol3/papers.cfm?abstract_id=2612715.

Wickens, Gerald E. *The baobabs: Pachycauls of Africa, Madagascar and Australia.* Berlin: Springer Science & Business Media, 2008.

Wiest, Amber L., David L. Andrews, and Michael D. Giardina. 'Training the body for healthism: Reifying vitality in and through the clinical gaze of the neoliberal fitness club'. *Review of Education, Pedagogy, and Cultural Studies* 37, no. 1 (2015): 21–40.

Williams, Apryl A. 'Fat people of color: Emergent intersectional discourse online'. *Social Sciences* 6, no. 1 (2017): 15.

Williams, Meredydd, Jason R. C. Nurse, and Sadie Creese. 'The perfect storm: The privacy paradox and the Internet-of-Things'. In *2016 11th International Conference on Availability, Reliability and Security (ARES)*, 644–52. IEEE, 2016.

Williamson, Ben. 'Algorithmic skin: Health-tracking technologies, personal analytics and the biopedagogies of digitized health and physical education'. *Sport, Education and Society* 20, no. 1 (2015): 133–51.

Williamson, Ben. 'Coding the biodigital child: The biopolitics and pedagogic strategies of educational data science'. *Pedagogy, Culture & Society* 24, no. 3 (2016): 401–16.

Willmes, Claudia Gisela. 'Celebrating molecular medicine'. *Trends in Molecular Medicine* 26, no. 9 (2020): 797–8.

Wills, John S. 'Missing in interaction: Diversity, narrative, and critical multicultural social studies'. *Theory & Research in Social Education* 29, no. 1 (2001): 43–64.

Winseck, Dwayne. 'Reconstructing the political economy of communication for the digital media age'. *The Political Economy of Communication* 4, no. 2 (2017). http://polecom.org/index.php/polecom/article/view/72.

Winston, Joel. 'Ancestry.com Takes DNA ownership rights from customers and their relatives'. *Think Progress*, 17 May 2017, https://www.geneticsandsociety.org/article/ancestrycom-takes-dna-ownership-rights-customers-and-their-relatives.

Winter, Lars, and Thomas Kron. 'Fuzzy thinking in sociology'. In *Views on Fuzzy Sets and Systems from Different Perspectives*, edited by Rudolf Seising, 301–20. Berline: Springer, 2009.

Wired. 'Know thy self: Tracking every facet of life, from sleep to mood to pain'. *Wired*, 22 June 2009, https://www.wired.com/2009/06/lbnp-knowthyself/.

Wodak, Ruth. 'Critical linguistics and discourse analysis'. In *Discursive Pragmatics*, edited by Zienkowski, Jan, Jan-Ola Östman, and Jef Verschueren, 50–70. Amsterdam: John Benjamins, 2011.

Woebapora, Lardi. 'Lardi Woebapora'. *Aduna*, 2021, https://aduna.com/blogs/our-producers-case-studies/lardi-woebapora.

Wolfe, Julia. 'Coerced into health: Workplace wellness programs and their threat to genetic privacy'. *Minnesota Law Review* 103 (2018): 1089.

Wolff, Jonathan, and Avner De-Shalit. *Disadvantage.* Oxford: Oxford University Press, 2007.

Wong, Julia Carrie. 'Revealed: Google illegally underpaid thousands of workers across dozens of countries'. *The Guardian*, 10 September 2021, https://www.theguardian.com/technology/2021/sep/10/google-underpaid-workers-illegal-pay-disparity-documents.

Woodall, Patrick, and Tyler L. Shannon. 'Monopoly power corrodes choice and resiliency in the food system'. *The Antitrust Bulletin* 63, no. 2 (2018): 198–221.

Worrall, Simon. 'Why race is not a thing, according to genetics'. *National Geographic.* 14 October 2017, https://www.nationalgeographic.com/news/2017/10/genetics-history-race-neanderthal-rutherford/.

Wright, Erik Olin. *Envisioning real utopias.* Vol. 98. London: Verso, 2010.

Wright, Jan, Jane Maree Maher, and Claire Tanner. 'Social class, anxieties and mothers' foodwork'. *Sociology of Health & Illness* 37, no. 3 (2015): 422–36.

Wylie, Charles M. 'The definition and measurement of health and disease'. *Public Health Reports* 85, no. 2 (1970): 100–4.

Yinger, J. Milton. 'Contraculture and subculture'. *American Sociological Review* (1960): 625–35.

YourSuper.com. '6 health benefits of baobab you need to know'. *YourSuper.com*, 2021, https://yoursuper.eu/pages/baobab-fruit-benefits.

Yoxen, Edward. 'Life as a productive force: Capitalising upon research in molecular biology' in Levidow, L. and Young, RM'. *Science, Technology and the Labour Process* 1 (1981): 66–122.

Yuval-Davis, Nira. 'Intersectionality and feminist politics'. *European Journal of Women's studies* 13, no. 3 (2006): 193–209.

Zavattaro, Staci M. 'Taking the social justice fight to the cloud: Social media and body positivity'. *Public Integrity* 23, no. 3 (2021): 281–95.

Zerzan, John. *Future primitive: And other essays.* New York: Autonomedia, 1994.

Zimmer, Michael, Priya Kumar, Jessica Vitak, Yuting Liao, and Katie Chamberlain Kritikos. '"There's nothing really they can do with this information": Unpacking how users manage privacy boundaries for personal fitness information'. *Information, Communication & Society* 23, no. 7 (2020): 1020–37.

Zuboff, Shoshana. 'Big other: Surveillance capitalism and the prospects of an information civilization'. *Journal of Information Technology* 30, no. 1 (2015): 75–89.

Zuboff, Shoshana. *The age of surveillance capitalism: The fight for a human future at the new frontier of power: Barack Obama's books of 2019.* London: Profile Books, 2019.

Zuboff, Shoshana. 'Panel for the future of science and technology – annual lecture 2020'. *European Parliament*, 9 December 2020, https://multimedia.europarl.europa.eu/en/panel-for-future-of-science-and-technology-annual-lecture-2020_20201209-1500-SPECIAL-STOA_vd.

Index

www.ingramcontent.com/pod-product-compliance
Lightning Source LLC
Chambersburg PA
CBHW071417290326
41932CB00046B/1976